The Mad Men of Hockey

The Mad Men of Hockey

by Trent Frayne

Dodd, Mead and Company
New York

ISBN: 0-396-07060-4

Dodd, Mead and Company
New York

TABLE OF CONTENTS

To June

PROLOGUE

Signs and slogans proliferate in Philadelphia.

"Let us take the shortest route to the puck-carrier and arrive in ill humor," Freddie Shero, the coach, chalks on the blackboard in the dressing quarters of his Flyers. A fan in the stands brings a lettered bedsheet to the Spectrum where the Flyers and the Boston Bruins are mugging one another in the Stanley Cup final in May of 1974:

> LADY BYNG DIED
> IN
> PHILADELPHIA

Television has created the illusion that the fun-loving Flyers are the first hockey club to bring a violent philosophy to the game, the first group of boys to engage in a sort of demolition derby on ice.

In truth, the Flyers have simply been in the process of restoring the game to normal, or what passed for normal prior to the enervating expansion of the National Hockey League from six teams to twelve in June of 1967. Until expansion, everybody played like Philadelphia began to play in the 1972-73 season when Freddie Shero found himself endowed with a handful of gifted players among a roster of good-sized

9

tough kids who shared a willingness to work hard and fight and follow a system and fight and to accept disciplined coaching and, of course, fight.

I remember talking to King Clancy one afternoon along about 1969 or 1970 when the Toronto Maple Leafs, for whom he'd toiled in one capacity or another for forty years, were being rudely treated in the playoffs by the Bruins. Francis Michael Clancy, then as now, is a laughing leprechaun of seventy-odd summers who played for the old Ottawa Senators, then the Leafs, then turned to coaching and refereeing and finally settled into a life-time job as a vice-president with the Maple Leafs, in charge of whatever came along and needed doing.

"The game's just not the same," Clancy lamented this day. "We don't have a soul who'll walk out there tonight when the whistle blows and hammer somebody into the seats. They're all thinkin' about their money, I guess. If we had some dirty son of a bitch like Sprague Cleghorn who'd just go out there and kick the bejesus out of somebody, I tell you we'd win the Stanley Cup." His scarred and mobile face was long and creased in gloom. "But we haven't an' we won't," King said. And he was right.

Television, taking the game to millions of new fans in the 1970s, vaulted the violence of the Flyers to a prominence in the United States unknown prior to expansion. Until then, it was simply taken for granted in Canada and in the four old-line American cities, Boston, New York, Chicago and Detroit. Expansion sapped the blood from hockey for a time, spreading the talent thin and turning the game into a form of Ice Follies, everybody skating around like a Peggy Fleming in shin pads. Then, in the fall of 1972 Freddie Shero began restoring the old philosophy of intimidation and, because he had a solid system of offence and defence and because he had two great centre players, Bobby Clarke and Rick MacLeish, and, more particularly, a superstar goaltender, Bernie Parent, he was able finally to challenge and often beat the best of the old established clubs, the first expansion club to win the Cup. One night in Toronto near the end of the 1974 season his Flyers toyed with the once vigorous Leafs. The Toronto owner, Harold Ballard, was sufficiently dismayed by what his eyes revealed that he publicly castigated his team by terming the players chicken. He even spelled it out: c-h-i-c-k-e-n. No one was appalled by the owner's outburst; indeed, his sentiments were shared by fans long since accustomed to the fact that hockey is a violent game.

In 1954 the Canadian novelist Hugh McLennan wrote a piece for *Holiday* magazine on hockey. "To spectator and player alike, hockey gives the release that strong liquor gives to a repressed man," he wrote.

10

"It is the counterpoint of the Canadian self-restraint, it takes us back to the fiery blood of Gallic and Celtic ancestors who found themselves minorities in a cold, new environment and had to discipline themselves as all minorities must. But Canadians take the ferocity of their national game so much for granted that when an American visitor makes polite mention of it, they look at him in astonishment. Hockey violent? Well, perhaps it is a little. But hockey was always like that."

Old-time hockey players laugh about the game they played the way old soldiers remember a war.

"I was seventeen when I turned pro," King Clancy says, looking across fifty-five years. "Before that, I played for St. Brigid's. We were the raggedy-ass Canal boys who played on the Rideau Canal in twenty-five degrees below zero. We used to play the Model School, kids of wealthy parents. They'd come in all dressed up in hockey uniforms and we didn't have anything but the clothes we wore to school an' it didn't make any difference. They played just as hard as we did an' they could fight *almost* as good. Andy Blair was the first fellah I ever played with who had an education. Jesus, he was a graduate of the University of Manitoba when he played with us on the Leafs. He could fight pretty good, too, come to think of it. Before that, when I was with the Senators, the practices were as tough as the games. That Sprague Cleghorn, why, he'd cut your heart out. Everybody had hard men. Like Sylvio Mantha; I remember one night with the Leafs we were playin' the Canadiens and Sylvio Mantha was the key to their defence. Dick Irvin was coach for us then, an' he called me over to the bench. 'Get that Mantha,' he told me. First chance I got I caught him with a cross-check and broke his jaw—I didn't mean to break it—and we beat 'em. A couple of nights later little Artie Somers who was with the Rangers gave me a butt-end in the face. It split my tongue halfway back and knocked out four teeth. The part that bothered me the most was the gum that stuck in the teeth. That was sore for a long time. It was all part of the game. I loved it all. You know?"

CHAPTER ONE: Are Hockey People People?

From earliest times the men who have involved themselves most deeply in hockey—the coaches, the managers, the owners, the players themselves—have shared a notable characteristic that has appeared in various guises. Sometimes it has been called dedication, sometimes sacrifice, and sometimes even religion. But really, when you come right down to it, there is only one way to describe the pain and the turmoil, the emotional toll and the shattering injury suffered by the people whose lives have become irrevocably entwined in this most violent of games: Sheer lunacy.

Consider the otherwise undistinguished February 18 of the year 1899. The Winnipeg Victorias have challenged the Montreal Victorias for the Stanley Cup. It is an era when teams are allowed to do that sort of thing. None of today's draining four-of-seven finals in the steaming rinks of early summer coming in the wake of other marathon semi-final playoffs and quarter-final playoffs which in turn come in the wake of eighty-game schedules which in turn come in the wake of weeks of pre-season exhibitions—no, just a simple challenge any time a team feels an uncontrollable urge to take on the current Cup-holder on a two-game total-goals basis when the weather is a sensible twenty degrees below zero.

Anyway, Montreal has handled Winnipeg by 2-1 in the opening game and now, with three minutes to play in the second game, Winnipeg is striving to overcome a 3-2 deficit. A man named Paul Gingras rushes out of his own end of the rink with the puck and outwits a man named Bob McDougall straining to check him. Clearly beaten, the chagrined McDougall does what comes naturally in hockey: he turns and slugs Gingras across the calves with an axeman's swing; and Gingras also does what comes naturally: he topples to the ice and lies there meditating. He wonders if he'll ever walk again.

Whereupon the referee, one J.A. Findlay, announces he will impose an appropriate penalty after he has assessed the damage. Rolling down Gingras's long woollen stockings and examining the rising welts across his calves, Findlay is not impressed.

"Two minutes," he says.

"What!" shriek the Winnipeg players, approximately. They argue that McDougall deserves a match penalty, if not life imprisonment, and their coach orders them from the ice, refusing to continue. This does not intimidate Referee Findlay. He merely declares that he has been insulted and goes home.

Meanwhile, McDougall goes to the Winnipeg dressing quarters and apologizes to poor Gingras, explaining that he had lost his temper and imploring the Winnipeggers to continue. They demur. Two officials set off with a horse and sleigh to Referee Findlay's home to try to persuade him to accompany them back to the rink where eight thousand people have been waiting with admirable, if inexplicable, patience. At length Findlay is placated, and when he arrives back at the rink, an hour and five minutes after play had stopped, he gives Winnipeg fifteen minutes to return to the ice. But the unrepentent Winnipeggers refuse, and Findlay awards the game to Montreal. Thus, the Victorias are winners and still champions.

Or consider the raffish odyssey of seven carefree young souls from the Yukon who, weary of the long Klondike nights of Dawson City, decide to challenge the mighty Silver Seven in far-off Ottawa. They raise $3,000 for their expenses by sponsoring dances and selling raffle tickets over a six-week period, and on December 19, 1906, they set off by dog-team for Skagway on the first leg of a four-thousand mile trip to Canada's capital city.

At Skagway they board a passenger boat for the long haul down the Pacific coast to Vancouver where they pile into a day-coach for the 2,500-mile train trip through the Rocky mountains, across the deep-freeze of the prairies, along the snow-packed rock and brush north of the Great Lakes, and finally into Ottawa on January 11. There, their travail has just begun. They are greeted by this account of their opponents in the *Toronto Globe*:

> Ottawa players slash, trip and practise the severest kind of cross-checking with a systematic hammering of hands and wrists. They hit a man on the head when the referee isn't looking, and they body-check a man into the boards after he has passed the puck. The rubber is not the objective; the man must be stopped at all costs. If he is put out altogether, so much the better.

Two nights later, before 2,200 spectators, the visitors from the far, far northwest are lashed by the Silver Seven 9-2. But the night is not entirely without reward; one of their forwards, Harvey Watts, opens Tom Moore's scalp for six stitches. However, the incident serves merely to strip the Silver Seven of any vestige of mercy; in the second game Ottawa savages the men who'd once moiled for gold by 23-2, and the Silver Seven's Frank McGee accomplishes scoring feats that stand to this day. He scores fourteen goals—eight in a stretch of eight minutes and twenty seconds—and the battered Yukoners undertake the long voyage home the moment the hospitals sound the all-clear.

Time has wrought vast changes on the face of hockey but its basic elements have gone unchanged for generations. To paraphrase Mr. Churchill, it is a game of blood, sweat and madmen. In the days before the World Hockey Association came along in the summer of 1972 and began making waves in the National Hockey League's financial structure, the crazy players absorbed their contusions and abrasions for next to nothing while the tyrannical owners grew ever richer. In the days *after* the WHA's arrival, the crazy owners thrust hundreds of thousands of dollars upon any boy who knew (a) a lawyer and (b) how to skate, and often his ability to skate was waived so long as any combination of his arms, legs, and head added up to five.

The men who play hockey are a breed apart, and although the *nouveau riche* are lighting their cigars with $50 bills these days, money has little influence on a hockey player's attitude towards hockey. Before the bell rings he wants his lawyer to extract every dime he can steal from competing NHL and WHA owners, but after it rings the money's as far from his mind as his Lamborghini. The hockey player wants only to climb into his harness, to feel the ice cutting beneath his long strides and, if the need arises (and the need almost always arises), to belt somebody in a different coloured sweater. There are even times when the colour doesn't matter. When Bobby Baun and Eddie Shack were team-

15

mates on the Toronto Maple Leafs in the mid-1960s, Baun drew Shack aside one time for a little chat. Eddie the Entertainer had an egg-beater skating style, all knees and elbows and flying hair. No one was safe when he decided to overwhelm a loose puck and upon occasion he knocked down his own teammates in his single-minded ebullience. This particular night he bowled over Baun early in the game, and then knocked him into the boards a little while later. Baun climbed slowly to his feet and skated close to Shack, who was jumping up and down like a horse in a starting gate.

"Eddie, hear me," Baun said, fingering the Maple Leaf tunic he wore with distinction and vast amounts of sweat. "Eddie, it's blue, same as yours. For Christ's sake, Eddie, I'm on *your* side."

And the nature of the game is such that sometimes it's even brother against brother. No two brothers had more admiration for one another than Lionel and Charlie Conacher. Lionel, nearly ten years older, was a strong and gifted athlete in many sports and though hockey was not his best game—he was an awkward skater, and slow—he enjoyed a long and distinctive career with the Chicago Black Hawks, the New York Americans and the Montreal Maroons. Because of the age difference, he was almost like a father to young Chuck, guiding him to a lucrative contract with the Toronto Maple Leafs, and theirs was a warm relationship. Nonetheless, one night when Lionel and Toronto's Red Horner engaged in a vicious brawl on the ice, there were unexpected repercussions. They were assessed major penalties and they continued to jaw at one another as they entered the penalty box. In a twinkling, they were at it again, standing in the aisle back of the penalty bench punching, with Lionel clearly in command. Whereupon Charlie, a big strong youngster who served as a Leaf policeman, hopped over the boards and shoved his brother away from Horner. "Do you still want to fight?" he rasped. Lionel responded with a looping right hand that caught Charlie high on the head and Charlie retaliated with a short hard uppercut to Lionel's chin. Then they grabbed one another with their left hands and began pummelling with their rights. Blood smeared both their sweaters, and the fight became so violent that four policemen were needed to pull them apart.

Afterwards, they went to their parents' home on Davenport Road in Toronto, not far from the downtown rink, and sat in the kitchen eating cold cuts and home-made bread.

"You've got a hell of a right hand," Lionel said. "You're gonna be all right, Chuck."

When a hockey player gets into his game, his money, his wife, and every girl he knows from Atlanta to Los Angeles, from Vancouver to

Montreal, flies from his mind. He'd play for nothing; he really would. This is a hard point to make with people who haven't spent time around hockey players, but it's true. It was true in the days of the boys from Dawson City, it was true of King Clancy, of Eddie Shore, of Red Dutton, of Sprague Cleghorn, of Howie Morenz, of Rocket Richard, of Bobby Clarke, of Bobby Orr. It is, perhaps surprisingly, even true of the instant millionaires. If they weren't getting their hundreds of thousands a year, the Parks and Hulls and Cournoyers and Espositos, for playing with the pros, they'd be playing for nothing in a corner rink somewhere. If you don't believe it, how do you explain Ken Dryden?

Some say Ken Dryden is the best goaltender to wear the tools since Terry Sawchuk was driving wild men wilder in the mid-1950s when he was at his absolute peak; and this is an opinion Dryden, who is a quiet, intelligent and realistic man, has no cause to refute. In the early summer of 1972, a few weeks *before* the birth of the WHA, Dryden signed a two-year contract with the greatest name in the hockey business, the Montreal Canadiens, for $80,000 a year. Comes the WHA revolution, and suddenly Dryden grows aware that goaltenders who would have difficulty carrying his cup have jumped to the new league and are being turned bow-legged by the largesse of grateful owners. And even goaltenders who haven't jumped but whose contracts are up for renewal are receiving undreamed of sums to stay put.

In the circumstances Dryden suggests a renegotiation of his own contract with his employers, but it turns out they have a deaf ear on both sides of the head. Foiled and quietly chagrined, Dryden uncomplainingly continues to guard Montreal's goal for another season, guides the Canadiens to another Stanley Cup, and between times completes his final year of law at McGill University. In the autumn of 1973, with still a year to go on his contract but now armed with a sheepskin in law, Dryden again introduces the subject of renegotiation, and when it turns out that his employers are once more prepared to enjoy the music while failing to appreciate the lyrics, he turns his back on the loftiest goaltending job on either side of the Iron Curtain and joins a Toronto law firm for a year of articling.

"In any line of work," he says later, blinking slowly behind big gold-rim glasses in a downtown Toronto tower, "if you see the guy next to you doing the same thing you do and getting twice as much for it, you're discontent. Maybe it's difficult for people to understand my situation because of the amounts of money involved, but, really, the principle is the same even after you go beyond a certain level. I mean, you might sign your first contract for a quarter the money you're making now, but you'd be happy with it because you know it's fair. Later, you might get a lot more money and be dissatisfied because you know it's unfair."

He reports that in the early days of retirement many people stopped him on the street, saying things like "Is it really true?" and "You're not going back?" and then walking away from him muttering, "This guy must be crazy." Then he grins shyly, "Maybe I am."

But wait. Crazy is just beginning.

As Ken Dryden plods through this year of purgatorial articling, earning $6,968 from a firm called Osler, Hoskin and Harcourt instead of $80,000 from the Canadiens, what he seems to be saying is that law is worth $73,032 more to him than the sweaty pursuit that made him famous. But what he's really saying is that the game means much more than money because no sooner is he settled into the law firm than he is out getting lumps and bruises on a hockey rink. No longer playing for tens of thousands of dollars with the world's champions as one of the great goaltenders, he turns in spare hours to play *for free* as one of the world's worst defencemen with the commercial-league bunch called Vulcan Industrial Packaging. In fact, it costs *him*; he lays down two dollars a week as his share of the fee for ice rental for a one-hour practice session every Friday night.

And any Sunday night during the winter of 1973-74 his hulking six-foot-four figure can be seen on the ice at a community rink called Lakeshore Arena. There, in the purple and gold trappings of Vulcan Packaging he glides about with ponderous strides like some prehistoric bird, No. 2 in a huge white plastic helmet, squinting through contact lenses, feet like twin watermelons in bulky black boots and long flat skates with closed pointed ends front and back, instruments of the puck-stopper's trade.

In his first game he is whacked over the eye for seven stitches. He rushes to a hospital nearby for hem-stitching and is back on the Vulcan bench before the game ends. In his second game he is dumped into the boards and misses the Friday night practice because of damaged ligaments on both sides of the collarbone. But he is there for Sunday's game, the injured shoulder strapped. When he comes to the bench for a rest, an army of small boys leans across a low enclosure to pat his padded shoulders, pluck at his sweater, lend high-pitched encouragement. "Hey, great," chirp the thin soprano voices. "Good shift, Ken, really great shift. Way to go." He gives them an occasional small smile, squinting and blinking, aware of the intent of their encouragement, then lurches to his feet for the next shift.

At twenty-six, Dryden is a man who likes new experiences and he knows goal is no challenge to him in this league. "I've never been a forward or a defenceman, even as a kid," he says. "I've always wanted to try it."

The spectre of a crippling injury that could ruin his return to pro hockey never occurs to him. By the fall of 1974 he is worth a fortune as an NHL goaltender in Montreal, but that fact means nothing in this commercial league in Toronto, and everyone playing with him understands that that is next year—this is this, and hockey is hockey.

One night he is dumped by a severe bodycheck; he turns a complete somersault and lands prone. He lays still. After a moment he comes to his knees, his hands supporting him, too, and shakes his head. Then he skates heavily back to his position. Later, he reflects on what has been, for him, a new experience, the somersault and the jolt of landing.

"It was very interesting," Dryden says. "It's not so bad at all. You're down, and then you're up and rushing on, and you think, 'So that's what it's like.' And, of course, Canadians have this long tradition, especially in hockey, of getting up and getting going, no matter how badly they're hurt. It's part of the game's tradition; you never show that you're hurt if you can help it, and if you can walk, why, then, of course you continue to play. I suppose people like to differentiate themselves, to find something unusual about themselves; this is a Canadian way of expressing it."

Punch Imlach, the former Toronto coach who became Buffalo's general manager, had a somewhat more succinct way of imparting his philosophy of injuries. "If he can fuckin' walk, he can fuckin' play," Punch used to say of the wounded, the halt and the lame he'd be compelled from time to time to send to the Leaf physiotherapist Karl Elieff, "but I don't want you sendin' him back to me unless he can fuckin' walk." A lot of people thought Punch had no compassion but, obviously, he was brimming with it.

There was a vivid illustration of this stoicism-under-duress in Stockholm in mid-September of 1972 when Team Canada, a collection of NHL players, was in the midst of its emotionally charged and marvellously matched eight-game series with the Russian national team. The NHLers spent nine days in Stockholm en route to Moscow, stopping off to grow accustomed to the larger playing surfaces of Europe in the Johanneshovs Isstadion, twelve feet wider and slightly longer than North American rinks. Between workouts they played two games with the Swedish national team to help celebrate the fiftieth anniversary of hockey in Sweden. Boston's Wayne Cashman and Sweden's Ulf Sterner crashed into the boards early in the second game and Sterner, bringing up his arms to protect himself in the crash, caught Cashman in the mouth with the blade of his stick. Blood spurted from Cashman's mouth. The stick had split his tongue down the middle. He gave no sign that the injury was painful, simply skated to the bench, stayed there for the rest of the period, and then skated with the other players toward the dressing room. Team doctors treated his swollen and inflamed tongue. The coach, Harry Sinden, told him to change into his street clothes, that there were several players on the large roster to fill his position. So Cashman changed and stood behind the bench as a spectator, and although his tongue continued to swell he refused to leave the rink for a hospital until the game ended. It's doubtful if half a dozen spectators were aware he'd been more than superficially injured.

By contrast, in the third period, Canada's Vic Hadfield, jostling with Lars-Erik Sjoberg in front of the Canadian net, high-sticked the Swede and cut his nose severely. Some of the world's great actors would be proud to duplicate Sjoberg's performance over the next five minutes. He waved off the team trainer and skated in small stilted steps toward the Swedish bench, blood streaming unchecked from the cut and dripping onto his yellow sweater with the three blue crowns. Nearing the bench he changed direction and skated slowly past the penalty box where Hadfield had gone as a matter of course, knowing he'd high-sticked his check. Hadfield damned nearly collapsed when Sjoberg dramatically waved one hand at him while pointing to his bleeding nose with the other.

Eventually Sjoberg reached his team's bench, then stood leaning against the boards for a moment, head down, before taking a seat. Play resumed. At the next whistle Sjoberg emerged slowly from the bench and started across the ice toward the dressing-room exit, holding a bloodied towel not to his nose but cradled in his hand near his face. The crowd cheered every stride, then poured high-pitched whistles of scorn upon Hadfield, the cad, who by now was frustrated to the point of throwing up. Sjoberg still had a drop to drain; he paused at the foot of a ramp before making his tortured way to the dressing room while a half dozen photographers caught the nose in every pose. Next day it made most of the front pages in Stockholm and Team Canada players became "barbarous animals". Ulf Sterner, whose stick had carved Cashman, had a by-line on a newspaper piece in which he called the Canadians "gangsters". Sterner is a guy who'd had a cup of coffee with the New York Rangers a few years earlier, then later failed again with the Chicago Cougars when the WHA came along. Meanwhile, the forgotten Cashman was having trouble breathing. By now there were nineteen stitches in his tongue and it had swollen so large in the hospital that he was being fed intravenously. Still, five nights later he was humming up and down his wing in the Moscow Sports Palace, jaw and elbows thrust defiantly outward, a graceful long-limbed man with wispy hair, keeping his mouth closed over a blackened tongue.

It's the tradition of the game as it's played in Canada that turns most hurt men mute. A year later when two members of that Swedish national team, Borje Salming and Inge Hammarstrom, made marvellous impressions as rookies with the Toronto Maple Leafs, other clubs' players took untiring runs at them, seeking to intimidate the "chicken Swedes". No such luck. Salming and Hammarstrom, performing in NHL rinks, absorbed every hurt and indignity without complaint or backward step.

Nothing unusual about the Cashman episode; hockey's had any number of hard tough men over the decades to whom physical warfare is endemic to their livelihood. Nor is it only those who live by the sword who die by it. Skinny little guys find their heads in the meat-grinder too. There's not a man among them who doesn't accept the likelihood of shattered bones, gaps in the gums and gut-stitched pelts from this tumultuous exercise they're engaged in, although no one should run off with the notion that *every* man who plays the game in the pros is fearless; indeed, some of them ride with fear as a companion, can be intimidated, and thereby generally ride along with a loser.

"There are guys who rush into corners determined to come out with the puck," says the solemn, talkative, analytical, little worrywart who runs the tempestuous Flyers of Philadelphia, the most penalized team in the history of the game. This is Freddie Shero, peering through dark hornrims from behind the Philly bench at the mayhem that almost always ensues when his orange-clad gang goes hunting. "On the other hand, there are guys who always make sure they're late arriving in the corners. Intimidation is a big part of the game. A lot of guys would be better off if they'd fight but they're afraid. If there's skating room they look just great and they score a lot of goals against the easy teams. But in tight, in the tough games, they freeze. It's a thing you're born with, and there's nothing a coach can do about it; you can't make chicken salad out of chicken shit, my friend." Freddie Shero taps his chest a lot when he talks. "They got to have it in here," he says whenever he taps it.

But size is not what determines what's inside a man's chest, although with people who skate around on skinny frames it's not often prudent to start challenging the enforcers. The trick is, however, not to back away when challenged, and not to expect that clean play alone will preserve the teeth, the bones, and the pelt. As Billy Harris discovered.

There is no finer gentleman anywhere than Billy Harris; quiet, polite, intelligent and six feet tall. But look quickly or you'll miss him for he is a mere hundred and fifty-seven pounds. Nevertheless, Harris lasted fourteen years in the pro game, living by his wits, and then turned to coaching the Toronto Toros in the WHA, his wavy stand of hair growing ever whiter though he would not be forty until mid-summer 1975. As a player he was rarely penalized. He turned ferocious one season with the Leafs in the late 1950s and piled up thirty-two minutes, which is nothing. Some guys on the Broad Street Bullies pick up thirty-two minutes just walking into their rink in Philadelphia.

At any rate, one night Billy Harris was minding his own business against Detroit, hoping to freeze the puck along the boards to force a face-off, jostling with Gordie Howe. Howe was squeezing him and the puck into the wood when Leaf defenceman Allan Stanley jammed against Howe. Harris was trapped in the middle, his arms pinned to his sides, and as Howe and Stanley brought up their sticks, shoving one another, Howe's stick cracked Harris across the right eye, above and below it, causing damage worth twenty-two stitches, and that's not all. A problem developed below the eye where hemorrhaging spread all through the cheek, and swelling pressed upward into the sac and blurred the vision. Harris didn't mind the broad cut above because the surgeon's skill soon had narrowed it to a slit, but by dawn of the following day the cheek where all the blood was trapped had grown increasingly painful. The kindly coach, Punch Imlach, told Harris to stay home in Toronto for treatment in the morning while the team flew off to Detroit for a return game with the Red Wings, and Harris went to the infirmary in mid-morning so that one of the team doctors, Jim Murray, could examine the eye. By then it was swollen completely shut, and the cheek had turned all shades of purple.

"We've got to bring down that swelling," Dr. Murray said.

"Yes," said Billy Harris.

"But I don't want to cut it," the doctor said.

"No," said Harris.

"I was thinking of Charlie," said the doctor.

"Oh," said Harris. "Charlie, eh?"

"Yes," said the doctor. "Do you mind?"

"I don't know," said Harris. "I've never tried him."

"No," said the doctor. "Neither have I."

"Will it work?" said Harris.

"We can try," said the doctor.

"Well," said Harris. "Okay then."

Now it turned out that the club trainer had been keeping this leech in a solution in a jar on the infirmary shelf, a leech the players had named Charlie. The doctor took Charlie from the jar with a pair of tweezers and placed him close to Billy Harris's eye. The leech reached over, examined the lump under and around the eye and then vacated the tweezers and clamped onto the lump.

Minutes passed.

"What's happening?" enquired Harris at length.

"Charlie's getting fatter," said the doctor.

"I can feel him pulsing," said Harris.

They walked to a mirror and stood staring, watching the leech pulse. The swelling in the eye was decreasing rapidly. The swelling in Charlie was increasing rapidly. By now the leech was almost round.

"I'll level with you, Bill," the doctor said. "I don't know how to get the damned thing off. Or when."

Then the problem was solved for them. Suddenly Charlie fell from the wound and lay on the dressing-room floor, dead. He had supped so long and so well that he had eaten himself to death.

Whereupon Harris and Murray put on their hats and coats and drove to the airport. That night in Detroit Billy Harris took his regular shift.

Sylvia Harris, Billy's wife, didn't mind his eye injury as much as a mouth injury he ran into later. At home in Toronto, Sylvia had been listening to the broadcast of a game in Boston. It was late in the game and the Leafs were leading the Bruins 5-2 when Sylvia decided to go to bed. She had to be up early to feed the baby and she knew the Leaf charter wouldn't get Bill home until the early hours of the morning.

At seven o'clock when the alarm awakened her she gave her sleeping husband a warm pat and got out of bed. She turned on the kitchen radio as she prepared the baby's formula. She heard the news and the weather and when the sports followed the man said the Leafs had beaten Boston 5-2. Sylvia Harris yawned. And then her mouth just stayed open.

"But it was a costly win for the Leafs," the man was saying. "They lost centre Billy Harris for at least a month. Late in the game Harris was hit by a flying puck and suffered a fractured jaw. He was taken to a Boston hospital for overnight observation."

Sylvia Harris fled to her bedroom. There was a body in the bed, the head buried in a pillow. She turned the head. The pillow was soaked in blood. She looked at the face. It belonged to her betrothed, all right, but what a mess. "My God," she cried. "Bill, Bill, what happened?"

What happened was that with only moments left on the clock in the Boston Garden, Harris endeavoured to check an attacking Bruin who was in the act of shooting. The zooming puck was merely ticked by Harris and, changing direction, it caught him full in the mouth, jamming his lower lip into his teeth and flattening three of the teeth at the gum line, laying them along his tongue, held in their moorings by strays of gum and gristle. He had gone to a hospital as the sportscaster had reported but he hadn't wanted to stay. He flew home with the other players, the pain dulled by pills. But their effect was wearing off as the plane touched down and when Harris got home he found a bottle of scotch. He sipped tentatively as the liquid explored the open wounds in his mouth, and paced the floor between sips. At six o'clock he tottered off to bed and fell into a painful sleep. By ten o'clock he'd had x-rays that showed the jaw wasn't fractured, only severely bruised and the lower gum mangled, and shortly afterwards he was in a dentist's chair having the roots of three teeth cleared away. The following evening Harris caught a flight to New York with the Leafs and played that night against the Rangers, a clever, clean, skinny stickhandler looking like a guy a good stiff check would break in two.

Injuries often send the men who manufacture equipment back to the drawing boards. The aforementioned Bobby Baun, whom teammate Eddie Shack kept running into, was responsible for two items of apparel that are now standard: metal toe caps in all hockey boots and small white plastic plugs that cover the rear points of all skates. Baun had so many broken toes—or, at least the normal ten toes were broken so many times thanks largely to Bobby Hull's slapshot—that he finally induced a manufacturer to come up with a piece of shoe equipment to protect his toes.

The play that ultimately produced plastic plugs for skate tips almost cost Baun his life. He was casually massaging the ears of Camille (the Eel) Henry one night in New York, trying to remove him from the danger area in front of Toronto's goal. Henry didn't do everything all that well for the Rangers but he had a wonderful facility for scooping rebounds into the net or deflecting shots past goaltenders. When Henry sprang for a loose puck in the goal-mouth that night Baun knocked him down and stood over him looking for fresh people to assault. But he didn't see a Ranger swerving up behind who crashed into him and spilled him over Henry whose feet were in the air. The rear tip of Henry's skate caught Baun in the throat as he fell, penetrating skin and muscle and coming to rest against the under side of his tongue. So much blood gushed from the wound and from Baun's mouth that he was fearful his jugular had been sliced. He pulled himself free of Henry's skate and wobbled to the bench. He stuffed a thick white towel against his throat and headed for the Garden infirmary. There, the Ranger team physician, Dr. Kazuo Yanagisawa, was playing gin rummy with three men, all of them puffing on cigars, filling the air with heavy layers of smoke.

Yanagisawa casually finished the hand of gin before turning to Baun standing in the middle of the room, the bloody towel clutched to his throat. With the cigar still clenched in his teeth, the doctor sewed up Baun. "There you go," he grunted, and turned back to the gin game. Baun returned to the bench.

That was near the end of the first period. By the end of the second Baun was having trouble breathing. The hole under his tongue was hemorrhaging and the blood was pressing against his windpipe. He was taking his turn on defence but by the end of the game he was feeling like last month's laundry. He passed up the couple of beers the boys usually gulped at a nearby bar before their bus took off for the airport, and went alone to the bus. He realized sitting there in the darkened bus that the hemorrhaging was gradually pushing his tongue down his throat, so he staggered to his feet, struggled to the door, started out of the bus, and collapsed at the foot of the steps.

It turned out that his defence partner, Tim Horton, had had enough beer and was returning to the bus early. Finding Baun he flagged a cab and got him to a hospital. The nurse on emergency was working on a ledger. She looked up briefly. "Stabbed, huh?" She continued writing.

By now the club president, Harold Ballard, a big florid bombastic guy with small patience, had caught up to Baun and Horton. He hailed another cab, found another hospital, and he and Horton led Baun into it. An intern cut under Baun's tongue and put a tube down his throat to help his wheezy breathing, but the incision induced more bleeding. Baun was put to bed and given three transfusions through the night and a drain plug was placed in his neck for air. By morning Baun was ready to take off; he reasoned that removal of the drain would reactivate the bleeding, which he needed like another hole in the neck, and he'd had enough of this road trip. He wanted to get home. Ballard, who'd sat with him through the night, found a men's shop and bought Baun a shirt to replace the blood-soaked one he'd worn into the hospital, and the two men walked out of the hospital, went to the airport and caught a flight home. They took a cab to the East General Hospital where Baun was greeted by his wife who'd just produced their third child. "This is nice," Baun croaked to Ballard.

That was a Monday morning. On Thursday the Leafs opened the playoffs. Playing right defence, and taking his regular turn, was Bobby Baun. Naturally.

All sorts of fascinating things happened to Baun during sixteen seasons plus in the NHL—with Toronto, with Detroit, with Oakland and, finally, with Toronto again. He tore ligaments in both knees, one requiring surgery. He broke two fingers. A thumb. A leg. A nose. A cheekbone, He lost teeth. He had a separated shoulder several times. His body was black and blue most of the time in winter. Until he got new shoes he broke all kinds of toes, of course. He stopped counting stitches early on, already past a hundred. At five foot nine, a black-browed, skimpy-haired fire-plug, he was just the right height to catch stray sticks and butt-ends and elbows in the eyebrows and nose from taller rangier forwards. Oddly, he found the simple act of falling on the ice caused more pain than most of his injuries. That's because he usually landed on his elbows. "They'd split from the inside out," he said once. "I'd get them sewed but they'd get infected and swell up like footballs. Then they'd have to be drained."

Once, in a practice, his teammate Frank Mahovlich whacked a slapshot with a stick that had a plastic blade. The stick exploded and a three-inch sliver of wood and plastic, longer and broader and harder than a sharp toothpick, penetrated the skin a quarter of an inch from Baun's eye, sliced through the side of his head behind his right sideburn, and reappeared behind his right ear. Some might say he was fortunate the sliver didn't slice through his eye but Baun never saw it that way. "Our reflexes are pretty good," he said matter of factly, speaking of hockey players generally.

Early in the 1972-73 season, Baun went into a corner in his fearless way to dispute Mickey Redmond's claim to the puck. Redmond caught him coming in, flailing with his arms high, and one arm caught Baun and flipped him. He landed heavily on his head and neck, severely straining some vertebrae. He'd had neck injuries before, and had worn an inflated neck brace upon occasion. This time the doctors told him he could incur permanent damage if he continued to play hockey. So he stopped. He went back to his wife and their five children and their thousand-acre farm, and now he raises corn and hay and has five hundred steers and two hundred heifers and cows to occupy the time he used to spend in hospitals.

Why did he always come back? "Oh, I don't know," he said mildly once. "Before expansion there were always far more players than there were jobs. If you didn't come back, some guy took your place and you'd wind up in the minors. I remember once that Moose Vasco of Chicago hit Larry Hillman on our club and Larry went from us to the Rochester farm and he didn't get back for five years."

Of all the injuries endured by Bobby Baun there was one in particular that perhaps best illustrates the nature of the unique and curious fibre that motivates so many hockey players. It was incurred on the night of April 23, 1964, in the Detroit Olympia in a game that, had it been won by the Red Wings, would have given them the Stanley Cup by four games to two. In the third period of that sixth playoff game, with the score tied 3-3, play was deep in Toronto territory. Gordie Howe rifled a low shot toward the net, hoping to use Baun as a screen to block goaler Johnny Bower's view. But Baun stopped the shot, taking the puck on the side of his leg just above the ankle bone. When the puck hit, Baun heard a sound like a small firecracker exploding. Moments later he moved into the face-off circle to oppose Howe in an important draw. The puck went to the corner from that face-off and Baun spun on his right leg to go for the puck. He heard a crack like a *loud* firecracker, felt fire race up his leg, and fell to the ice. He was taken to the dressing room on a stretcher. There, his stocking and pieces of soft padding were cut away from the ankle, which was already beginning to swell.

"Can I still play?" Baun asked Dr. Jim Murray. Baun is a low-key man, speaks softly. He didn't ask the question as a fiery-eyed college player might, all do or die. It was simply that he did not want to miss a very important part of a very important game.

"Well," the doctor said, fingering the swollen area, "there are no jagged edges."

"Can you freeze it?" Baun asked.

"I could."

"Will I hurt it more if you do?"

"I don't think so."

"Then you better freeze it."

Murray inserted the needle, freezing the area, and tightly taped the ankle, leaving a hole in the tape in the event further freezing were needed.

Baun returned to the ice for the remaining moments of the third period and with the score still 3-3 the teams rested and then took the ice again for sudden-death overtime. Baun was taking his regular turn at right defence. After nearly seven minutes of overtime he was playing the point at the Detroit blueline as the Leafs pressed, and when the puck came to him near the line he fired a low shot that found its way through jostling players into the corner of the Detroit net. Baun's goal sent the teams back to Toronto for the seventh and deciding game of the Stanley Cup final.

Dr. Murray packed ice around the ankle and fixed it firmly for the flight home. Baun walked on crutches to the bus, then from the bus to the plane, and then from the plane to his car at the Toronto airport. He stayed in bed all the next day. On the morning of the final game he drove to a friend's farm and talked about cattle. The conversation kept his mind away from thoughts of his ankle. His ankle burned sharply when he took his weight from his crutches and put it tentatively on his right leg. He adopted the attitude that his ankle was severely bruised, although, really, he knew better.

At six o'clock that evening Bobby Baun drove the forty-five miles to Maple Leaf Gardens where Dr. Murray was upset because Baun had not appeared for an appointment to have his leg x-rayed. Murray had phoned an orthopedic surgeon in Chicago, a friend of his, Dr. Bill Stromberg, and had asked him to come to Toronto. Now, in the absence of an x-ray picture, Stromberg probed the ankle thoroughly with expert fingers and said he thought it would carry the strain of one more game. Before the game, and between each period, the ankle was pierced with a hypodermic needle pressed into the tiny hole left by the careful taping. Baun played his regular shift. Toronto won the game 4-0 and with it the Stanley Cup, kept alive by the goal he'd scored in Detroit. In the morning Baun went into the hospital and the leg finally was x-rayed. As he'd known all along, ever since he'd heard the first small firecracker, the bone was fractured. It had been broken for more than sixty hours. The leg was placed in a cast from the heel to the knee. Baun wore the cast for two months that summer.

CHAPTER TWO: What Kind of a Crackpot Is a Goaltender?

Once, the goaltender's hutch was a pleasant place to pass a winter, a not overly strenuous retreat where a man had time to think. Guys like Tiny Thompson and Lorne Chabot and the squirt Roy Worters took their lumps, God knows, but in an era of forty-eight game schedules and small travel they usually had time to bend an elbow, put the feet up now and then, and rest their contusions between acts of derring do.

Then came rule changes that turned the rinks into shooting galleries. Goaltenders became the most vulnerable men in the game, emotional as well as physical victims of screened shots, deflections, five-man attacks and rush-hour traffic in every goalmouth. Later, expansion took jet lag and netminders to such outposts as California and Georgia. There was even a whole new league, the WHA, stretching from Quebec to Texas and across the Canadian prairies, and the schedules jumped to eighty games a season. The day of the *regular* goaltender was fast disappearing; only a rare Tony Esposito or Bernie Parent among a legion of goalers that had grown to more than sixty members were physically and mentally tough enough to handle the job in extended stretches. And even they were compelled to take occasional time off to rest an aching back, a gaping cut, or a tortured mind.

On a delightful winter day, cold and bright, in early 1974, Eddie Johnston sits on a rubbing table in the Maple Leaf dressing room, his legs dangling and his burgeoning pot nicely contained by the wide band of his jockstrap. As a goaltender growing long in the tooth at thirty-eight, however, E.J. is reflective. He is recalling an October night in 1967 when he was Boston's goaltender and the Bruins were visiting the Detroit Olympia, taking their pre-game warm-up. He remembers being aware of two pucks. Bobby Orr cradled one, moving in for a practice shot. Another player, E.J. has forgotten who, was farther out, across the rink. Johnston set himself for Orr. Then he flicked his eyes to the second puck, not turning his unmasked face, simply stealing a glance. In that split-second Orr cranked a slapshot and that was the end of hockey for Eddie Johnston for seven weeks.

Now he fingers his temple, his legs swinging idly. "It hit me here," he says. "It knocked me down. I was in a hospital in Dee-troit for three days and then they flew me to the Massachusetts General in Boston. Players came around for the first couple of days and then quit; I didn't know they were in the room. My weight went from one ninety-four to one fifty-five in that first week. There was a blood clot at the back of my head. They kept taking me to the operating room in case the clot moved and they had to drill a hole. They never had to, though. When I got back playing I put on a mask, you better believe it."

The black-haired heavy-shouldered goaltender, acquired from Boston by the Leafs in the summer of 1973 after eleven seasons with the Bruins, taps himself solemnly on the head for luck—knocking wood, you see—and says he hasn't had a serious injury upstairs since that night when Orr knocked him senseless. Not that he needed any new facial adornment; by then, his nose had been broken seven times, he'd picked up 175 stitches in his face, and he'd almost lost an ear lobe. It was sliced by a flying puck and left dangling by a thread of skin. It was stitched back on and now it fulfils every purpose ever designed for the lobe of an ear.

From a goaltender's viewpoint, the mask is the most revolutionary development in hockey history. Without it, there is little question the species would have grown extinct, and hockey would have become a sort of basketball on ice, topping even roundball's outrageous scores. The threat was very real until a November night in 1959 when Jacques Plante of the Canadiens defied his coach and hung a mask over a bent and bleeding nose, pumping life back into the netminding trade.

By then, goaltenders were undergoing strains that had been unknown to the Tiny Thompsons and Lorne Chabots who had gone before with their life-time leases on the cages they guarded. In their time, goalers got their work done in rocking chairs and substitutes were next to superfluous. Lester Patrick is still revered for his part in the Stanley Cup final of 1928 for leaving the Rangers' coaching bench and playing goal for part of a game when his man Chabot was disabled by a puck in the eye. He went because there was nobody else; it never occurred to the Rangers to burden the budget with an additional goaltender, or, if it did, they thought better of it.

In the 1940s the war disrupted the careers of later iron men such as Turk Broda, Frank Brimsek, Prince Charlie Rayner and Sugar Jim Henry but, more significantly, one spectacular rule change started making fierce inroads on the goaltender's life expectancy: the centre red line, introduced in 1943. It turned the game around; it permitted teams to pass the puck onside half the length of the rink, opening up what had been a tight, sock'em game and setting the stage for five-man offences keyed to chilling slapshots through mazes of players cruising and crowding in front of screened-off goaltenders. Compared to goalers, sitting ducks led leisurely lives.

Development of the slapshot by which people like Bobby Hull and Bobby Orr came close to turning the puck into a speeding bullet was the final straw for the beleaguered goaltenders. Well, *nearly* the final straw; Chicago's Stan Mikita added a refinement. By using a stick whose blade carried a half-moon curve, Mikita began to produce an action on the puck similar to that of a knuckleball's, dipping and flipping as it flew through the air, practically a frisbee in flight. Then the league stepped in to limit the degree of curve on the stick before Mikita and his emulators produced a full-blown boomerang. That cut the flipflops but it didn't eliminate them altogether. "The bastards cheat," says Eddie Johnston. "They still sneak the odd stick in."

Still, the mask has made survival possible; without it, the goaltending job would approach the impossible. It propelled patriarchs like Johnston, Jacques Plante, Terry Sawchuk, Les Binkley, Glenn Hall and a few others into the expansion era of 1967, abetted by the policy of alternating goaltenders. However, it is not an all-purpose panacea; it has not solved the problem of direct hits. Dunc Wilson, one of three goalers employed by Toronto through the 1973-74 season, says the jolt of a puck cracking into a mask is stunning, carrying the impact of a sledgehammer. Wilson remembers a night when he was with Vancouver being knocked out by the first shot of a game; it hit him right between the eyes and kayoed him, or at least its concussion did.

But direct hits leave the facial bones intact, so only the rarest of big-league birds skate into the goal-mouth unmasked these days. Indeed, by the spring of 1974 only two were left: Joe Daley, whose

31

nomadic career took him from Pittsburgh to Buffalo to Detroit to the Winnipeg Jets; and Andy Brown, who toiled infrequently for Detroit and then Pittsburgh. Gump Worsley, another nomad, held off until he reached forty-five in a marvellous career with the Rangers, the Canadiens and the Minnesota North Stars. Then in the fall of 1973, coming out of one of many retirements to give another season to Minnesota, he finally strapped one on.

Eddie Johnston can't agree with the side of Gump that went maskless so long, and he simply feels Brown and Daley have lost their marbles.

"Only a crackpot plays without a mask today," E.J. insists. "The slapshot has changed everything. It used to be there were maybe half a dozen big shooters in the league but now nearly everybody can crank it. There's no finesse; they just come across the line and unload. Nearly everything's tip-ins and deflections now. Hull has the biggest shot in our league—Dennis. He shoots a heavy puck, a bruiser. Lemaire and Cournoyer can crank it for Montreal. Hadfield's is hard and so is Gilbert's in New York. Cowboy Bill Flett has an excellent shot, something like Dennis but from the other side of the rink. Pappin can shoot, the son of a bitch; a lot of those Chicago guys can. I guess Orr can rifle it as good as anybody, and Hodge bothers you because he doesn't know where the hell it's going."

Goaltenders were a long time accepting the mask partly because pride prevented them from hiding their beautiful kissers even while pucks were mashing them. Usually it took a serious injury such as Eddie Johnston's Orr-inflicted concussion to persuade a guy he needed help, either a mask or a psychiatrist. The slapshot and deflections off it, both lethal weapons, eventually convinced most of the species that covering up was necessary, but it was still ten years after Plante wore the first one in public that they became commonplace.

Truth to tell, Plante was *not* the first masked man although it was certainly he who popularized the plastic adornment and persisted in wearing it. But thirty years before Plante's time, Clint Benedict experimented in the Montreal Maroons net with a mask made of leather that left only his eyes exposed. Benedict, the Praying Netminder, dropped to his knees once too often in a game against the Canadiens in January 1930 and caught a blast from Howie Morenz directly on the mask. The shot slashed open Benedict's forehead and smashed shut his nose, and it sidelined him for seven weeks. By then Benedict was an old hand at the puck-stopping trade; he'd been at it as an NHLer for seventeen years during which his teams had won the Stanley Cup four times, three of them the Ottawa Senators and once the Maroons. He was thirty-four by then and soon after, when his improvised mask was jammed against his tender nose in a goal-mouth collision, he decided to call his hockey pursuits to a halt.

And so goaltenders went maskless for another twenty-nine years. Then, on November 2, 1959, Plante got permission to wear one from his flint-hearted coach Toe Blake, and he got it the hard way. He was with the Canadiens then, trying out masks in practice, but Blake had refused to let him wear one in games, presumably on the grounds that somebody might think his goaltender lacked courage. Far better that Plante accumulate facial stitches until he resembled a baseball than *that*.

At any rate, the Canadiens went into Madison Square Garden on the night in question, and Andy Bathgate of the Rangers rifled a puck at the Montreal cell that smashed Plante's nose. Seven stitches were taken in his bloodied horn. No spare goaltender, of course, so there was a delay while Plante was hemstitched. Because of the wound and the swelling, Blake didn't protest—well, he didn't threaten to throw Plante out of the rink—when Plante reached resolutely into his locker and brought out his mask. Luckily, the Canadiens won that night, so Plante was allowed to wear the mask in succeeding games. Nothing so influences the inflexible judgment of an inflexible coach as victory.

Still, physical pain is endemic to this game and for a long time masks were resisted; they represented a concession in this long heritage of toughness. Eddie Johnston remembers that he picked up three of his seven broken noses in one stretch of ten days. "I broke it in New York and took eighteen stitches. There used to be this little doc at the Garden there, Yanagisawa, who we all called Kamikaze, and he'd just reach up and give the nose a quick twist to bang it back into place. The next night in Boston I broke it again for twelve more and then we went into Montreal and I broke it again. But did I have sense enough to put on a mask? No way."

Johnston's former goaltending sidekick, Gerry Cheevers, believes he understands this enormous disdain of pain as something beyond vanity—although he readily admits to the vanity, too. "Goaltending is a very lonely and difficult task so we tend to be very proud bastards," says Cheevers, who jumped from the Bruins to the Cleveland Crusaders when the WHA came along carrying money in wheel-barrows. "Everybody says we're a different breed and I guess they're right. But sooner or later, when you start adding up the scars, you realize if you don't start wearing a mask you may not survive." Cheevers has the wildest mask in hockey. He paints the stitches on it that he knows he'd be carrying in his face if he hadn't switched. Or used to; after he hit 250 stitches the mask became so crowded with chicken tracks that he gave up the practice.

Facial injuries were common enough for the veteran Toronto Toro goaltender Les Binkley in the days before he wore a mask. Now he has difficulty remembering them and finds it impossible to recall who inflicted them. Bink is not a man whose trade you'd quickly identify when he's not in his working clothes. An accountant, maybe, or the clerk in bedding. He's a skinny guy with a long pale face cast in sadness and he wears hornrims (contact lenses when he's playing). By the spring playoffs of 1974 with the Toros he was an eldering old lad of thirty-nine, talking quietly in a laconic way. Queried once about his injuries before he began to wear a mask, he studied his questioner as though he'd been asked to reveal his net worth. He was sitting on a rubbing table in the Toro dressing room wearing a set of long johns, his glasses and a toothpick which rested at the corner of his mouth through fair words and foul.

"Couple broken noses," he said at length.

"How did they happen?"

"Shots."

"Do you remember who shot?"

"Let's see. No, I guess I don't. Broke a jaw once."

"How did that happen?"

"Shot."

"Have you got all your teeth?"

"Most of 'em."

"How many are missing?"

"Oh, a few." He placed an index finger against an upper bridge at the front. "These two," he said.

"But wearing a mask ended all that?"

"You kiddin'? First mask I had, a shot cut me for fifteen right below the eye. I switched to a different type mask. Course, who knows, without that mask maybe I lose the eye."

Binkley's buoyant sidekick in the Toro net that spring, Gilles Gratton, too young to know goaltenders didn't always wear masks, fought off muscle strains by doing a fifteen-minute program of calisthenics before each game and each practice, including a series of upside-down pushups. In upside-down pushups Gratton retired to the gentlemen's shower and stood on his head in a stall, raising and lowering himself with his arms.

"Clears the brains," explained the twenty-one-year-old Gratton, a tousle-haired boy from LaSalle, Quebec. "Sometimes I bring the body to the rink but the head she is somewhere else."

All goaltenders undergo a kind of tension that's unique in sports. The very nature of their work prevents them from giving free rein to their emotions. Defencemen can rid themselves of tension by knocking down an opposing forward, and forwards can tear up and down dodging defencemen, offsetting pressure with physical outlet. Goaltenders stand there. They have time to think.

"They look impassive but they boil inside," Muzz Patrick used to say. Patrick coached the Rangers for a couple of seasons after a boisterous career. "They play a different game, you know. The closest approach might be the catcher in baseball, but at least he does some things that *are* baseball; goes up to hit, chases pop flies. But the goaltender does nothing that the other hockey players do. Except for his jersey he doesn't even dress the same."

Lloyd Percival used to say that for twelve hours before a Stanley Cup game goaltenders carry a tension load an average citizen faces only two or three times in a life-time. Percival was director of a national research organization called Sports College, ran an incredibly sophisticated health club, and was an internationally recognized authority on the stresses and strains of the games people play. He said that through tests and interviews over a ten-year period his researchers concluded that it's the same tension load as carried by a patient before an operation or a man in an interview for a job vital to him.

One of the first goalers to succumb to the shakes after the centre red line turned the tranquil ponds into nut houses was Frank McCool, an anguished chattel of the war-time Maple Leafs who ran up a record three straight shutouts over Detroit in the 1945 Stanley Cup playoffs. The Leafs scored only four goals in the first three games yet managed to win them all, with a large assist going to the grim McCool. But each tight fit brought him corresponding misery for he was nursing an ulcer.

The series went seven games when Detroit came back to win three in a row themselves, and the deciding game was played in the Olympia. Halfway through McCool called time and skated to the Toronto bench, white-faced. He walked past the coach Hap Day, clomped to the Leaf room and sat in front of his locker, his elbows on his thighs, and stared at the floor. As Day arrived McCool reached for a bottle of stomach powder, mixed it in a paper cup, gulped it down and stared some more.

"How about it, Frank?" Day asked.

McCool didn't answer.

"There's nobody else," reminded Day.

McCool nodded. Then he got to his feet. "Okay," he said. Few men walking the last mile ever went more reluctantly. Halfway through the third period Toronto got a goal and McCool hung on until the end, bent double and clutching his stomach whenever action moved to Detroit's end. That was the only full season for McCool who'd played all fifty league games and thirteen more in the playoffs. The next season he lasted twenty-two games. When Turk Broda returned from the army McCool retired happily.

By then coaches becoming aware of the growing strain on their anguished serfs began handling them differently than they did normal humans. Tommy Ivan was excessively careful in pre-game conversations with Terry Sawchuk when they were at Detroit. "I used to sit beside him before we went on the ice," Ivan related. "He'd shake his head unconsciously, a little twitch, over and over. I'd put my hand on his arm, and I'd talk quiet about anything but hockey."

Goaltenders have snapped under tension in public. One night in Montreal Dave Trottier scored for the Maroons on a long shot that eluded Wilf Cude in the Canadien goal. Trottier circled the net after his shot, laughed in Cude's face and pointed to the puck lying behind him. Cude took off in pursuit of Trottier, swinging his big goaler's stick around his head, an ice-bound helicopter. However, as he'd missed Trottier's shot, so he missed Trottier's head. Finally the laughing Maroon was out of range and fellow Canadiens led Cude mumbling back to his cage.

The most celebrated victims of high tension in the 1950s were Bill Durnan and Gerry McNeil, both of whom quit the game rather than face another season in the padded cells. Both had big careers with the Canadiens, a hard place to work, Durnan as one of the all-time all-timers. He was a big man with great hands, built along the rangy lines of a latter-day Habitant, the six-four Ken Dryden. Durnan survived seven seasons with the Canadiens, rarely missing a game, won the Vezina Trophy a record six times, and was No. 1 among NHL goaltenders with six all-star elections to the first team. However, after he'd won both prizes again in 1950 he called a halt to the whole thing.

"The Vezina got to be a matter of personal pride after I'd won it a couple of times," Durnan said. Originally this bauble was awarded to the goaler who allowed the least goals over a season, but as the goaltending mortality rate rose the wording was changed to accommodate the man who played the most games in goal for the *team* allowing the least goals. "The thing was always hanging over my head. Every time I blew a soft shot I suffered. The fans were murder, too. Winning is great in Montreal; losing is a federal offence."

Durnan set himself in one game to stop a routine shot by Reggie Hamilton, a Toronto defenceman who needed a seeing- eye dog to find the net. The sliding puck hit an ice chip, changed direction, hopped, and avoided Durnan's outstretched foot. Hamilton tried the same shot later and Durnan was taut as a violin string bracing for the stop, replaying the earlier accident.

"I was ready for that puck to hit any piece of ice in the building," Durnan remembered. "So what happened? It didn't hit a damned thing; it went through my feet into the net again. I didn't sleep all night. I played the two shots over and over and I made the right move every time. Then I'd think about it and start making the stops all over again."

Gerry McNeil was twenty-four when Durnan retired after the 1950 playoffs, and he was the regular Canadien goaltender for four seasons. In the spring of 1954 an injury took McNeil out of a few games and rookie Jacques Plante came up from the Buffalo farm to fill in. But Plante was hot and kept the job even when McNeil was ready. In the playoffs, though, Jake the Snake grew erratic against Detroit. When the Wings won three of the first four games Hab coach Dick Irvin called back McNeil who beat the Wings twice to square the series. In the seventh game Detroit's Tony Leswick fired a long shot in overtime. McNeil set himself to take the puck on his chest but his all-star defenceman Doug Harvey, six feet in front of him, reached out to catch it. The puck struck his hand, banked off and squirted into the net to end the series. McNeil played that shot all night, as Durnan had before him, and through most of the summer too. By fall he'd decided he didn't need the aggravation; he retired.

One thing Durnan remembered for years about playing goal was the sheer physical effort involved. "It'd be tiring for most people simply to *stand* through a game carrying about thirty-five pounds of soaking equipment. We were up and down like yo-yos."

Indeed they were—and are today. The nature of the job compels its tenant to hurl himself, legs and arms asprawl, to the rock-hard ice as many as thirty times in a sixty-minute game, then spring erect the next split second in the uncertain hope somebody isn't about to clunk him on the head with a frozen rubber cannon ball moving 120 miles an hour. Acrobatic goaltenders don't move so much as they explode into human pinwheels; down the glove, up the arm, over the stick, up the pads in a diving sprawl, all in incredibly swift succession.

"Another thing was the heat," Durnan often recalled of his seven years in purgatory. "In the spring the temperature in those buildings would climb into the eighties. If a game went into overtime a guy might be on his feet for three hours. I used to lose five to eight pounds every game; one playoff game I lost seventeen."

That was a Stanley Cup final in 1947 when Toronto's Gus Bodnar scored after seventeen minutes of overtime, ending an ordeal for Durnan in which he'd stopped seventy-two shots—to twenty-one by Leaf Turk Broda. Broda is still remembered as the most phlegmatic and one of the very best playoff goaltenders of all time. But he's perhaps even better remembered as the scapegoat of owner Conn Smythe's ploy early in 1950 when the irascible little boss was looking for ink. He blamed a Leaf slump on overweight lazy players and zeroed in on one of the few men in hockey who was fat when he was thin, the bulging Broda, who figured he was reasonably svelte at one ninety-seven. Smythe announced Broda was out of the line-up until he hit one ninety. It was an off-day for the newspapers at a diet-conscious moment in world history, so the story got a good spread. Unaccountably, as with a Susann novel, the public picked it up, diet charts everywhere, Turk's wife being interviewed for a calorie-by-calorie report on her husband's crash diet, pictures of Turk in steam baths, on stationary bikes, in whirlpools, on rowing machines, looking thoughtful. It lasted a week—during which, by an astonishing coincidence, the Leafs happened to be idle—and one day the *Toronto Star* came out with two-inch type on the front: BRODA HITS 190. The world was younger then.

By far the best goaltenders all through the 1950s and halfway into the Sixties were Terry Sawchuk, Glenn Hall and Jacques Plante, each of whom endured untold misery, both real and imagined, and none of whom had anything more in common with the others than their scars and their skills. In the fourteen seasons from 1951 when Sawchuk was the No. 1 goaler until 1964 when Hall was named, one or the other of this disparate trio made first-team all-star eleven times. Hall was the top selection five times and the others three times each. Also, in those fourteen years one or the other was the second-team pick ten times. But, oh, how they suffered.

Hall always hated the job. He endured twelve years with Detroit and Chicago and when expansion came in 1967 he took on four more seasons with St. Louis, and the only thing that kept him in the game, he said over and over, was the money. He was a scrawny-looking lanky jack-in-the-box with a pale drawn face and black hair that grew ever thinner in the late stages of his long ordeal. It was a rare night that he didn't vomit before a game. Rudy Pilous, his coach at Chicago in 1961, once recalled a particularly tense game against the Canadiens in front of the 20,000 lunatics who, then as now, filled every available seat and aisle in the Chicago Stadium, frequently littering the ice with debris. After one stoppage, while workmen impassively scooped up more trash, play could not be resumed; the Chicago net was vacant not only of overshoes and brassieres and programs but also of its regular tenant Glenn Hall. It turned out that he'd taken advantage of the delay to go bring up more lunch in the Hawk powder-room back of his cage and down a flight of stairs.

A few intrepid souls were wearing masks by then but Hall wasn't among them. Indeed, he didn't become a masked marvel until his last two seasons at St. Louis. He'd tried them before that, but couldn't find one that permitted him to see the puck at his feet. Maskless, he set a consecutive-games record that will never be approached—552 games without a break, 502 league games and fifty playoffs. By 1974, most goaltenders were looking for $100,000 salaries if they played 552 consecutive *minutes*.

In that stretch, Hall was dealt a dreadful blow in his second year with Detroit during a 1957 Stanley Cup semi-final against Boston. Vic Stasiuk zinged a rising shot at him just as somebody floated past his line of vision. The puck hit him in the mouth and he went down and out, cold as a Manitoba winter. He was carried to the infirmary and stretched on a table as a doctor bent to peer at the carnage below Hall's nose. When Hall came to, his eyes were blackening. He explored his mouth with a tentative sweaty paw.

"How many'll it take, doc?" he mumbled through the mashed flesh.

"A few, I'm afraid; you really caught one."

"Well," said Hall resignedly, "let's get it over with."

The doctor used no anaesthetic as he probed with his stitching needle; they never do. The theory is that the nerve endings around fresh cuts are already numbed. The doctor worked for half an hour. Then Hall climbed to his feet, wearing twenty-three new stitches in his bruised and swollen mouth. He put on his big mitts, picked up his stick, and clomped to the arena. The crowd stood applauding for nearly three minutes as he took a few long lobs from teammates to adjust himself, and then he finished the game.

At forty-four in the spring of 1973, closing out his career with the Bruins after noble service in Montreal, New York, St. Louis and Toronto, Jacques Plante was one of the most remarkable athletes of his time, not only outside where his muscles were lean and supple and tough as cable, but inside his head, too, where his brain ticked away like a self-winding watch, inventive, alert, questing.

There was nothing accidental about Plante's unusual success at that stage of his life; it was simply the product of a remorseless dedication to its physical and mental demands. To prolong his hockey life, he followed a routine as inflexible as the fiberglass mask he invented. In ten years with the Canadiens Plante won the Vezina Trophy six times and drove everybody crazy. His employers called him a hypochondriac. But Jacques said no, he really did get those funny itches and rashes and plugged noses from things like the material in his underwear and mysterious pollutants in the air. In New York, Emile Francis used to stare at him strangely, and finally sent him off to the farm club in Baltimore where at least Francis would be safe. Jacques retired for three years. Expansion brought him back and they loved him in St. Louis where he and Glenn Hall even combined for a Vezina Trophy. Scotty Bowman, the coach then, scratched his head as he pondered Plante and decided the best thing to do was send him to Toronto where at least Bowman would be safe. Toronto absolutely adored him. In forty games he compiled an unbelievable 1.88 and made the second-team all-stars behind Eddie Giacomin, perhaps in a miscarriage of justice; Giacomin's goals-against figure was 2.15 in forty-five games. In the spring of 1973 Toronto was going nowhere and Boston needed a goaltender. Since Plante was forty-four and had already been around forever, the Leafs were delighted to get Eddie Johnston and a first-round draft choice from the Bruins for good old, crazy old Jacques.

But crazy like a fox. Plante was a meticulous student of the game itself and of any game in progress. He had a mathematician's grasp of the angles of approach to the net, and when a puck-carrier confronted him Plante knew precisely how much open net was available and stationed himself to reduce the daylight to its absolute minimum.

"You never beat Plante with a flukey goal," Gerry Cheevers said once. "You only beat him where you should beat him—on the far side, or wherever there was that extra half-inch or inch to shoot at."

Plante paid his dues to the goaltenders' union. Before he covered his handsome dark features with his mask he had broken his nose four times, his cheekbones twice, his jaw once and had picked up a hairline skull fracture, a concussion and two hundred stitches in his face. He also had four leg operations for removal of cartilages from both knees.

Plante's speech was faintly accented with a French flavour and he often delivered long and detailed monologues on the art of puck-stopping in a sort of wide-eyed wonderment, as though he, too, was astonished by what he heard, a man awed by a miracle. He knew such things as whether rival players had black tape or white or none on their stick-blades.

"The black tape? Ah, if there's black tape on the stick, the black puck is harder to find in that fuzzy background, eh? So you must be ready when he shoot to look for the puck in the black tape. If you know he's a man with white tape, you know you will find the puck sooner. The same with no tape, yes?"

Plante kept his wife, Jacqueline, and their two boys home in Montreal while he lived and cooked alone in apartments in the towns where he played after the Canadiens sent him away. He'd sit on a couch with one leg on an Ottoman. Strapped to his shoe was a sixteen-pound lead weight. He'd read three pages of a book, then pause to raise the leg three times, then three more pages, then three more raises. Then he switched the weight to the other foot and, if necessary, he'd switch the book when he'd read it. At one point he was reading two books alternately, Jean-Jacque Marie's biography of Stalin in French and Mary Barelli Callaghan's biography of Jacqueline Kennedy in English.

"Lifting the leg is very boring," Plante would explain. "The reading takes away the boredom. Since I am reading, I make sure I am learning. I like biographies best—Eisenhower, Churchill, Kennedy, Lenin, Khrushchev, Marx, Mao, Lester B. Pearson, all of them."

Plante had a reason for everything he did.

"Feel," he'd instruct, indicating his thigh. It felt like a thigh. Suddenly he'd tighten the muscles and lift the sixteen-pound weight. The muscles of the thigh became pieces of steel.

"Pulled groin and hamstring muscles are the goaltender's most common injuries, eh?" Jacques would say, his eyes wide at the wonder of it all. "This prevents them."

Until he moved to Toronto Plante could not survive in the air of Toronto. Coaches tried various ways of getting him into Toronto at the last possible moment so that he'd breathe only a minimum of air he felt befouled his bronchial tubes. Once, Montreal's Toe Blake sent him to the Westbury Hotel while the rest of the Canadiens stayed at the Royal York. Did Plante feel better the next day?

"No," said Plante in his wide-eyed manner. "I slept well but I dreamed I was at the Royal York. When I woke up I was plugged."

When Plante was traded to Toronto he took an apartment in the extreme north section of the city where the air was sufficiently pure for him to retain life.

Of all the masters of this strange craft, none ever suffered more ups and down than Terry Sawchuk, whose trials were awesome during a twenty-year career at Detroit, Boston, Detroit again, Toronto, Los Angeles and New York. Injuries, illness, accidents and medical operations plagued him. His weight once soared to 229; he was admittedly overweight but a few years later he stepped on the scales after a particularly enervating playoff game, his body a mass of blue and yellow and purple welts and bruises, and the needle stopped at 157, a spread of seventy-two pounds on a five-eleven frame. He had some 400 stitches in his face and head before he adopted a mask in 1962, three of them in his right eyeball. He broke bones regularly, had concussions, arthritis, charley horses, mononucleosis. Surgery was necessary one time when he suffered a collapsed lung in a car accident. He developed a spinal condition called lordosis that was so painful he could sleep only in two-hour stretches. He believed he had suffered a stroke in 1966 when his left side went numb. It turned out to be two herniated discs in his back. An operation could have ended his career but he had it done anyway, and it didn't. He was believed to be on the brink of a nervous breakdown in 1957; he took time off, of course, and was back in the cage the following season, a morose, nervous, short-tempered young man who died at forty in May of 1970 after emergency surgery to remove a collection of blood from his liver. This, in turn, had followed an incident in which he and his teammate on the Rangers then, Ron Stewart, had wrestled on the lawn of a house they shared at Long Beach, Long Island. They'd been drinking and had begun horsing around, not in anger, and had tumbled to the grass. A grand jury ruled the death accidental, said no blows had been struck, and absolved Stewart.

I knew Sawchuk fairly well; I'd written a few pieces about him and we'd shared a few beers when he was with Detroit. The last time I saw him was only a few weeks before his death. He was leaving the Boston Garden after a game between the Bruins and the Rangers. It was the first time I'd seen him in two or three years, and our relationship had always been cordial. So I hailed him and went through the crowd to shake hands. I could see then that he didn't recognize me so I mentioned my name. His face contorted. "Won't you sons of bitches ever leave me alone?" he said, wheeling. "*Fuck off!*" He disappeared in the crowd, an anguished man.

CHAPTER THREE: Orr and Shore: Who Could Ask For Anything More?

By the purest coincidence the two best defencemen in the history of hockey, Eddie Shore and Bobby Orr, played the same position on the same team: right defence for the Bruins.

Shore had nothing like Orr's finesse and Orr nothing like Shore's power. Essentially, Shore's job was to stop attacks, Orr's to mount offences. On the occasions when Shore took the puck he was a great straight-ahead rusher, ox-strong. When he crossed the rival blueline he'd shoot the puck past the defencemen to the corners, then bull his way past them and go after it, battling for it there, trying to get it to his forwards in front of the net.

Orr plays *defence* when the moon is blue. When he isn't lugging the puck out of his own end in fluid twisting rushes, he is passing off in his own zone, flipping the puck rink-wide to his defence partner or gliding it ahead diagonally to a moving forward. His forte is a devastating shot from the enemy's blueline on power plays, a slapshot with a quick release that finds its own way to the net or is tipped by men at the goalmouth. At Orr's most boisterous he never knew the night he could knock a man bow-legged with a body-check; Shore was knee-deep in people he'd knocked bow-legged, a balding scar-face, breathing hard.

They were, in short, vastly different people playing vastly different games. Shore played when the defenceman's job was protective, knocking guys into the seats upon occasion, into the streets when possible, and of course being knocked there now and then himself. Defencemen rarely scored as many as ten goals a season. They weren't expected to; it wasn't their line of work. When they got the puck they often rushed with it, as Shore did, piling up assists, but more often they fed it to teammates in their own zone and then stood awaiting the next wave of attackers. In Orr's era nobody stands waiting for anything except maybe an airplane. It has become go, go, go, and Orr is the go, go, goingest of them all.

Defencemen, all defencemen, engaged in a great deal more bodily contact in Shore's time than in Orr's. There was less boarding then; indeed, the rules didn't allow it. Defencemen had to stand up to incoming attackers and stop them with tough hip-checks that often somersaulted them to the ice. And when big forwards were hurtling through, elbows high and sticks higher, defencemen took as much as they gave out. Attackers and defenders actually *hammered* one another; they didn't pinch people into the boards and hold them there until the play moved on. All that came later.

So it was a more physical game in the 1930s than forty years later when mobility was the essential ingredient. The drain in the Thirties was not the 1970s' strain of rushing both ways at top speed; it was the sheer man-to-man pounding. The difference was something like that between basketball and football, both demanding games physically but in different ways. This is not to say the game was more difficult or less demanding in the 1930s, only that it was different.

In his milieu, Shore was the master, a man who could deliver punishment and who, perhaps more notably, could absorb it. No one is quite sure how many injuries he endured in his fourteen-year career, not even Shore himself, but some statisticians claim he picked up 964 stitches in his face and body. He broke his hip, his collarbone and had a spinal vertebra cracked and displaced, putting him in traction for six months. His nose was broken at least ten times, his jaw five times, and he lost most of his teeth. Once, his ear was mangled in a collision, and the club doctor told him he didn't know how he could save it. Shore stormed from the Garden and trudged through swirling snow, searching out a doctor's shingle. He entered two offices but left when the physicians affirmed the opinion of the club doctor. Then he found one who said he'd try to save it. He wanted to give Shore an anaesthetic.

"Just give me a mirror, doc," Shore said. "I want to be sure you sew it on right."

In 1971 when Shore was in his late sixties he still cast a lean tough athletic shadow, with a huge pair of hands and wrists and forearms. He could drive a golf ball out of sight. He was taken to court in November that year by neighbours who swore out a complaint that he was annoying them by his golf, amplified music and bright floodlights. They claimed Shore was driving golf balls into a canvas net at all hours of the day and night. He desisted, a singular man with a long big-jawed face that was *unmarked*, the face that had absorbed hundreds and hundreds of stitches.

"I kept it smooth by rubbing the scars every day," he said once. "It takes five to seven years for a scar to heal, and the way I did it was to massage it."

Even in 1974 when he was closing on seventy-two Shore was a formidable figure. In June he attended the NHL's summer meetings in Montreal and, sitting in a hospitality suite in the Queen Elizabeth Hotel there one night, he tired of the comments of a minor-league coach, Aut Erickson, that hockey had passed him by. He warned Erickson to stop taunting him. When the warning passed unheeded Shore nailed the coach, who at thirty-six was half his age, with a right to the chin. Eyewitness reports said Shore also landed a left before Erickson hit the floor.

By then, Shore had survived three heart attacks and cancer of the bowel, and he was still active as the franchise owner of the Springfield Kings of the American Hockey League. Shore bought the Springfield club, then called the Indians, in 1940 for $40,000 when he was closing out his NHL career. In that final season he made an arrangement with the Boston general manager Art Ross that he'd play home games for both clubs, the Bruins and the Indians. Then, because he was the owner of the Indians, he wanted to play their road games, too, and when he and Ross wrangled Ross traded him to the Americans for rightwinger Eddie Wiseman and $5,000. In one stretch that spring Shore played eight games in eight nights, flying between various cities to maintain his commitments to both the Amerks and the Indians. He turned thirty-eight that year.

Shore's determination—or his stubbornness, whichever—was legendary. A famous story relates how a snowstorm prevented him from catching an overnight train to Montreal, stalling his cab on Boston streets. He phoned several friends looking for an automobile, finally found a rich one who loaned him his big car *and* chauffeur. After a few hours of swirling winds and inky icy roads the windshield wipers failed. Ice thickened on the glass. The chauffeur, alarmed by the constant skidding and vanishing visibility, insisted upon turning back. Shore said he'd drive. He lowered his window and curled his left hand around to the front of the windshield where the warmth of his hand kept a small space clear. Then the car skidded from the road, embedding the wheels in shoulder snow. The men couldn't free it, one pushing at the side and steering with his right hand on the wheel, the other shoving at the rear. Shore got the tire-jack and slashed small branches from a nearby grove of trees. He placed branches in front of each wheel, providing enough traction to free the car. They drove all night and all day through the stubborn storm, chilled to the point of freezing until they could get the wipers fixed in a small Quebec town and buy tire chains to reduce the skidding.

But in mid-afternoon the chains broke and the car skidded into the ditch. Shore hiked through the snow to a farm house and paid a farmer eight dollars to borrow a team of horses which pulled the car back to the road. Darkness had settled when they reached Montreal, sleepless and weary with strain. The Bruin players were almost ready to leave the Windsor Hotel for the Forum when Shore pushed his way through the revolving doors, eyes bloodshot, face frost-bitten and wind-burned, and legs aching from endless applications of the clutch and brake. He allowed himself a brief nap from which he had difficulty awakening, and went, bone tired, to the rink. Ross was reluctant to play him until Shore demanded he send him out. The Bruins beat the Canadiens 1-0 that night. Shore scored the goal. You could look it up.

In his fourteen years in the NHL Shore took a brand of rough-and-tumble to the rinks that has never been approached. He antagonized fans, fought opponents and stirred endless controversy. In a game against the Maroons in November 1929 Babe Siebert made a deliberate attack on him that was not seen by the referees. Play was stopped because Shore's blood had to be scraped from the ice. He was taken to hospital with a broken jaw, a concussion and missing four teeth. Siebert did this to Shore after Shore had hammered him while Siebert was prone back of the Boston goal. Siebert had a broken toe, bruised ribs and a black eye. In that same game, Dave Trottier claimed Shore had butt-ended him, causing a lung hemorrhage. A few days later, the president of the Boston club, Charles Adams, presented Shore with a cheque for $500 representing a hundred dollars for each facial scar inflicted by Montreal players.

In the spring of 1939 the Bruins and the Rangers finished one-two in the seven-team league and met in the first round of the playoffs. The Bruins won the first three games and in the fourth, in New York, the Rangers were playing it tough, trying to turn things around. Suddenly, Phil Watson slugged Bruin defencemen Jack Portland between the eyes with a right hand; Portland had cross-checked him in front of the Boston net. Players of both teams jumped into the fight, arms and sticks swinging savagely. Shore, nearing thirty-seven then, led the charge for the Bruins and became involved with Muzz Patrick, big and black-haired and once Canada's heavyweight boxing champion. The first time Patrick hit Shore, he broke his nose. The second time, he cut a gash under Shore's eye. The third time, he knocked Shore semi-conscious. When the referee got control he sent six players to the penalty box with major penalties. Shore went to the infirmary. He was back for the next period with only a strip of tape across his broken nose. For the rest of the night and for the rest of the series—the Rangers came back and won three straight to force a seventh game—he was the best player on the ice. Time after time he broke up Ranger thrusts, sent players sprawling, was as tough as he'd ever been. He was still there in the seventh game, breathing fire, when Mel Hill scored for Boston after forty-eight minutes of overtime, the fourth time a game went into extra play. It was an astonishing series that required a hundred and thirty-two minutes and eight seconds of overtime. A week later in the Stanley Cup final the Bruins completed a five-game conquest of Toronto, and Shore was still socking people when the last game ended. He did not score a goal in the twelve playoff games; indeed, the only defencemen who did in the dozen games were Art Coulter and Muzz Patrick. That's the way they played the game then.

Shore knew how to attract attention and stir people's emotions, and these things were very important when hockey was first burgeoning in the U.S. He was an actor with a flair for the spectacular. When he was knocked down he rose like a Barrymore, gestured and argued with referees while the crowds in Boston roared their approval and those on the road their abuse. "He could do a dying-swan act that would have aroused the envy of Margot Fonteyn," Baz O'Meara wrote in the *Montreal Star*. "He knew every nuance." Kyle Crichton in *Collier's* magazine called Shore the greatest drawing card in hockey. "What makes him that way is the hope, entertained by spectators in all cities but Boston, that he will some night be severely killed."

Ross and Shore worked out a ceremonial for Eddie's entrance before a game. The rest of the Bruins would be on the ice when suddenly the band would strike up "Hail, the Chief", and Shore would skate slowly onto the ice wearing a toreador's cape across his shoulders. A valet would follow him. When the valet lifted the cloak gently from his shoulders the crowd would go nuts. But all this ended one night when the Americans went into Boston with Rabbit McVeigh. After Shore made his theatrical entrance and doffed his cloak, Amerk players skated to mid-ice carrying a large rolled rug. They paused there. Amid silence, they unrolled the rug and disclosed McVeigh reclining in its folds much like Cleopatra in Caesar's tent, his head resting elaborately on his palm. Then he leaped to his feet, pirouetted daintily on the tips of his skates and tossed kisses to the crowd. In subsequent games Shore went out and warmed up with the others.

He was an ungiving man. Early in 1970 when everybody else was saluting Bobby Orr as the best forward-moving defenceman of all time, Shore flatly noted at a dinner in New York at which he was presented with a trophy for his contribution to hockey in the United States that he, not Orr, should have been the first defenceman ever to lead the NHL in scoring. "I could have won it lots of times; what stopped me was Art Ross," he said levelly. "If I carried the puck up the ice and shot instead of passing Ross'd fine me five hundred. Even if I scored." When he was asked if he thought Orr could skate so spectacularly in the brand of hockey played in Shore's day, he replied impassively, "I would rather not comment." He conceded Orr was "a good hockey player" but emphasized that the greatest he had ever played against was Howie Morenz. "Morenz is the only one I'll single out," Shore said. "The rest I won't discuss."

Shore was ten days short of his twenty-fourth birthday when he played his first NHL game, a 4-1 win over the Canadiens in the Boston Garden on November 16, 1926. By the time Bobby Orr reached twenty-four in March of 1972 he had been in the league for six seasons. Orr had been the league's most valuable player three times, the No. 1 defenceman on the all-star team five times and had scored more than a hundred points a season three times. During his fifth season, and not quite twenty-three, he was elected by *Sports Illustrated* magazine as Sportsman of the Year, the top man in *all* sports for 1971, and called "the greatest player ever to don skates; not the greatest defenceman, the greatest player at either end of the ice." Maybe he was and maybe he wasn't, but one thing was certain: *Sports Illustrated* wasn't even a twitch in the overgrown eyebrows of old Henry Luce when Shore was driving crowds crazy.

No question, Orr could have made it any time any where. For instance, when Gordie Howe was asked one time what he thought were Orr's best moves, he looked up from a stick he was taping and said wryly, "Just putting on those fucking skates." Still, it's a fact that Orr could hardly have arrived on the NHL scene at a more propitious moment. He turned eighteen in March of 1966 and had a year's exposure the following season to the misery of last place with a Bruin club that won exactly seventeen of its seventy games. The Bruins had no way to go but up when expansion came along a few months later, immediately providing them with six new teams, infinitely inferior. But the Bruins did much better than that. On May 15, just a month before expansion, Chicago's general manager Tommy Ivan was seized by a mind-boggling attack of the vapours and traded three big young tough forwards, Phil Esposito, Ken Hodge and Fred Stanfield, to the Bruins for Jack Norris, Gilles Marotte and Pit Martin, the dumbest trade since the white man caught up to the Indians. It turned Boston into an ugly bunch to meet on a dark night or in a bright arena, especially when the schedule permitted these long-hungry fellows to root around with a whole new division of callow youths and old jockstraps suddenly finding themselves designated as major leaguers.

It was a situation made for a player of Orr's particular gifts—swift, mobile, bright and clever, a dexterous stickhandler, deft passer, possessor of a big shot, and backed by a cast of ruffians who topped the league in penalties year after year. And almost all of their opponents—always excepting the Flying Frenchmen of Montreal—had too many left feet cluttering their line-ups to catch up to Orr. Old Jacques Plante placed a gnarled finger on another trenchant factor. "He can pick his spots," Jacques noted. "Being a defenceman on a team that stresses offence, he is trailing the play, and he never has to rush up unless he wants to. He can wait until the end of a shift. The players have been on the ice for two minutes while he's been laying back, and all of a sudden the other team is pressing. Orr gets the puck and just leaves those guys behind him because they are too tired to catch up. Many times he could beat them anyway, but he has that great advantage of being able to pick his spots.

"You watch him at the end of a period with maybe twenty seconds to go. He will rush right up to the opponent's net, right to the goaltender. He's not afraid of being caught out of position because he knows that even if they regain the puck, they won't have time to attack. He watches the clock, and then he goes. He is very smart. He is unbelievable."

He was born for his time, a man of marvellous offensive skills, remarkable puck control, instant acceleration, and a driving spirit. Whether he is the best player of all time is an argument he leaves to others. Indeed, he leaves all controversy that concerns him to others. He tries very hard to deflect attention; when a game ends he rushes to the Bruin medical room off the main dressing quarters, which is off-limits to newsmen, and waits there patiently while they talk to other Bruin players in the main room. When they've left, he emerges and dresses. "He's not trying to be exclusive," says Herb Ralby, ex-Bruin publicist. "It's just that whether we're home or on the road Orr's the man the writers want. They used to crowd around him five deep. He'd try to direct attention to the other guys. If the Bruins won by a shutout he'd talk about the goaltender. Even if he'd had an ordinary game and somebody got three goals, they'd still crowd around him. So now he ducks."

As a kid of fourteen he played with the Oshawa Generals in one of the country's two top junior leagues, the OHA Junior A. Almost all the players were eighteen and nineteen. His parents, Doug and Arva Orr, didn't want him living away from home so they or their neighbours drove him from the family home in Parry Sound, 140 miles north of Toronto on Georgian Bay, to and from the games in the various league towns. Sometimes the round trip would be more than three hundred miles, two or three nights a week and on Sunday afternoons. When he was fifteen he moved in with an Oshawa family in the winters, going to school and playing hockey. Although he played against older players for four years in a tough league, he was always the dominant figure.

I remember once talking to him when he was sixteen. *Maclean's* magazine wanted a piece on this junior phenomenon and, truth to tell, I wasn't following junior hockey and had never heard of him. I was prepared for a big outgoing kid, the hockey hero in a small town, when Wren Blair introduced us. But Blair, who later became the general manager of the Minnesota North Stars and was running the Oshawa team then for the Bruins, produced a skinny, crewcut, reserved youngster in the dressing room after a practice in Oshawa. Orr and I went to a restaurant and sat in a booth and I had a cup of coffee and he had a glass of milk and after twenty minutes there was simply nothing to talk about. He was very shy, though he tried hard to answer questions. We talked about his ambitions in hockey and his school work and what he did in the summer, and I remember he was concerned that people might think he was getting a swelled head.

"I don't look at any of the write-ups," he said, staring at his hands. "I used to read them but I'm afraid I might believe the things they write. I don't want that to happen. I've got an awful lot to learn, you know."

Through his years with the Bruins he managed to retain this remote quality, as though the Bobby Orr who piled up the unprecedented accomplishments on the ice were somehow unrelated to the quiet young man off it. His teammates respected his skills, of course, but more than that, they liked *him*. He had no side, no fits of temperament; he was one of the gang, not one to take himself or his gifts too seriously.

For all that, Orr was a tough man in a fight and his temper was balanced on a short fuse. He was tested early, as all rookies are, and he proved he could handle himself, and then some. Accepting him into the union, rival players began to leave him alone. Along about his sixth season he got involved with Rosie Paiement, a strong rightwinger for Vancouver, who decked him early in the game. Always thinking, Orr didn't want to take an early penalty, sitting out for five minutes while the game was close. So he growled at Paiement, "When there's a minute left, I'll be looking for you." The game ground on, with the Bruins pulling inevitably ahead of the expansionist Canucks, 7-3 in the dying moments. Sure enough, Orr and Paiement found each other, dropped their sticks and gloves, and began firing. One thing about it, Paiement flattened him again. For ten days after that Orr showed up in rinks around the circuit wearing a beautiful mouse under his left eye.

"It sure as hell surprised me," grinned Doug Favell, the Philadelphia goaltender then. "That shiner was the first real indication I'd had the guy was human."

Through his first eight years with the Bruins Orr scarcely picked up a facial scar and never lost a tooth but he had serious trouble with both knees and remedial surgery on them three times. Dr. Jim Murray, physician for Team Canada in its epic series with the Russians in September of 1972, ministered to Orr's right knee, which had been operated on the previous June, and came away with the opinion that Orr's career would be foreshortened.

"He has osteo arthritis," Murray noted in the spring of 1974. "When you get an arthritis it sort of perpetuates itself. I don't know how long he'll last as a hockey player but, whatever it is, he'd have gone ten years longer without this problem. When you look at x-rays you'd think you were looking at the knees of a man sixty-five; the surfaces of the joints are very ragged. Now he has to get all of his skating power from the quadriceps, the big muscles in the thigh. They get smaller after an operation and he has to work very hard to keep them built up. It's a thing that gets worse with time."

Eddie Shore turned forty-six the year Bobby Orr was born and by then he had owned the Springfield Indians for eight years and had begun accumulating a reputation as bizarre as anything in the history of sports.

Once, when Don (Nip) O'Hearn was playing goal for Shore, his wife gave birth to twin girls.

"If you'd come to me you'd have had boys," Shore told him.

"What do you mean, Mr. Shore?" O'Hearn asked.

"I'd have shown you how to screw by the moon," replied his employer.

O'Hearn is not entirely convinced that this is not so. "My wife had five children," he noted once. "Shore told me to tell Molly to rub cocoa butter on her stomach and hips to avoid stretch marks. Molly did. She hasn't got a stretch mark."

One time Shore had a rightwinger named Otto Schmidt, a big

51

strong kid who kept drifting from his position. The Indians were training at Saskatoon and Shore arrived early at the rink one morning with a canvas harness, a piece of rope, a huge length of wire, a hammer and some nails. He strung the wire the length of the arena ten feet above the ice surface and a couple of feet inside the boards. When the players arrived for their morning workout Shore called Schmidt aside. He fitted him into the harness and attached it, by means of the rope, to the length of wire. Whenever Schmidt wandered from his rightwing position, the harness and rope gently lifted him off the ice.

"That man will make an excellent rightwinger if he learns to play his position," Shore commented, viewing the dangling player. But Shore was wrong; Otto Schmidt did not fulfil his promise. Or perhaps he just never learned to play his position.

One Saturday night, Springfield, with Norm Defelice in goal, shut out Cleveland 6-0. When the players boarded the team bus for a Sunday game in Buffalo Defelice cheerily climbed the steps. But as he walked past Shore, who always sat in the front seat on the right-hand side of the bus, the owner stopped him.

"Mis-ter Defelice, what are you doing?"

"Gettin' on the bus," replied the puzzled player.

"You're not making this trip, Mis-ter Defelice. You'll be on the ice here at 8 a.m. on Monday."

"But my family's coming from St. Catharines to see me in Buffalo," protested the goaltender.

"They'll have a long wait, Mis-ter Defelice. Eight o'clock Monday morning."

On Monday morning at 8 o'clock Defelice was there, the only man on the ice of the West Springfield Armories arena. He was in full goaltending gear. For the next four hours he engaged in an exercise Shore called visualizing, used frequently and unpredictably by the owner on his goalers. What they did was make imaginary stops of imaginary pucks fired by imaginary attackers. They stopped long shots and close-in shots and slapshots and flip-shots and rebounds; every conceivable kind of stop. Except, of course, there was no puck. They were being developed into stand-up goaltenders, and one thing they could not do was drop to the ice making non-existent saves from non-existent forwards. Shore had no patience with goaltenders who flopped. "When you flop you're helpless," Shore used to say.

After four hours of this, Defelice took off his skates and pads and walked across the street to Claude's Snack Bar for a bowl of soup. He was back at 12:30 for another long session of visualizing.

"You could always tell when Shore was in the rink, although he used to try to hide behind the boards and surprise you," Defelice recalled one time. "He wore a brown five-gallon hat. When he'd stoop behind the boards, spying to make sure you were making your saves, you'd see the crown of this hat every once in awhile as he ducked along."

Defelice was exposed to the owner for the first time in 1958. After two seasons with Hershey in the American League he had been elevated to Boston in the NHL for ten games and then shipped to Shore at Springfield where he played out the season. In the fall Shore sent him to Three Rivers in the old Eastern pro league and presented him with a $3,900 contract. Defelice revolted and went home to his wife and family at St. Catharines. Each morning, as he remembered it in later years, the phone rang.

"Good morning, Mis-ter Defelice. How is your wife?"

"She's fine, Mr. Shore."

"And the kiddies?"

"They're fine, too."

"Are they eating?"

"Yeah, they're eating."

"Are you going to Three Rivers, Mis-ter Defelice?"

"No, I'm not."

"Mis-ter Defelice, unless you go to Three Rivers you'll sit home on your ass until you can bark like a fox. Have you ever heard a fox bark? Goodbye, Mis-ter Defelice."

"Goodbye, Mr. Shore."

Finally, Defelice phoned Clarence Campbell, the NHL president, and got himself reinstated as an amateur. "I played another ten years," Defelice recalled. "There was never a year that I didn't make more money in the amateurs than I ever made from Shore."

Shore may be the only owner in history who traded one of his players for two hockey nets, and he is definitely the only owner in history who traded one of his players for two hockey nets and then lamented that he'd made a bad deal. The party involved was Jake Milford, a stocky philosophical forward who, having been exposed to Shore, was perfectly suited to labour under the mercurial Jack Kent Cooke, the former Canadian entrepreneur who moved to Los Angeles in a snit in the early 1960s when the Toronto City Council declined to build him a baseball stadium to accommodate his dreams of owning a major-league ball club. Milford became general manager of Cooke's Los Angeles Kings during the 1973-74 season.

"Eddie called me in one day to tell me he'd sold me to Buffalo," Milford recalled once. "As I stepped off the train my eye caught a headline in the Buffalo paper—Milford Acquired for Two Hockey Nets.

I wasn't surprised, but Shore complained later that the Buffalo team had led him to believe they'd be *new* nets. Apparently the ones they sent him were used."

Edward William Shore came out of Fort Qu'Appelle, Saskatchewan, where his father was a prosperous farmer. He and his brother Aubrey could ride almost as soon as they could walk, but even at seventeen he hadn't played much hockey. When Aubrey went to college in Winnipeg and made the hockey team, Eddie said he guessed anybody could. "Anybody but you," jeered Aubrey. So Eddie went to college in Winnipeg and determined to play hockey. He played in all kinds of weather, Winnipeg being Winnipeg.

"Our ears, noses and cheeks used to freeze regularly," he recalled once. "You'd be playing only a little while when you could scrape the hoar frost off our backs and chests, from the sweat hitting the cold air. I remember one game when it was fifty-five below. Our eyelashes froze so stiff we had to quit, we couldn't see. I scored two goals."

He never wearied of trying to improve, of studying techniques that would better utilize his abilities. In everything. Anatomy fascinated him in later years; he learned to identify every bone in the human body, even fancied himself as a chiropractor and impelled his services upon every unsuspecting hockey player who confessed to an aching back or a headache. He could never understand the laissez-faire attitude of most players. Even as a pro in the Western Canada league with Regina and Edmonton (he became known, inevitably, as the Edmonton Express) in the early 1920s, he worked to improve his posture, his approach, his stride, his stance.

Bep Guidolin, who became Bruin coach in 1973, played for Shore's 1959 Springfield club and once recalled that crucible. "He harped on three points," Guidolin said of Shore. "He wanted the hands two feet apart on the stick, the feet eleven inches apart on the ice, and you had to skate with the body erect but in a kind of sitting position, bent at the knees. You had to do it exactly right."

During a scrimmage Guidolin completed a pass that resulted in a goal; he had done everything right, he thought. Shore blew a whistle and summoned him.

"Mis-ter Guidolin, would you explain that manoeuvre."

"Jeez, Mr. Shore, the pass was perfect. My hands were right, I was in the sitting position and the guy scored."

"Not good enough, Mis-ter Guidolin. Your legs were too far apart by *at least* two inches."

Out of his own experience Shore felt every man should apply himself fully and develop all his assets properly, as he himself had done. He also believed every man should earn his keep, meagre as it was, and dash off in all directions at his whim, even family men hoping to be settled. Nipper O'Hearn, the goaltender, married and father of five, toiled all over hell's half acre as a Shore serf; from 1948 to 1957 he hit New Haven, Fort Worth, Oakland, Vancouver, San Diego, Fresno, Springfield, Syracuse, Troy and Halifax. One year at Springfield Shore piled $3,300 on him for the entire season. That wasn't bad; he worked for seventy-five dollars a week in San Diego. If players were injured or benched, thereby joining the Awkward Squad or the Black Aces as these temporary non-combatants were called, Shore expected them to work, selling programs at the games, hawking peanuts or stuffing popcorn boxes. One time the skating show Ice Capades hit Springfield with an act in which hundreds of balloons were dropped from a net in the ceiling, floating to the ice in the show's finale. For as many nights as the ice show was in town, Shore had the Awkward Squad spending that many afternoons at the rink blowing up balloons.

"We blew 'em up in a dressing room," O'Hearn laughed in recollection. "We had that room floor-to-ceiling in balloons. You could open the door, stand 'way back in the corridor, and then run and jump feet first into so many balloons that you'd bounce right back out on your ass in the corridor."

Few of the hundreds of chattels who toiled for Shore over the years argued that his theories were unsound; it was simply that he left them no dignity. He rarely praised any effort by any player, although, perversely, he often bailed them out of sudden financial binds or helped in domestic crises. Once, O'Hearn beat Buffalo 2-1 in a game he regarded as one of the best he had ever played. "You'd have had a shutout," Shore rasped afterwards, "if you'd stayed on your feet." Another time, after a 3-2 win over Cleveland, Shore wasn't satisfied with *how* the team had won. Before the rink had emptied of fans he had his players back on the ice for a full one-hour drill, including a scrimmage. When the players left the rink after midnight, three of them, Norm Gustafson, Danny Summers and O'Hearn, returned to their rooms at the YMCA ("Where the hell else would we be staying on what the Old Man was paying?" sighed O'Hearn, relating the saga) to watch a communal television set in the scruffy dormitory.

"Jesus, I'd like a drink," mumbled Summers. It had been a long night.

"Let's go have one, just one," suggested Gustafson. "It's still ten minutes to curfew."

So the three of them went to a neighbourhood bar and ordered three beers.

In reconstructing the scene, O'Hearn remembered they'd gone down the fire escape so they wouldn't be seen by anyone in the lobby.

"We haven't been in there ten minutes, haven't even had one beer, the foam from my first sip is still on my lips when who opens the door and walks to the cigarette machine and then disappears out the door but the club's coach, Frank Beisler. We think maybe he hasn't seen us so we gulp our beer and rush back to our rooms.

"The next morning at practice, not a word from Shore. It's a tough practice, too, but then we know he's nailed us; the three of us have to stay on the ice for an extra half-hour of starts-and-stops which, you know, just tear your guts right out. Ah, well, what the hell, we figure. But that's not all. When we get back to the Y there's an envelope for each of us. We've been fined *one hundred bucks each*."

In March of 1970 Eddie Shore, going on sixty-eight, an all-star NHL defencemen seven times in his fourteen-year career, the Hart Trophy winner four times, is pontificating.

"Hockey players today slow the blood circulation to their brains by bending over when they skate," he says.

He stands erect, bald, *smooth*-faced, still looking fit.

"When you're like this," he says, "the circulation can go from the spinal column to the brain. But players today, they bend forward. That makes the brain react a split second slower."

Not his; not Eddie Shore's. Eddie Shore has a brain that reacts as fast as a man's forty-six years younger. A man like Bobby Orr, say. What a pair they'd make. On the ice, of course.

CHAPTER FOUR: The Bootleg Baron of Broadway—and Other Vanished Americans

There have always been crazy hockey players, just as there have been crazy psychiatrists, left-handed pitchers and blondes, but the New York Americans were something special: the whole team was crazy.

The Amazing Amerks, who pre-dated the Amazin' Mets by nearly forty years, were imported from Canada by a man who knew all there was to know about importing, William V. Dwyer, the biggest bootlegger in New York in the early years of Prohibition. Dwyer, called Big Bill, was a tall red-faced quiet fellow who paid $80,000 for the troubled franchise of the Hamilton Tigers, whose players had won the NHL title in the spring of 1925 and then gone on strike and been suspended. Dwyer relieved Hamilton owner Percy Thompson of his financial burden and transferred the whole package to Manhattan in the fall and rechristened it the Americans.

Dwyer operated out of a small, neat and nicely furnished hotel he owned called the Forrest located on 49th Street half a block from the old Madison Square Garden, which had just been built on 8th Avenue. Most of the Amerks lived there in their early New York days, sharing the run of the place with Dwyer's henchmen, gang bosses such as Legs Diamond and Dutch Schultz and Owney Madden, and the columnist Damon Runyon who shared a suite at the Forrest with a tall bosomy blonde and a small yappy fox terrier which the blonde compelled Runyon to walk every evening. To the vast amusement of loitering players, he used to lead the dog on a short leash through the lobby for these nocturnal constitutionals, and perhaps because the players regarded him as a dandy Runyon never wrote favourably about hockey. Or maybe he simply thought it was a dumb game. At any rate, he called it glorified shinny and wrote that "the business left me palled" after one foreshortened visit to watch the Americans and the Montreal Maroons. "Neither team scored while I was in the building, largely because of the agility of the two goaltenders, who were padded like stuffed sausages."

In the beginning Dwyer shared Runyon's lack of enthusiasm. He had bought the franchise because a friend of his, Bill MacBeth, a native of Windsor, Ontario, who worked on the *New York Herald-Tribune* and was enthusiastic about hockey, had convinced him that it was a cinch to be successful in New York. But he grew to like the game as he gained an understanding of it. He was a devoted family man who delighted in escorting his wife and children to a loge box back of the Americans' bench. Dwyer was forty-five when he acquired his hockey bauble, a not unkindly man who for years had had more money than he could spend. He operated eighteen ocean-going ships, owned trucks, warehouses, a nightclub or two in New York, a casino in Miami, and a piece of a couple of race tracks in Florida and Montreal.

The inaugural hockey game for Dwyer's Amerks in New York on December 15, 1925, was sponsored by—in retrospect one might say fittingly—the New York Neurological Institute, and such lofty auspices turned the event into a social gala. The list of patronesses alone filled a page in the official program and named, among others, Mrs. Franklin D. Roosevelt, Mrs. Julius Ochs Adler, Mrs. Vincent Astor, Mrs. Charles L. Tiffany, Mrs. William Woodward, Mrs. George Whitney and Mrs. Charles Scribner. Nowhere in the program, however, was there to be found the name of William V. Dwyer who, almost overnight, became the most silent owner in the history of professional sports. In fact, for several months into the new season Dwyer got what his mob would call the big ignore from the Garden and, curiously enough, the newspapers as well, presumably bowing to the Garden's wishes. What happened was that seventeen days prior to the opening game Big Bill had been thoughtless enough to get himself some publicity he could really have done without. As the *Times* of December 4 headlined it on Page 1:

BIGGEST LIQUOR RING SMASHED BY ARRESTS OF 20 HERE
WILLIAM DWYER SEIZED AS HEAD OF INTERNATIONAL GROUP
WIDE BRIBERY CHARGED ; OPERATIONS RAN TO MILLIONS

Suddenly, the Garden had never heard of Dwyer. The hockey club became "Tex Rickard's Americans". And, with a sellout crowd headed by the social elite in attendance at the opening game, the lavish seventy-two page program listed one Thomas J. Duggan as the hockey club's chairman of the board, Colonel John S. Hammond as club president, and Thomas P. Gorman as general manager and coach. The honour roll of Garden executives was headed by the name of the new arena's president, George L. (Tex) Rickard, who was running the Garden when Dwyer's hockey club became his tenant. Duggan, the hastily invented chairman of the board, was a beefy hustler and promoter out of Montreal who had helped Dwyer acquire the Hamilton franchise that launched the Americans. Gorman was a fast-moving executive of the celebrated Ottawa Senators who sold an interest in that club in order to accept Dwyer's five-year contract to run the Amerks. For his part, Hammond was a suave greying quiet man, a friend of Rickard's who took on the presidency of the Americans for one year; when the Rangers were born he became their president, hired Connie Smythe of Toronto to recruit a team for him, then fired Smythe a few weeks before the season opened and replaced him with Lester Patrick.

Dwyer, for the indiscretion of getting caught, was sent to penitentiary in Atlanta for a two-year stretch in June of 1927, and he departed apparently saddened and contrite. "I wish I had never seen a case of whisky," he told reporters. "I spent years in daily fear of my life, always expecting to be arrested, always dealing with crooks and double-crossers, and now look at me. My wife is heart-broken and I am worse than broke. I owe $150,000 although I never was a millionaire but just a figurehead for a bunch of rich guys."

Big Bill's penitence barely outlasted his sojourn in prison. He was paroled in the fall of 1928, but when Federal agents knocked over a brewery on 10th Avenue at 25th Street in May 1931 the operators were revealed to be the one-time Public Enemy No. 1 Owney Madden and none other than William V. Dwyer, joined in a business venture representing an investment of $2,500,000. Meanwhile, though heavily involved in other matters, Dwyer had not given up his interest in his hockey club. Upon being sprung from Atlanta he returned to the NHL's board of governors in the fall of 1928 and remained there until 1937. Eventually, though, the government won a $3,715,907 action against him and it cleaned him out. He died broke in December 1946 at sixty-four, a decade after he had been forced by dwindling finances and mounting debts to give up the Americans. Big Bill was a man who came in with Prohibition and went out with it.

The men who wore the startling star-spangled suits of the Amerks were a considerably less sophisticated crew than the men who ran the operation. "The first thing I did when I saw the bright lights of Broadway was I noticed the lovely underwear," Jumping Jakie Forbes, the goaltender, recalled not long ago, a man of seventy-five smiling across nearly fifty years. "Mine was long in the sleeves and legs and woollen and I got into them short silk ones straightaway."

The rest of the players were a long way from beautiful downtown Hamilton, too, by the time they reached New York, and the rollicking life of Manhattan generally and the Forrest Hotel specifically took a terrible toll. Unlike Jake Forbes, many of the players found that the silk underwear they were climbing into was rarely men's. Gunmen's molls and Dwyer's booze were never far away at the Forrest and both held their charms. Sometimes the newspapers would announce that players were out of the line-up through injuries but, in truth, they were more often drunk in bed, unable to move more than a searing eyelid. Players who were on their feet and mobile used to carry trays of food to supine teammates, sometimes every day for a week. The previous year as Tigers in Hamilton they'd topped the NHL standings, but as Amazing Amerks they succumbed to the bright lights. Occasionally they'd play marvellous games, beating the powerhouse teams from Montreal and Ottawa, but more often they simply weren't in shape to endure the long season, and inevitably they'd sink ever deeper in the standings.

But the opening game was a marvellous spectacle, and the next day Al Dayton of the *New York Sun* wrote:

It was the night of nights. Never has a more glittering spectacle surrounded a sporting event in this city. The new Garden, already a thing of beauty, was decked out in its finest. Flags from Canada and the States vied with each other from the boxes and tiers. But as ornate as was the arena, the crowd actually added color to the scene. Society was out in force and the gorgeous gowns of the women blended a picture at which even an artist would have marvelled. The white line of men in evening dress around the edge of the rink served to create the impression of snow, which is banked around the sides of the outdoor rinks in Canada, so even the players were treated to an eyeful.

But this was merely a preliminary eyeful. Once the magic wand was waved and the festivities set into motion, this colourful throng was presented with a sight which rivalled their own. The Montreal Canadiens were the first upon the ice. They were accompanied by the Governor General's Footguards Band, decked out in crimson jackets, black trousers and tall bear hats. Around the rink they paraded, exhibiting various formations, and finally drew up at the 49th Street side of the Garden facing the centre of the rink. Then there was a blare of trumpets and the Americans glided to the ice, led by the West Point Cadets Band. More manoeuvres of a martial nature and finally with a fancy twist the cadets and the star-spangled players lined up opposite their rivals from the north. National anthems of both countries were played and the prologue was called a draw, the bands and the crowd finishing on even terms.

The strong and flashy forward line of the Montreal club—Howie Morenz, Aurel Joliat and Billy Boucher—furnished a combination play that New York's high-priced sextet led by Billy Burch and Bullet Joe Simpson could not solve, and but for the sterling network of Vernon (Jakie) Forbes in the home citadel Canadiens winning margin of 3 to 1 might easily have been increased. Their victory, however, was no more decisive than that of hockey itself, for as play after play went ranging down the ice the uninitiated New York crowd that filled almost every available seat in Tex Rickard's new Garden, paying prices ranging from $1.50 for the uppermost balcony seats to the lofty toll of $11.50 for the choice box seats, was sent into wild demonstrations of enthusiasm. If the opener is to be taken as any criterion the winter sport as fostered by the NHL has found a firm spot in the heart of Gotham's sportdom.

The prices, by the way, were scaled high purely for the Neurological Institute benefit; seats ranged from $1.10 to $3.85 for the balance of the Amerks' eighteen-game home schedule in the thirty-six game season. The opener made its impression on, for one, Ed Sullivan, who wrote for the *New York Chronicle* in those pre-television days, and sought out this feature on the Amerk goaltender:

The more we see of Vernon Jakie Forbes, also called Cowboy Forbes because his goaltender's garments resemble cowboy's chaps, the more we are impressed by the large ears of this little fellow.

Forbes has a pair of underslung ears that look very much like mudguards. When he speeds down the ice at practice he keeps his ears at half-mast, and the wind gets behind them and propels him forward, much as a sailboat is driven ahead.

Mr. Forbes loaded his ears in an upper berth last night and departed for Pittsburgh where the Americans face the Smoky City entry Saturday. Yesterday before departing Forbes told us why New York lost to the Canadiens in the opening game. "Red Green is still suffering from the ankle he injured in training," explained Forbes, "and Mickey Roach is out of the game with an attack of appendicitis. Furthermore, Bullet Joe Simpson is not yet in his best form. You see, Simpson is a coast player, and out there a player is not able to breathe properly until Christmas."

The Americans, in fact, seemed to inspire purple prose wherever they went. Later in the season, in Montreal, they were edged 1-0 by the Canadiens, eliciting this outburst from one G.D. Lawrence in the *Montreal Herald*:

Today's hero: Vernon (Jakie) Forbes, who saved Tom Duggan's star-spangled crew from a pasting that would have rung down the corridors of time, though looking over the high spots in the bataille one must not overlook Morenz and Joliat. Howie exploded a line of wares that sparkled with brilliancy, while Aurel scored a goal that proved him to be a Napoleon of strategy. If you don't believe it, ask Simpson.

As Aurel swung through the American breastworks, Simpson made a dive for him. Joliat made a fake pass that completely fooled Joe, who stopped in his tracks and started to streak for Aurel's imaginary teammate. Forbes also whirled around, and Aurel had a clear field. He promptly punched the twine with deadly precision, and the whole New York outfit gazed at each other with slants that made an African Honking Gander look like a professor of philosophy.

Jakie Forbes, Tommy Gorman, the Statue of more or less Liberty, Volstead, and a couple of New Yorkers seated near the pressbox loudly howled that the goal was offside. Tommy appealed to the writer. The writer referred Tommy to Louie Larivee, the mad and merry Frenchman, who said, "Et ton viellard aussi," which, translated into the jargon of the Anglo-Saxons, means, "So's your old man." Far be it from us to take away any credit from the Americans but it must be admitted they were outclassed.

For their time the Amerks were a highly paid crew. Jakie Forbes and Billy Burch, who had led the revolt of players in Hamilton in the spring of 1925, each got $20,000 for three-year contracts in an era when $5,000 was an excellent annual salary. In fact Forbes was a hold-out until two nights before the Americans opened their season in Pittsburgh on December 2. He had taken a summer job as a salesman with a fine-china wholesale company called Cassidy's in Toronto, working on a commission and going his rounds on a bicycle until he accumulated enough money to buy a Model T Ford. He was an excellent salesman but he wanted a regular income.

"If you'll give me fifty dollars a week I'll sign for ten years," he told his boss, a man named McKay, one morning late in November when he was endeavouring to decide whether to continue with hockey or settle down in business. McKay soon helped him make up his mind.

"What the hell are you talking about?" McKay snapped. "The bank manager next door isn't making that kind of money."

Each payday in New York, Forbes and most of the other Amerks—Bullet Joe, Burch, Alex McKinnon, the Green brothers, Red and Shorty—collected their money at Dwyer's office in the Forrest, stepping past the owner's expressionless corral of hoods right out of central casting in wide-brimmed hats, smoking cigars and playing cards, guns stuffed into their waist-bands or bulging under their armpits. When the players had their pay they walked to 8th Avenue and took a subway ride to Wall Street where they paraded from bank to bank, seeking the best exchange rate on their U.S. dollars and transferring the money to banks at home in Canada. In that period the rate was always highly favourable. Once, Forbes got 31.2 percent.

After the first season, with the Rangers setting up competition in the Garden, Tommy Gorman decided he couldn't manage the Americans and coach them, too, so he confined his duties to administration and hired a coach. In Edouard (Newsy) Lalonde he could scarcely have found a more colourful or celebrated figure. For twenty years Newsy had been one of the truly remarkable lacrosse and hockey players in Canada, scarred and gnarled and mean, a fearless fighter with a fiery temper who chased fans, opponents and even teammates when the black mood was on him. He played hockey for ten seasons with the Montreal Canadiens through 1922 and then he had a falling out with the owner, Leo Dandurand, and was traded to the Saskatoon Shieks of the Western Canada Hockey League for the brilliant little Aurel Joliat. As a playing coach with the Shieks, Lalonde scored twenty-nine goals in twenty-six games and led the league in scoring although he was then thirty-six years old. Lalonde played sparingly the next season when his star pupil, Bill Cook, took over the scoring leadership but he went into the line-up for a New Year's Day game against Regina who had a new and talented goaltender named Red McCusker. Lalonde led an assault on McCusker in which the goaler was felled wearing a long gash in his forehead that bloodied the ice beneath him. He had cuts on his nose and cheek too, and when the game ended Regina's manager, Wes Champ, announced his team would not play Saskatoon again if league action were not taken against Lalonde for "leading this deliberate assault" on McCusker. Lalonde got a one-game suspension, at which the playing coach merely snorted, "Did you notice we beat those bastards four to nuthin'?"

When Lalonde moved to New York in the fall of 1926, Jakie Forbes, for one, remembered him from his eruptive years with the Canadiens when Forbes had toiled for the Toronto St. Pats. Even fifty years later Forbes still recalled him vividly.

"He was the dirtiest son of a bitch I ever played against," stocky little Jakie said.

One night in Montreal, Lalonde broke clear on Forbes and was beaten by the goaler on a close-in try. Lalonde circled the net as play swept up the ice and veered sharply in front of the Toronto goal. As he sped past Forbes he belted him with a right hand squarely across the face. Blood spurted from the goaler's nose and he took off after Lalonde, brandishing his stick like a lariat. In his frenzy he bowled over the referee, Cooper Smeaton, who jumped to his feet and threw his arms around Forbes.

"Get back in the goal, you crazy little bugger," he shouted at the five-foot-five goaltender, "or you're out of the game."

Forbes retreated to his cell. But he was determined to even the count with Lalonde and he got his chance near the end of the game when the Canadiens were leading 4-1 and were clearly the winners. As Lalonde neared his net cradling the puck, Forbes gripped his stick in both hands readying an axe-swing at Lalonde's head. But at the last instant the flying Lalonde spat a long stream of tobacco juice into Jakie's face, circled the net laughing, and pushed the puck into the goal past the sputtering Forbes.

Still, Lalonde was no match for the rollicking, roistering Americans, whose quaint training methods soon were assisting them into the familiar cellar, both in the standings and the speakeasies. He tried fining them, cursing them and suspending them but nothing dissuaded their ways. On one road trip Lalonde banged on a hotel-room door where the players were partying after a loss, and when he was admitted he began shouting at the players. Alex McKinnon, swaying on his feet, told him he was a lousy coach. Lalonde swung a short vicious punch and knocked McKinnon down and out. The punch closed both of McKinnon's eyes and he couldn't play for a week during which the papers noted that he was injured. The papers were entirely correct.

As McKinnon lay on the floor in the hotel room, Lalonde stared from face to face. "Anybody else?" he invited. There was nobody else.

The Amerks played their best games against the Rangers whose arrival in the Garden had split the hockey crowds down the middle.

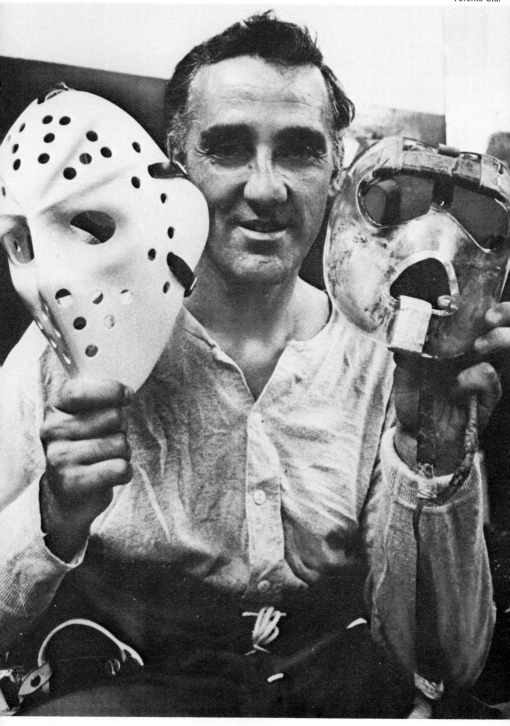

The man and his masks, Jacques Plante with the oldest and the newest.

At his peak with Detroit, Terry Sawchuk *(above)* may have been the best goaltender of all time. Teammate Gordie Howe prepares to belt Toronto's Billy Harris.

Clint Benedict of the Montreal Maroons *(right)* with hockey's first mask ever. Jacques Plante made mask-wearing respectable, but Benedict's facial adornment pre-dated Plante by forty years.

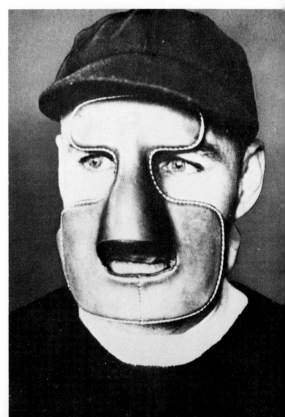

Death claimed Chicago's great Charlie Gardiner *(above)* at his absolute peak. He was glib and acrobatic and he once wore a derby hat in goal.

Someone once noted that Montreal's imperturbable Ken Dryden *(above)* greeted each stoppage of play by folding his arms over the top of his stick and leaning there like a street-cleaner resting on his broom.

The Chicoutimi Cucumber, George Vezina *(above),* who sired twenty-two children and found time to become a hockey immortal.

Gentlemanly Billy Harris *(above)* absorbed abnormal abuse before turning to coaching the W.H.A.'s Toronto Toros.

"Heh, heh," chuckles Chicago's great Glenn Hall *(above)*, "gotcha that time."

(Left) The all-time champion voice of hockey, Foster Hewitt.

(Below) Rocket Richard's goal-mouth fervour was a tangible thing reflected in black eyes that literally glowed when he approached a rival goaltender, in this case Toronto's Johnny Bower.

The master, Montreal's Howie Morenz *(above),* who could skate a hole in the wind.

(Below) "I was never hurt in hockey," Clancy always said. "Oh, I lost my teeth and bust my nose, but I never was what you'd call handsome."

Lionel Conacher *(above)* was Canada's greatest athlete of the half-century in a 1950 national poll, and yet hockey was merely his third or fourth best game.

(Above) "I'll drink it, but I won't like it," Gordie Howe acknowledges, drinking a toast with Punch Imlach after Imlach's Leafs edged Detroit in the 1964 Stanley Cup.

When Conn Smythe (below) was young and sprightly, he organized the first Ranger club, and then went on to win Stanley Cups for Toronto. Excess baggage here is Eddie Powers, farm-club coach at Syracuse.

Toronto Star

Miller Services

No one suffered more terrifying
injuries than Bobby Baun, but on
the ice no one knew of his pain.
Off the ice though . . .

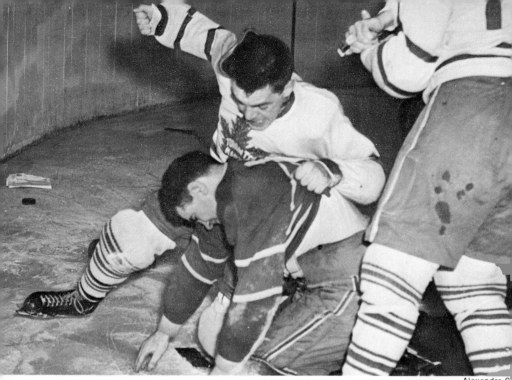

The puck lies unnoticed as Toronto's Howie Meeker *(top)* gets down to the basics with a a friend from Montreal.

(Above) Duels between Maurice Richard and Turk Broda were classics. The Rocket won this one.

(Top) Mayhem was far behind them in 1942 when Sprague Cleghorn *(left)* and Newsy Lalonde *(right),* two of the meanest who ever carved a skull, were reunited at this benefit.

(Above) Ace Bailey *(left)* accepts Eddie Shore's apology following a near-fatal accident which ended Bailey's career.

Jolly Jawn Adams *(above)* ran the Detroit operation for nearly thirty-five years. He was a man who laughed a lot, but he didn't have much humour.

Little Frank Selke *(above)* invented the farm system for Montreal that kept the Canadiens flying for decades.

The thinking man's coach, Freddie Shero *(far left),* brought a new kind of life to Philadelphia. His Flyers became the first expansion club to win the Stanley Cup, in the spring of 1974.

The elegant Major, Frederic McLaughlin *(left),* made a bizarre imprint on Chicago. He once fired a coach who had won the Stanley Cup for his team.

(Right) Frank Patrick, the great innovator, contributed so much to hockey that the rule book still carried twenty-two pieces of his legislation in the mid-1970's.

(Below) Lester Patrick with sons Muzz and Lynn. The Silver Fox's persistence made them both stars in New York.

Taking the shortest distance between two points, Eddie (the Entertainer) Shack finds a road-block in Oakland's Gerry Ehman.

(Top) The star-spangled splendour of Red Dutton and the New York Americans. They both teemed with colour.

(Above) Aurel Joliat looks undressed without his black cap. Rivals used to try to knock it off in the goalmouth because the Montreal ace would always stop indignantly to retrieve it.

Toronto Star

(Left) When the Eagle speaks the hockey world listens. It was Alan Eagleson who organized the players' union that revolutionized incomes.

Defeat does not rest easily on Bobby Orr *(below)*.

Toronto Star

There were almost always fights in the gallery, and one night after the Americans had lost by one goal, Amerk fans chased a referee down 50th Street calling him a thief and threatening to kill him. He escaped in a cab.

Halfway through the season Tommy Gorman made a deal with Chicago that brought Lionel Conacher to the Americans. Conacher helped the defence, and he also fit right into the team's social pattern. Indeed, Conacher showed the Americans a drinking capacity that, experienced as they were in that area, they found awesome. He and Joe Simpson sometimes missed games and practices for a full week, drinking just short of constantly, and Newsy Lalonde could do nothing to curb them. It was a sad denouement to a long career for Newsy, who quit the Americans after just one season. One day during a practice in the arena at Princeton University—the Amerks rarely were given ice time at the Garden—he walked into the dressing room and found his goaltender Jakie Forbes there alone. Forbes had caught a puck and then left the ice.

"Get back out there," growled Lalonde.

"Jeez, Newsy, I can't go back out there," Forbes protested. "Look." He held up his hand and showed Lalonde his bent and swollen index finger. "I've broke it in three places."

"Aw, for God's sake, what's that?" Lalonde said resignedly, dropping wearily onto a bench. "Look at me, look at my eyes, look at my face. I got scars all over 'em. Do you think a busted finger ever stopped me?"

With Dwyer's problems occupying him elsewhere Tex Rickard turned his hand to hockey promotion. Rickard, the Garden president, was a fight promoter without peer. In September of 1926 on the eve of the Amerks' second season he had staged the Jack Dempsey-Gene Tunney championship fight in Philadelphia, attracting 120,000 people and a gate of $1,895,723, and now he saw in hockey a heartier version of his favourite sport. He worked hard to capitalize on the game's bone-crushing aspects. Two men in a fight was one thing; twelve guys carrying spears offered unlimited possibilities, the way Rickard saw it. As people milled past the Garden on hockey nights, he'd send fleets of ambulances, their sirens wide open, screeching up to the curbs outside the arena. He figured the implications of their flashing red lights and white-uniformed attendants would hustle the crowds through the turn-stiles, and he encouraged the players to fill the waiting vehicles as rapidly as possible. Of course, once the games were underway, the hired ambulances and their attendants would drive off into the night.

When Lalonde departed, Gorman elevated Shorty Green to the coach's position. Green was an epileptic sometimes taken by seizures during a hockey game. On such occasions, three or four players hurried to his assistance, holding him until the seizures waned. His affliction did not detract from his zeal for the game, a grim intense little fellow, a hot-eyed fighter on the ice, mild and soft-spoken away from it. He was one of the few Amerks with a passion for winning—or, at least, with a passion that endured past the end of a game. Whatever passions most of the others took to the ice, they soon waned once a game ended and the night life of New York beckoned.

One night Shorty took a heavy beating in a Garden match-up with the Rangers and a couple of hours later in the apartment he shared with his brother Redvers he awakened Red and told him he felt as though he was bleeding inside. Red got him to a hospital where the doctors discovered Shorty had made an excellent diagnosis of his condition. He *was* bleeding inside, and was quickly wheeled to an emergency operating room.

Next day the hockey writer of the *New York Journal*, Max Kase, wrote a hair-raising story under the heading:

SHORTY GREEN, HOCKEY STAR, DYING FROM INJURIES

"He is dying in the Polyclinic Hospital," Kase wrote, "as a result of injuries he suffered after a collision with Taffy Abel, the burly Ranger defenceman. Dr. Henry O. Clauss announced he had dislocated his kidney, and a priest was summoned who administered the last rites."

The report of Green's imminent demise was somewhat exaggerated, though his playing days were now over and he turned himself full time to coaching. But the Americans baffled him, as they had baffled Newsy Lalonde, although Frank Graham, who had become a columnist for the *New York Sun*, recounted a night that Green enjoyed thoroughly. It was a game against the Canadiens in the Garden and Green exhorted his players to stop Montreal's marvellous Howie Morenz.

"Every time he gets the puck, knock him down," Green cried to his men. And it was one of those nights when they were successful against the Habitant centre star who usually skated rings around his opponents. He was knocked to the ice a dozen times, butted and shoved and manhandled. When the final bell sounded with the Americans ahead 1-0, the weary Morenz stopped at the Amerk bench. "If there's any son of a bitch who hasn't had a shot at me, you've missed your chance," Morenz said. "I'm going home."

But one season was enough for Shorty Green, as it had been for Newsy Lalonde, for the joyous times had been rare. There was one happy night in Ottawa to cheer him when the team beat the Senators, who had fallen upon bad times and who were soon to be shifted to St. Louis for one final fling before the franchise was closed down. The following day Green telephoned the owner, Bill Dwyer, who had served his time in the Atlanta penitentiary and was now back in full swing in New York, to tell him the good news and also to advise him the team would arrive in New York the next morning on the overnight train after a three-hour stop-over in Montreal. Dwyer was delighted to learn of the rare victory on the road.

"When you get to Montreal," he told Green, "take the boys to dinner. Tell them to have all they want to eat and all they want to drink. If they've got any friends who can make the party, tell them they're welcome." As long as he had money, Dwyer was an expansive owner.

The Americans finished last in their division with twenty-eight points, sixteen less than Toronto who also failed to make the playoffs, and that was too much for Green. He was succeeded by Lionel Conacher as coach and one of Conacher's first moves was to convince Gorman that what the team needed most was Conacher's tiny drinking pal from Pittsburgh, goaltender Roy Worters. Gorman made the deal and Worters succeeded Jakie Forbes in goal. Forbes, in turn, became the NHL's spare goaltender, filling in for any team when the occasion arose.

That season of 1928-29 was one of the few successful ones for the Amerks when Conacher put together so strong a defensive club that the team yielded only fifty-three goals in forty-four games and finished second to the Canadiens. That qualified the Amerks to meet the Rangers in the playoffs, and their two-game total-goals series, attracting 35,000 fans to the Garden, was one of the more remarkable ones in Stanley Cup play. The first game was scoreless through its sixty minutes and the second game was unproductive in regulation time so that the teams embarked on sudden-death overtime play. Finally, after twenty-nine minutes and fifty seconds, Butch Keeling beat the gutsy shrimp Roy Worters, only five-foot-three and a hundred and thirty pounds, and that was all the Americans were to see of the playoffs for nine years. As a coach Lionel Conacher followed up his successful debut by finishing absolutely last in his second season and was removed as coach and traded to the Montreal Maroons. Shocked by this turn of events and then buoyed by the birth of the first of five children, Conacher phoned his wife in a Toronto maternity ward from Montreal. Towards the end of their talk, after a short pause, he said, "From now on, Dot, things will be different." From that November day in 1930 until his death in 1954, Conacher never took another drink, returned to top form and later helped the Maroons and then the Chicago Black Hawks to the Stanley

Cup. For their part, the Amerks were to benefit hugely from the trade, too, for in return for Conacher they acquired the rambunctious and thoroughly unrestrained Red Dutton. Dutton was one of the greatest things that ever happened to the Americans. For a decade, Dutton *was* the Americans.

Nowadays, and for many years, the Americans have been only a memory. But sometimes, even now, they come alive. They come alive when Red Dutton is talking. The last time they came alive for me was in December of 1973 and, of course, it was because Red Dutton was talking. He remains an astonishing figure of a man, ramrod erect, six feet tall, full-chested and expensively tailored. When I think of him now he is standing at the window of my hotel room in Calgary, the once flaming hair a white crown on a man of seventy-five who is still filled with the fire he took to a hundred rinks, vigorous and restless. He had come to the hotel from his ranch, a millionaire with a hundred and twenty acres of rolling land in the foothills of the Rockies. Turning suddenly from the window and in a quick impulsive gesture so typical of him, he drops his pants.

"It was high explosive," Red Dutton says earnestly. "It took ten pounds of meat out of my ass. Right here. Look. Shrapnel hit me right here in the ass, in my thigh, and all down the calf. . . ." His finger traces tiny pock marks on his leg as he talks, his pants half-mast at his knees. He hikes them up, never missing a syllable. "I'd been twenty months in the front line. I was eighteen. A couple of years before, I'd lied about my age when I enlisted. I was still a buck private. We were carrying ammunition to the front line at Farbus Wood. I had this ammo over my shoulder. I remember the quiet. So still. And then suddenly the German guns opened up, and a shell exploded and the shrapnel hit seven men in a row, killed 'em right there, and then hit me. I crawled into a gun emplacement and lay there. I was in hospitals for eighteen months. The doctors wanted to take the damn leg off but I said no way. When I got back to Canada in the spring of 1919 I was determined to play hockey. I took a job on one of my dad's railway construction projects. I wore the heaviest work boots I could find and I *ran* from construction gang to construction gang to strengthen my leg. At freeze-up I went back to my folks' place in Winnipeg and skated every day from early morning until late at night. By God, I played hockey in *seven* different leagues, sometimes two leagues on the same night, playing well past midnight."

This ebullience and enthusiasm carried Dutton through fifteen tumultuous seasons; he was a defenceman for Calgary in the old Western Canada Hockey League and then the Maroons and the Americans in the

NHL. He spent six more years as coach and general manager of the Amerks and then, though he was on his way to becoming a construction tycoon in the West, he returned to Montreal as NHL president from 1943 to 1946.

Dutton first became celebrated in the spring of 1924 when his Calgary Tigers engaged the Montreal Canadiens in the Stanley Cup final and he repeatedly tangled with the cold-eyed bad man of the NHL, Sprague Cleghorn. The Canadiens beat the westerners in two straight games, but eastern papers glowed with accounts of Dutton's fearless retaliation when Cleghorn jabbed him with his stick, elbowed his head, tripped him up and butt-ended him. Cleghorn is renowned to this day as one of the meanest men who ever played the game, overt and covert, but there was nothing surreptitious about Dutton's responses; he simply threw down his stick, tossed off his gloves and sailed into Cleghorn. Blood flowed like wine.

In another exchange, this one between Montreal's meteoric Howie Morenz and the Calgary defence of Dutton and his sidekick Herb Gardiner, Morenz swerved to avoid Dutton and was crushed by Gardiner; ligaments in his left shoulder were torn and the collarbone was splintered. Fifty years later, in a hotel room in Calgary, Dutton remembers the collision with blue eyes aglow. "Morenz was in the hospital for three months," he says. "Jesus, it was a lovely check."

Dutton and Gardiner were cherished chattels when the Western league folded in 1926 and its players parcelled to teams in the expanding NHL. Lester Patrick and his brother Frank, who owned the Vancouver and Victoria teams, were hustling the signatures of western players to be delivered to NHL clubs at handsome profits, but Dutton refused even to talk to Lester. He was convinced he could make a better deal for himself, one of the few players, apparently, to whom that thought occurred. Most of them were under the impression their contracts were simply being transferred to the expanding Eastern league, and were quite content to go. But Dutton and Gardiner agreed neither would sign with the Patricks, and Dutton went off to a job shipping hay in southern Saskatchewan, loading it into boxcars. One day a station agent from Moose Jaw interrupted his haying to tell him two men had been enquiring after him in the town.

"Was one a tall fellah and the other a little stout?" Dutton asked. "That's them."

Dutton went to his brother Jack and told him, "Jack, I don't want to talk to these fellahs; I'm afraid I'll weaken. When they come, the tall one is Lester Patrick and the stout one is Lloyd Turner, the Calgary owner. Jack, you tell 'em I'm not around here anymore."

And then Red ran to a bunk house, picked up a pair of field glasses and set off for a hillock a mile away. He watched through the glasses as his brother talked to the visitors, and then he saw them drive off.

That night he phoned his friend Herb Gardiner.

"You dirty son of a bitch," shouted Gardiner. "You signed a contract."

"I *didn't*," cried Dutton. "I hid."

There was a silence, and then Gardiner said resignedly, "Those bastards. They told me you'd signed. So I signed for four thousand. I hear I'm going to the Canadiens."

A week later the station agent showed up at Dutton's haying field again to tell him there'd been a long-distance telephone call for him.

"From where?" Red asked suspiciously.

"Montreal."

"Did you get a name?"

"Gerard. Eddie Gerard."

He drove twelve miles into town and called Eddie Gerard, coach of the Montreal Maroons, the Stanley Cup holders.

"I want to ask you two questions," Gerard said. "Have you signed a contract?"

"No," Dutton said.

"Are your legs sound?"

"Sound as a bank. I'm a hundred and seventy, lean as a rail and hard as a board."

"I'll meet you this Monday in Moose Jaw."

In the intervening days Dutton pondered ways that he might get a $5,000 contract from Gerard. He was twenty-eight years old, had a wife and two children living in an apartment while he toiled in the fields, and he had his eye on a home he could buy if he landed a good contract.

When Gerard arrived he got quickly to the point.

"I want you with the Maroons," he told Dutton. "I'll give you five thousand dollars for signing with me, I'll give you five thousand dollars a year for three years. I'll give you a five-hundred-dollar bonus if we make the playoffs, another five hundred if we go to the Stanley Cup final and another five hundred if we win it. And I'll pay your transportation both ways."

Dutton was stunned. All his dreams had come true. Now he could buy the home for his family. He couldn't speak, and Gerard misinterpreted his silence.

"All right, Red," he said. "I'll make it six thousand across the board but I can't go a cent higher."

"Eddie," Red managed to croak. "You've got a deal."

Dutton was lonely in his early days with the Maroons. The players weren't interested in the newcomer from the west. "They were a clannish bunch," he remembered, "up to their ass in the stock market. I used to sit in a corner of the dressing room; nobody talked to me. I sat next to the guy I played defence with, Reg Noble. He'd drink a case of beer the day of a game. His breath would knock you down."

On the ice, though, the Maroons were a hard team to beat. Nels Stewart, an ungiving man, was in his prime; Babe Siebert, Dunc Munro and Punch Broadbent were stars; and Praying Clint Benedict, who was always on his knees, was the goaltender. A year later Hooley Smith joined them from Ottawa, a bulldog in a fight. By then Dutton had penetrated the social barriers. One fall day the club's owner, Jimmy Strachan, turned over to some of the players a hunting lodge he owned on an island in the St. Lawrence River. Munro and Stewart got to drinking with both hands and Dutton had a few too. They decided to shoot some ducks. Munro hung back in a thicket of bushes close to the cabin and began tossing pebbles at Stewart, who was concentrating on the ducks. When Stewart didn't turn, Munro tossed another handful of pebbles to distract him. He succeeded. Stewart turned and calmly fired a shotgun blast into the thicket. He put twenty-seven pellets into Munro's leg, one of which lodged under his kneecap. Red, Nels, Babe and Hooley got him to a hospital where Munro said the wounds were accidentally self-inflicted. An operation was required to remove the pellet from beneath his kneecap and he missed the first two months of the season. The papers reported that he had torn his knee ligaments in practice.

Dutton spent four unrestrained seasons with the Maroons, a man easily taunted into reckless penalties, happiest when the games were thunderous and the bodies flying. Once, eager for a game with the arch-rival Canadiens to begin in the Forum, he chafed at the blueline as the referee searched vainly for a puck. None was immediately available at the timekeeper's table, and as the referee waited for someone to provide him with one, Dutton grew increasingly impatient. "Never mind the damn *puck*," he grated finally. "Let's start the game."

At one time he held the NHL record for penalties—139 minutes in a forty-four game schedule—and was taking so many that Eddie Gerard benched him for three games. Dutton was shocked. He stormed into Gerard's office and demanded he be reinstated or traded.

"If I put you back into the line-up, do you think you can control your temper?" Gerard asked.

"*Temper*," cried Dutton. "There's nothing wrong with my temper. It's my *enthusiasm* I can't control."

Gerard went off to the Americans as general manager before the

1929 season began and a year later was instrumental in acquiring Dutton. Disenchanted by the outlandish training methods of Coach Conacher, Gerard was able to persuade his superiors to trade Con to Montreal for Dutton and Hap Emms, a workman-like forward.

"You know Roy Worters, don't you?" Gerard said, introducing Dutton to his new teammates and stopping in front of the pint-sized goaltender. Worters looked up at his new defenceman.

"No, I don't think I know him," the goaltender said. "He's never been down at my end of the ice."

Dutton and Worters had great years. The goaltender yielded only seventy-four goals in the forty-four games and won the Vezina Trophy, and Dutton, finally getting a leash on his temper—or his enthusiasm—cut his penalty output to seventy-one minutes. One night after the Amerks had beaten the Rangers, Bill Dwyer, happy with the victory, walked into the dressing room and when he stopped beside Dutton he told Red to take his wife to a nightclub and have dinner on him. Dutton invited Worters and his wife Al to join them. When they were seated Worters immediately spotted the six-foot-seven heavyweight fighter, Primo Carnera, and his eyes began to twinkle.

"C'mon, Al," the tiny goaltender said to his equally tiny wife, "Let's dance."

Dutton, having seen the twinkle, turned to his wife. "Let's dance, too, Phyl. That little bastard is up to something and I don't want to miss it."

So the Duttons watched as Worters guided his wife close to Carnera's table. The giant Italian, who had won the world's heavyweight championship by beating Jack Sharkey, was seated at a ringside table in a conversation with three people. Suddenly, his face contorted and he reached frantically for his enormous foot. Worters, dancing close, had stepped heavily on it, and then had shouted at Carnera before darting away, laughing fiendishly, "You big bum, who did you ever lick?" Then he was lost in the crowd of dancers.

As the Amerks struggled for a playoff position, the delighted Dwyer invited several players to his thoroughbred farm in New Jersey one day early in March. Soon they were into Dwyer's bootleg whisky, which they called Jersey Lightning, and they decided to take his race-horses for a romp on the training track. George Patterson, one of the more productive Amerk forwards, fell off his horse and broke an arm. He was out for the season, "the victim of a freak accident in practice," the *New York Sun* reported.

By 1935, the Volstead Act repealed and government agents constantly hounding him, Dwyer was hard-pressed for money. The players often went a month without pay. Bullet Joe Simpson had become coach but the team won only twelve games in the forty-eight that season and crowds were poor. By then, Dutton was a sort of team banker, a hundred here, a hundred there, to tide the players over, and he was carrying a sheaf of N.S.F. cheques from Dwyer from the year before. At the end of the season the club treasurer Marty Shenker, a friend of Dwyer's, told him Dwyer wanted to see him.

"By Jesus," Dutton said, "I want to see him, too. He's into me for about four thousand dollars."

Dwyer was apologetic. He said he was getting things straightened around and that he'd soon settle up with Dutton and the players. In June, Dutton got a call from Shenker asking him to go to New York to see Dwyer.

The harassed owner had moved from the Forrest and they met in a nightclub he still owned. He lost no time with formalities.

"Will you take on the job of managing this hockey club?"

Dutton was startled.

"What about Simpson?" he asked.

"He's not going to be here," Dwyer said. "And we've got to get some players."

"I'll tell you, Mr. Dwyer; I'm worried about the finances of this club. What about those post-dated cheques?"

"Shenker tells me we owe around $19,000," Dwyer said. "If you'll lend me $20,000 we'll clean everything up."

"What about collateral?"

"I've got the hockey franchise and a race track in Montreal. That'll easily cover your twenty thousand."

Dutton returned to Calgary and conferred with his brother Jack. They decided to lend Dwyer the money, borrowing it from a Calgary bank against their construction machinery. Dwyer had gone to Florida, so Red sent the money to Shenker in Montreal where he was running Dwyer's race track. Shenker, in turn, forwarded the money to Dwyer. Dwyer took it to a crap game and lost every dime.

In this emergency, a matter of days before the Americans were due to open training camp at Oshawa, Dutton went to Montreal. There wasn't enough money even to get the players to camp. Dutton was standing in the lobby of the Mount Royal Hotel late one evening when Shenker burst through the revolving doors.

"Come to the room," he said excitedly to Dutton, heading for the elevators. "I've been in a crap game. I scored."

In the room he dumped bills on the bed. He had $4,300. Dutton grabbed four thousand, and headed for the telegraph office. He wired every man on the roster the money to get to camp.

In Oshawa, the players did their calisthenics in a field near the arena. Then they ran to the rink where their hockey equipment had been stored. A sheriff was standing by the door. The Doug Laurie sporting goods firm in Toronto had put a seizure on the equipment; the Americans owed him $1,900 from the previous season.

As it happened, Dutton knew Laurie, a peppery little guy who operated his store in Maple Leaf Gardens and was a hockey fan. Dutton implored Laurie to withdraw the writ, or at least to postpone issuance. Laurie finally agreed.

It turned out to be a big season for the Amerks. Longtime stars Normie Himes and Rabbit McVeigh had retired, but Dutton, who played, coached and managed the club, acquired his old friend Nels Stewart from Maroon days, and added Carl Voss, Cowboy Tommy Anderson, Baldy Cotton, Joe Jerwa and Al Murray to go with rising young stars Sweeney Schriner, Lorne Carr and Art Chapman. The Americans made the playoffs for the first time since 1929, drew $223,000 at the gate, paid their bills, including the $1,900 to Doug Laurie, and wound up with a $1,100 profit. They even eliminated Chicago in the first round of the Stanley Cup playoffs before submitting to Toronto in the semi-finals.

But in spite of this modest success, the league governors were moving to oust Dwyer, whose troubles with the U.S. government were endless and rising. In September 1936 league president Frank Calder advised the governors, who were, in essence, the club owners, that the Americans had failed to discharge certain obligations provided by league by-laws. The owners decided to pull the plug on their old partner, the bootlegger, cancelling his franchise and instructing Calder to operate it on behalf of the league. Which Calder did, incorporating the team as American National Hockey Club, Inc.

Dutton was unaware of this decision, though he knew from his own experience that Dwyer was in deep financial trouble. He also knew that he'd received none of his $20,000 loan. He was advised by his lawyer to foreclose on Dwyer, so he called the owner and arranged a meeting in his office in the Garden. It was not a meeting whose memory he relished.

"Dwyer had his wife with him when he came in," he recalls. "She was a fine woman, a genteel lady. I didn't want to talk in front of her but when I mentioned this to Dwyer he said it was all right. So I asked him if he had my money and he said no, he didn't. I told him my lawyer had advised me to foreclose.

"What happened then shook me. Tears began to run down Dwyer's cheeks. 'Don't do that, Red,' he said to me. 'My hockey club's the only legitimate thing I've had in my life. The NHL is starting to squeeze me, you know.' I asked him how he'd got himself into this mess. 'Well, Red, I've spent time and not much has gone right since. Today the internal revenue people have eight million against me. Red, I want my hockey club.' I pointed out to him that if I didn't foreclose on him, the NHL was ready to. He told me he could fight the NHL; he wanted me to hold off. I thought about it, but I finally said I couldn't do it, that my brother Jack and I had to answer to the Calgary bank."

A few days later Dutton got a call from Calder, asking him to meet him in Toronto. There, Calder told him the league was taking over the American franchise, that the owners wanted Dutton to continue running the club, working now for the NHL, not for Bill Dwyer. Calder gave him $5,000 of the $20,000 Dwyer owed him and Dutton decided to retire as a player and take on the job full time.

In November of that year the owners appointed the Toronto and Boston governors, Conn Smythe and Art Ross, to try to reach a settlement with Dwyer who had by now initiated a suit of his own against the league for loss of the franchise. They drew up a proposal, accepted by Dwyer, which gave him an option to buy back the Americans provided (a) he paid the league $130,000 by the following April 15, (b) paid the league the $20,000 he owed Dutton, (c) paid another $20,000 towards the current season's expenses, (d) dropped all litigation against the league, and (e) remained as a league governor and became a director of the new club. Dwyer did not turn up at the league's semi-annual meeting in early May. And since the April 15 expiry date on his option had come and gone without word from him, William V. Dwyer was drummed out of the regiment.

When Dutton retired as a player he lost none of his flair. In the clearest picture of him as a coach, he is restlessly prowling behind the Amerk bench wearing a pearl grey fedora, shouting at his men, jawing at rival players, and in a frequent impulsive gesture leaning far across the boards, thumping his hat viciously against them, to berate an official. Other times in his zeal he'd leap onto the ice, slipping and bouncing toward the referee, seeking to bawl him out at the closest possible range, often concluding his argument by sweeping off his hat and thumping it against his thigh. Apparently he had an inexhaustible supply of identical pearl grey fedoras; he was forever attacking things with them, yet in his calmer moments they were always impeccably tilted on his head.

Referees were always his target. One night in New York, Rabbit

McVeigh, a former Amerk teammate, made a call that enraged him.

"Rabbit, God dammit, is the government still paying you that pension for your ears?" he cried.

"Huh? Why sure, Red," replied puzzled McVeigh, who had been partially deafened by shelling in World War I.

"They should be paying you for your eyes, too," roared Dutton, slamming his hat on the boards. "You're blinder than you're deaf."

Talent was in short supply for the Amerks who had no farm system to speak of. The other clubs sponsored junior teams throughout Canada, giving them an endless chain of young talent, and Dutton started from scratch to try to build a supply line. Mostly, he made do with other team's cast-offs, and sometimes he truly prospered. In his second season as a bench coach he moulded a second-place finish largely out of other teams' discards—Nels Stewart and Hooley Smith from earlier high-living days, Ching Johnson, the bald-headed grinning veteran from the Rangers, Red Beattie and Johnny Sorrell from Detroit, Hap Day from Toronto. With them were the younger stars, the Chapman-Schriner-Carr line, Cowboy Tommy Anderson and Eddie Wiseman, and Earl Robertson, a goaltender Dutton had picked up from Detroit to replace Shrimp Worters. Halfway through the previous season Worters was found to be suffering from a severe hernia. Although he underwent an operation, his gritty and colourful career was ended, and Dutton made do in goal with veterans Lorne Chabot and Alfie Moore.

So, second in their division in the spring of 1938, the Amerks faced the hated Rangers in the first playoff round, attracting the year's largest crowd to the Garden, 16,340, for the deciding game. The Rangers got off to a 2-0 lead but Carr got one back and when Old Poison, Nels Stewart, tied the score the crowd turned delirious. Then they went berserk after a full hour and forty seconds of overtime when Carr scored again, and the Rangers were dead.

The Amazing Amerks *almost* made the Stanley Cup final that spring, something they never did accomplish. They beat Chicago in the opener of a two-of-three game semi-final, and with mere seconds remaining in regulation time in the scoreless second game Nels Stewart put the puck in the net. But the referee, Clarence Campbell, later the NHL president, disallowed the goal, ruling that Eddie Wiseman was in the crease when Stewart shot. So the teams went into sudden-death over-time, and after thirteen minutes Cully Dahlstrom scored for the Hawks to save them from elimination. Two nights later, another full house of Amerk fans streamed into the Garden for the deciding game and their mood grew joyous when Carr scored first for the Amerks. Then Chicago tied it. In the third period Hawk defenceman Alex Levinsky fired the puck past Earl Robertson but the red light back of the Amerk net did not go on and wild confusion ensued. Referee Ag Smith skated to the goal judge to consult with him on the shot and discovered the poor wretch's arms were pinned to his sides by Amerk fans refusing to allow him to turn on the light.

In succeeding seasons everything went downhill for Dutton and the Amerks. Most of the players were old, and as they retired Dutton was compelled to trade his stars, one by one, to fill their sweaters. He sent Sweeney Schriner to Toronto for Busher Jackson, Murray Armstrong, Buzz Boll and Doc Romnes. Always down, he never stopped believing things would be better next year. But the 1940-41 season was a disaster; the Amerks won only eight of their forty-eight games. Still, Dutton went into the dressing room for the last game of the season urging his players to give their best.

"You're still being paid," he cried. "There's nothing at stake except your God-damned pride, so go out there and keep punching." The Amerks were playing the Rangers in their finale, and in the first period a Ranger player slipped the puck between the feet of defenceman Joe Jerwa, stepped around him and scored. Dutton was livid, convinced Jerwa had purposely allowed the puck to slide between his feet. Moments later, the same thing happened. Dutton threw his hat to the floor and jumped on it. When the period ended he could barely wait to close the dressing-room door before sailing into Jerwa.

"God dammit, Joe," he yelled, "you did that on purpose. That'll cost you two hundred and fifty."

"Why don't you double it?" hollered Jerwa.

"It *is* doubled," cried Dutton.

"You can't do it," said Jerwa, beginning to grin.

"Why the hell can't I?"

"Because," laughed Jerwa, "there ain't that much comin' in my pay."

Dutton proclaimed the passing of the New York Americans, as such, for the opening of the 1941-42 season on November 13, and announced the birth of the *Brooklyn* Americans. The team played in the Garden but practices were moved to a small arena in Brooklyn. Dutton and his wife moved into an apartment there, and the players were urged to find places to live in Flatbush. But it was a dying gasp, a transparent effort to attract fans from across the bridge.

Dutton hung in. He had high hopes that season for a young brawler named Pat Egan, a heavy-duty fire hydrant who could skate and shoot and fight. Earlier, Red had signed a working agreement with Eddie Shore's Springfield club in the American Hockey League for the placement of players and their development. He and Shore were seated together in the stands in Calgary watching some rookies in a workout, and they were both impressed by Egan, who seemed to have the puck all the time. Dutton knew instantly that Shore would want him for Springfield, and he suspected he might be able to use him, himself. So there was a certain jockeying between them.

"Who's that lunkhead?" asked Shore innocently.

"Which lunkhead?" parried Dutton.

"That lunkhead with the puck."

"I dunno," said Dutton. "Must be a new boy just off the boat from some far-off land." Then he snorted. "God dammit, Eddie, that boy might just be good enough to make my club, and you know it."

"Now, Red, you'll have to admit he needs a little seasoning. If I take him to Springfield I'll make him the greatest hockey player who ever lived."

After a few more workouts it was decided Egan would go with Shore. Dutton brought him up to the Americans when injuries sidelined a couple of Amerk defenceman. Egan had a great game against the Canadiens. "He scored three goals and hit every son of a bitch on the ice," Dutton remembered.

So in the fall of '41, with the incubation period over, Red had high hopes that Shore had indeed turned Egan into the greatest hockey player who ever lived, or any facsimile thereof. But soon after the season began the suspicion grew in Dutton's mind that, as had happened two or three million other times in Amerk history, the bright lights of Broadway were getting to young Pat. He drew him aside one day in practice.

"Son, you've got a great future but you've got to watch yourself," he told the young defenceman. "Three days out of four you're in a coma. Now, my boy, a bottle of beer once in awhile never hurt a hockey player, but the hard stuff'll kill you. Pat, lay off that booze."

A few nights later, playing Boston, Egan had another bad game. "The worst damned game I ever saw played," Dutton cried afterwards. "God dammit, I want to see you in my office tomorrow at ten a.m."

In the morning when Egan appeared, Dutton sailed right in.

"What in the name of Christ was wrong with you? You played like a plumber."

"I don't understand it," Egan said. His brow furrowed. "Mr. Dutton, do you know Jack White?"

"You mean Jack White's bar? That Jack White?"

"Yeah, him."

"Of course I know Jack White. God dammit, everybody knows Jack White. What's he got to do with it?"

"Well, I went over to see him yesterday and, like you told me, I wouldn't drink that whisky. I only drank beer. Then I ate and I was at the Garden in plenty of time for the game."

"I'm not sure about beer *before* a game," Dutton said. "How many'd you have?"

"Oh, a dozen or so," replied Egan. "But no booze."

Bearing his crosses, Dutton fought on. Before the season was a month old he had been fined three times for rushing onto the ice to upbraid the officials over decisions adverse to the Amerks. He launched a full-throated campaign around the league in praise of his defenceman, Tommy Anderson, and was rewarded at season's end when the Cowboy was awarded the Hart Trophy as the league's most valuable player. The Amerks finished last that year; God knows where they'd have finished without a most valuable player.

That was the end for the Americans. The league's governors decided to dispense with their ward when the war began making serious inroads into the manpower supply, and they were none too sure how long the NHL itself would survive. Besides, Madison Square Garden wanted the Americans out. The Garden-owned Rangers were a power then and prospering—though the war was soon to turn the tables on them—and the corporation felt it had more profitable uses for the Amerks' twenty-four home dates. So the league shut down the franchise. Players who didn't qualify for military service moved to other clubs, and Dutton returned to his contracting business in Calgary which by now was in full boom, laying down twenty-two airports across the prairies for aircrew training in the British Commonwealth Air Training Plan. In the summer of 1942 he was offered two executive jobs in hockey—General John Kilpatrick, president of the Garden, wanted him to become vice-president in charge of hockey for the corporation, and Senator Donat Raymond, president of the Montreal Canadiens, offered him the job eventually taken by Frank Selke as managing director of the Habitants—but he rejected both.

However, when Frank Calder collapsed of a heart attack during a governors' meeting in Toronto on January 25, 1943, Dutton agreed to fill in for him for the balance of the season. When Calder died soon afterwards, Dutton agreed to keep the job until a successor was chosen. In June of 1945 when a successor finally was selected it turned out to be Dutton himself. He liked the job, which was partly why he took it, and also he wanted to stay close to the scene because he'd been assured by three governors, Senator Raymond, Major Frederic McLaughlin of Chicago and James D. Norris, then of Detroit, that if he could build a rink in Brooklyn he'd get a franchise there when the war ended. It turned out that Dutton's association with hockey didn't hurt his contracting business either. His Calgary partner, Reg Jennings, later observed that their multi-million dollar Standard Holdings Limited owed much to Dutton's hockey reputation and name on the door of the presidential suite at NHL headquarters. "Red's name opened doors for us in Ottawa when we were looking for federal government contracts," Jennings said. Nonetheless, Dutton's life had its setbacks. He lost his two eldest sons, Alex and Joe, flying over Germany with the RCAF. The youngest son, Norman, who falsified his age as his father had done and joined the Royal Canadian Navy, survived the war but died of a fall late in 1973. And, finally, Dutton was shut out of the promised franchise by the governors when World War II ended.

More than a quarter of a century has passed but that rejection by the league governors still rankles. From the hotel window Dutton looks again across the gleaming snow at the distant mountains. He inhales deeply on a cigarette. His blue eyes narrow and although he's seventy-five the fires still burn.

"It was at the league's annual meeting in June of 1946 at the Commodore in New York," he reconstructs. "I'd long since told them I was leaving, that by staying on any longer I wasn't being fair to my partners out here. Campbell was coming in to be the president, and I said I'd stay on to help him until he got settled in. Then, I said, there's this other matter; the franchise in Brooklyn.

"Well, there was this long stony silence. Finally, Connie Smythe says, 'Yes, Red, we've talked about that.'

" 'So?'

" 'There are complications.'

" 'Like what?'

" 'Well, for one thing, Madison Square Garden wants two franchises.'

" '*What,*' I say. 'But I've talked to people in Brooklyn. They've got a site and they're ready to put up a $7 million building as soon as I get the word from here.'

" 'Yes. Well, the Garden wants two.'

"I look around the room and nobody's looking at me, and I get the message. 'Gentlemen,' I said to the governors, 'You can stick your franchise up your ass.' I gathered up my papers and left."

CHAPTER FIVE: Oh, How the Frenchmen Fly

Tradition and nostalgia are not precisely the words that leap to mind when one thinks of big-league hockey. It's a mere fifty years since the NHL poked a tentative toe into Boston and New York, and it was only last week or the week before that expansion sent the game into several well-populated settlements in the south and far west. As for the WHA, by the autumn of 1974 when the new league launched its third season it was understandably less concerned about a glowing historic imprint than simple survival.

But then there is Montreal, a place apart. As the sports historian Herbert Warren Wind once observed of Montreal: "It is doubtful if there is any group of sports addicts anywhere which year in and year out supports its team with quite the supercharged emotion and lavish pride expended so prodigally by the citizens of bilingual Montreal on their hockey team, *Les Canadiens*—the Canadians."

Uniquely, the Flying Frenchmen pre-date the NHL itself. They were founded in December of 1909 and the league did not come into being until eight years later. The Habitants, as they're often called (that's what the H stands for within the large flat C of their emblem) have known a few dark moments in their history but most of the time they have been the most colourful team in hockey. Even their names are delicious to roll around on the tongue: Battleship Leduc, Rocket Richard, Aurel Joliat, Pit Lepine, Georges Vezina, Wildor Larochelle, Boom-Boom Geoffrion, Jacques Laperriere, Sylvio Mantha, Newsy Lalonde, Didier Pitre, Leo Lamoureux, Rogatien Vachon, Jean Beliveau, Jacques Lemaire, Yvan Cournoyer, and more.

These, obviously, are the Gallic heroes, but there have been plain stolid Anglo-Saxon names like Tom Johnson, Doug Harvey, Ken Dryden and Jim Roberts, too, and other non-French names with their own special ring: Goldie Prodgers, Amos Arbour, Skene Ronan, Sprague Cleghorn and his brother Odie, Frank Mahovlich, the Big M, and his brother Peter, Toe Blake, Gus Rivers and, of course, the immortal No. 7 Howie Morenz, the Stratford Streak. Although Morenz was of German origin and born in Ontario, the fans who soared vicariously with him into every success and suffered his every lump embraced the inspired fiction that he was a Swiss with a French spirit. He became a part of the national folklore, a symbol of an era now just a memory, a time when the players were a boisterous hard-living bunch, fiercely loyal to their teams. The rinks were smaller then, hung heavy in smoke and sweat and noise, and the teeming throngs were as much a part of the action as the game itself. Morenz was more than a flashing figure of great skill to the legion of factory workers, industry hands and railroaders who ebbed and flowed in one end of the Forum, calling themselves, with a nice ironic touch, the Millionaires. They identified with him as an expression of their own emergence and as he dashed across the brilliantly lit ice in his scarlet uniform with its white and blue trim, they toasted him in home-brew and bathtub gin and hoarsely echoed his name, *"Ow-ie, Ow-ie!"* or raised their battle cry, *"Les Canadiens sont là"*.

Still, it has been since Morenz's time that the Canadiens have taken hold of the Stanley Cup and made it into something very close to their own private bauble. Morenz was on three Cup-winning clubs (he died tragically at thirty-five in 1937) but it was in the early 1950s that *Les Canadiens* really began to *sont là*. In the twenty-year period between the springs of 1953 and 1973 they won the trophy an even dozen times, including a run of five straight, 1956 through 1960. More recently, in the decade ending with the playoffs of 1974, they won it six times, and it is not just by coincidence that they were led in these two decades first by Frank Selke and later by Sam Pollock, two of the shrewdest and in some ways weirdest managers in hockey history. This pair, neither of whom ever played their riotous game to any account, had the demeanour, manner and dashing elan of undertakers.

Selke was hired by Senator Donat Raymond in the summer of 1946 when both he and the Canadiens faced a bleak future, and held it until the summer of 1964 when Senator Hartland de M. Molson, whose family's brewery assumed control of the club in 1957, kicked him upstairs to a vice-presidency. Molson replaced him with Pollock, who had learned whatever he knew about hockey to that point at Selke's tiny knee. Each of them, in his own way, contributed enormously to Montreal's enduring success by putting his thinking apparatus to work at crucial moments in the game's development while his peers were sitting around counting their money.

Until he moved to Montreal, Selke took little but abuse from the irascible Connie Smythe at Toronto from the time Smythe bought the franchise of the old Toronto St. Pats in 1927 and later renamed them the Maple Leafs until he quit under the burden of Smythe's impossible rancour nineteen years later. In July of 1946 he became managing director of the Canadiens. A trim and gloomy man of perhaps five foot three, with a funereal mien, a soft high voice, a habit of rubbing his hands while he talked, rimless glasses and thin short-cropped hair, he sounded like a pastor visiting a covey of spinsters. I remember sitting with him on the porch of his daughter's home in Toronto one time after he had gone to Montreal to run the Canadiens. I was researching a piece on Rocket Richard and stayed to hear him pour out a litany of woe concerning life with Smythe. Yet, a year later when I asked him for permission to use some of that conversation in a piece about Smythe, he claimed to have no recollection of any such conversation. He felt only warmth toward his old pal Conn, he said; I must have been talking to somebody else.

Selke showed a side of himself in a paragraph of his memoirs when he wrote of his relationship with Dick Irvin, who coached one of his Stanley Cup teams before Selke brought in Toe Blake to handle that job.

"Hockey has provided me with hundreds of wonderfully staunch friends, but amongst these Dick Irvin was certainly the most intimate. We were about the same age; neither of us had any use for tobacco or liquor; and we cared even less for gambling. We shared the same lovely hobby of raising exhibition fowl. We had been very close, working under Conn Smythe at Toronto; and we were even more friendly and happier under kindly Senator Raymond at Montreal."

Selke did a superb building job for the Canadiens, a team that was brought out of the worst period in its history by World War II. From the mid-1930s when Morenz was traded to Chicago and age began to catch up with the Flying Frenchmen until the fall of 1943 when the manpower crunch of the war began to be felt most acutely, the Canadiens languished in or near the cellar. There was little discipline in the dressing room. Players smoked and drank beer beside their lockers, shaved when the mood struck them, and generally took small pride in their work or themselves. The Habs finished last or second-last six times during that eight-year span, and in the late 1930s crowds dwindled to three thousand a game.

With the war, though, the Canadiens did not suffer the player losses that eventually caught up to the other clubs because most of their players took jobs in essential war-production plants that kept them out of the armed services and permitted them to play hockey. They finished on top of the standings four straight years through the end of the war and the immediate post-war period, destroying humpty-dumpties. And by that final year Selke had arrived on the scene.

In spite of the string of successes, it was not a scene to exhilarate him, however, and soon after he'd assessed the line-up at training camp he asked Raymond for a meeting. He told the senator that no other team could come up with six players as good as his top six—goaltender Bill Durnan, defencemen Ken Reardon and Butch Bouchard, and the Punch Line of Elmer Lach, Toe Blake and Rocket Richard—but he said there were no reserves in sight. When Raymond asked for his solution Selke put forth an idea he'd evolved at Toronto in the early 1940s when Smythe was overseas. Sensing then that most young players in service would return stripped of their ice skills, he'd scouted kids' leagues and signed the best sixteen-year-olds he could find.

"I'd like to inaugurate a farm system here," Selke told the president. "I'd like to put a team in every province to build up young reserves. I did this in Toronto and the players there will be haunting us for years."

Raymond gave him *carte blanche.* In an era long before the NHL's junior draft Selke began tossing Montreal money into teams clean across Canada for the rights to their young players. He spent $300,000 one season to keep the system going since many affiliates lost money; $70,000 alone to bail out the farm team in Quebec City. As Selke predicted, the kids he'd recruited for Toronto haunted him for years: the Leafs won the Stanley Cup four times in the next five years. But then the fruit began to fall on Montreal. Beginning with the spring of 1951, the Canadiens reached the Stanley Cup final through ten straight seasons and won the old basin six times. They finished high in the standings in each of the next four years, but they won no Cups; indeed, they didn't reach the final in any of them. Whereupon Senator Hartland Molson moved the seventy-one-year-old Selke aside and brought in Pollock, Selke's thirty-eight-year-old disciple.

Samuel Patterson Smyth Pollock, son of an English immigrant haberdasher, brought to the job much of Selke's forward-looking acumen. He also brought a facial expression even more lugubrious than that of his predecessor. Then, as now, sad Sam squints and broods and stews,

84

a blocky man of five foot eight and a hundred and eighty pounds, with a circle of dark hair surrounding an ever-widening bald crown. The effect is of a monk with ulcers. Often he chews on a handkerchief in an interview or at a meeting. All that aside, Pollock learned his lessons well in twenty years in the organization as a coach and then manager of junior affiliates and later, under Selke's supervision, director of the highly fruitful farm system. Not long after he got the top job he proved he knew how to look ahead; it was none other than Sad Sam who supplied the blueprint for the NHL's expansion program in 1967. By it, the old-line clubs with full rosters and legions of reserves absorbed no loss of strength while supplying surplus players to the six new expansion teams. Nobody had a larger surplus of bodies than the Canadiens, thanks to Selke's full-blown Pollock-administered farm system, and none could now more easily afford to lop off a few expendables and feel no pinch whatever.

But Sad Sam was just getting started. When the NHL introduced the junior draft it adopted a method designed to help the weakest teams by giving them first crack at the junior graduates each year. The lower a team finished in the standings, the higher its order of selection in the annual draft; the worst got the first pick, the second-worst the second pick, and so on. Enter wily Sam Pollock: he began to trade off veterans from his vast resources to expansion teams in exchange for their draft choices far into the future. Expansion teams, eager to attract and hold fans immediately, couldn't afford to wait years for the fresh legs they'd eventually be able to draft.

So, then as now, they trade them off to the rich-in-talent, and since no one is richer in talent than Sam the Canadiens have acquired high draft positions for years to come. As an illustration of this, between 1968 and 1973 Montreal had a total of fourteen first-round draft choices while the poor downtrodden California Golden Seals had two and the rich but mired Los Angeles Kings only one; the California teams had traded away the future trying to find patches for the present. At the June draft meeting of 1973 the Canadiens, who had won the Stanley Cup a few weeks earlier, owned seven of the first twenty selections, including the No. 2 pick acquired from California three years before. Sam's cupboard was already so stuffed that he traded *this* off to the Atlanta Flames for their first pick in *1978*.

"People criticize my tactics, sure," Pollock said after that meeting, as the rich got ever richer. "They claim I take advantage of other general managers. That's not correct. If you take advantage of people, they won't deal with you again. Look, I've made countless deals with Minnesota, St. Louis, California, Los Angeles. So why do they keep coming back? Obviously I'm giving them something good in return."

Who can argue with that kind of logic? Or not see through it? It's not for nothing that Sam's sobriquet, picked up in the early 1970s when his benevolence was becoming universally recognized, is the Godfather.

Sad Sam stews many of his schemes in the back seat of a chauffeured Lincoln or while he squints at some of the hundred or so paintings that hang in his home. "Riding in the car lets me relax and concentrate," he says. He refuses to climb into an airplane. During playoffs he'll sit in his car from Montreal to Chicago if necessary, some 850 miles. "I stopped flying after making two hundred and sixty-two plane trips one year."

Oddly, the Flying Frenchmen had their genesis in a conversation between a Scottish baker and an Irish contractor one December night in 1909. In the whole world there was only one professional hockey league then, the Eastern Canada Hockey Association, and it was not flourishing. Hoping to strengthen it, James Strachan, the manager of the Montreal Wanderers, a Montrealer whose family was prominent in the baking industry, made a thoughtful remark to young Ambrose O'Brien whose father had made a fortune as a railway contractor.

"A club composed entirely of French-Canadian players in Montreal, with its seventy percent French population, is bound to be a success," Strachan said.

But O'Brien wasn't interested in the conversation. He wanted his home-town team, the Renfrew Millionaires, to win the Stanley Cup and he made application to the one pro league, the Eastern Canada, for its admittance. But, for whatever reason, the application was refused. O'Brien, fuming at the rebuff, remembered Strachan's remark and set out to form not just a French team for Montreal but a whole new league to challenge the men who'd rebuked him. He financed and founded the Canadiens on December 10, 1909, depositing $5,000 in a St. James Street bank to guarantee players' salaries. They got a series of postdated cheques that could be stopped at the bank if any player defected. He commissioned Jack Laviolette, an itinerant hockey player and owner of a restaurant in Montreal called Jack's Café, to put together a team for the five thousand.

To round out his league, O'Brien persuaded James Strachan to transfer his Montreal Wanderers to it, brought in the Renfrew Millionaires, and financed two more teams at Cobalt and Haileybury in the booming mining belt of Northern Ontario. He called the league the National Hockey Association, and it turned out to be the forerunner of the NHL, formed in November of 1917.

O'Brien's move caused an upheaval out of which the Ottawa Senators and the Montreal Shamrocks withdrew from the Eastern Canada league and joined O'Brien's NHA bringing an end to the tottering Eastern league. The new NHA season began on January 5, 1910, with the Canadiens playing Cobalt in a tiny noisy smoky firetrap called the Jubilee Rink in Montreal. They attracted just under three thousand customers who watched seven-man hockey in two thirty-minute periods. And the Canadiens were indeed comprised entirely of French-Canadian players, among them Jack Laviolette, the café owner; goaltender Joe Cattarinich, who later with Leo Dandurand as his partner became co-owner of the club; Newsy Lalonde, then the greatest lacrosse player anywhere; and Didier Pitre, who'd been paid $2,000 for a season with Renfrew a few years earlier but who signed for considerably less in order to join his teammates in shouting imprecations in French at referees. For that first game, Lalonde was the highest-paid Canadien on the ice; he got $1,300 for the season, which the Canadiens launched with a 7-6 victory.

O'Brien made a fifty percent profit on the Canadiens even before the season ended. He sold the franchise for $7,500 to a Montreal wrestler and fight promoter who called himself George Kennedy. Actually, Kennedy's name was Kendall, but his father, a dour Scottish sea captain, was so enraged when his son told him of his wrestling ambitions that George altered his surname.

To promote his team in the French-speaking townships east of Montreal, Kennedy arranged occasional exhibitions in the little towns, one of them Chicoutimi, a thriving lumber town on the Saguenay River. These were welcome workouts for the players, giving them a chance to sample the local beer and causing them no undue effort. But it didn't work out that way at Chicoutimi. They outplayed the local amateurs, of course, but as they swept in droves upon a pale slender young man in the Chicoutimi goal they were thwarted by his fast-moving legs and, more particularly, his magic wand of a stick which he used to deflect the puck as deftly as a man bunting baseballs or a batsman in cricket. Into the third period the Canadiens still had not cracked him, and when a Chicoutimi player broke free long enough to score for the amateurs they redoubled their efforts. But to no avail. The game ended with the professionals still scoreless. It was, of course, their introduction to Georges Vezina, who during the next fifteen years became celebrated as the Chicoutimi Cucumber, the coolest goaltender in hockey and one of the most accomplished.

From this exhibition, Vezina joined the Canadiens for the following season, which opened on New Year's Eve, the last night of 1910. Ottawa beat the Canadiens 5-3 and went on to win the league championship in the sixteen-game season. In an era of high-scoring games when goaltenders were not permitted to leave their feet, Vezina led the goalers with a 3.9 average.

He was a tall slim solemn man with sleek dark hair who never learned English. One must presume he never had time to; he sired twenty-two children and died at thirty-seven after fifteen years of pro hockey. He played his final game in Pittsburgh on November 28, 1925, the year the Pirates joined the NHL. He'd played on five championship teams, two of them Stanley Cup winners, and had not missed a game in 367 from the moment of his debut until the second period of that game in Pittsburgh. His temperature was 103 at the end of the first period and he suffered a slight hemorrhage during the intermission. But he went back onto the ice. Just as the referee dropped the puck for the start of play he slumped in front of his net. He was carried from the ice; later, his illness was diagnosed as tuberculosis. He died in Chicoutimi four months later.

Long before that, the Canadiens had won their first Stanley Cup; that was in 1916 when George Kennedy, "without once raising his voice or using an oath," as Newsy Lalonde phrased it, cajoled the Canadiens to their first of an endless chain of Cup acquisitions. In the spring of 1919 the Canadiens were involved in the only Cup final ever suspended. They were playing the Seattle Metropolitans in the Pacific Coast city during an influenza epidemic, and Kennedy and all but three of his players caught the flu in varying degrees of severity. Joe Hall, a brilliant and ferocious centre player, was seriously ill. Bad Joe was next thing to a surgeon with his stick; it sometimes caressed the skulls of opposing players more often than it encountered the puck. In one game against Toronto en route to the final, Bad Joe carved up Alf Skinner so severely that he was taken over by the cops as he arrived at the bench with a match misconduct penalty. He was booked at a downtown jail and charged with assault. The case was dismissed.

Hall became ill in the fifth game in Seattle. It was an exhausting series. The fourth game, a scoreless tie in which Vezina weaved his wand in wondrous fashion, went through an hour and forty minutes of overtime. The Canadiens won the fifth game to tie the series at two wins each but by then they were so short-staffed that Kennedy suggested a group of replacements be brought in from Victoria. The Seattle team refused that move and the series was abandoned. On April 5, six days after he'd been hospitalized, Joe Hall died. Kennedy himself never fully recovered. He died two years later, at forty-one.

The club was put on the auction block in October 1921. Out of a flurry of bidding that started at $8,000 Leo Dandurand, Louis Letourneau and Joe Cattarinich, who were then operating a racetrack at

Cleveland, had their representative, Canadien coach Cecil Hart, buy the club for them for $11,000. It took them three years to build another Stanley Cup winner, employing the haphazard scouting methods of the time. Sylvio Mantha, who became a Hall of Famer, was found in Montreal idly playing shinny on the school rinks of a working-class district called St. Henri. Dandurand happened to run into George Boucher, an Ottawa star, at a racetrack in the summer of 1922. Boucher said he'd been impressed in a game against the Saskatoon Shieks of the Western Canada league by a tiny elusive rookie named Aurel Joliat, a fellow Ottawan. Dandurand incensed Canadien fans by trading the idolized Newsy Lalonde for the unknown Joliat. He got so many telephone threats that he had the phone disconnected.

But of the trade Lalonde said, "I was getting $2,000 a season at Montreal. Leo knew I was over the hill, but he made Saskatoon pay me $4,500 to be the playing coach. I was delighted."

As casually as he'd met George Boucher at the track, Dandurand dropped into a restaurant for a mid-morning cup of coffee and encountered Ernest Sauve, who refereed amateur games and who, indeed, had worked a junior game the night before. Sauve bubbled with praise for a young Stratford player, Howie Morenz, and urged Dandurand to see him. The Toronto St. Pats were interested in him too, it turned out, and Morenz later admitted he signed with the Canadiens because Dandurand paid a forty-five-dollar tailor's bill and gave him another three hundred to clear up a number of small debts. A salary of $3,500 for the twenty-four-game NHL schedule was signed July 7, 1923, and because the seventh was Dandurand's birthday the owner assigned young Morenz sweater number 7. Eleven years later, in the autumn of 1934 when Dandurand traded Morenz to Chicago, he threw a going-away dinner for him and announced that no other player would ever wear Morenz's number. None ever did. Morenz was shattered by the trade, and Dandurand took more abuse for it than he'd absorbed in sending Newsy Lalonde to Saskatoon twelve years earlier. He insisted in later years he made the trade for Morenz's own good. "Howie was fading fast," the suave and handsome owner told me one day in his Montreal apartment, a sick man then but still strikingly dark-featured with thick sleek white hair. "The fans had already begun to boo him in the Forum, and I knew it would get only worse. At least in Chicago he was not the hero he was in Montreal."

Morenz drifted to the Rangers from the Hawks and when Dandurand sold the Canadiens for $165,000 to the Canadian Arena Company, headed by Senator Raymond, Howie was brought back to the *rouge, blanc et bleu.* He had begun to show flashes of his old Forum form but a crash into the boards and a broken leg finished him. He was still in hospital when he died on March 8, 1937, apparently of a heart attack. His body was placed at centre ice in the Forum where Canadien players formed a guard of honour as fifteen thousand people moved slowly and silently into the rink for the service. It was the eeriest of moments in Forum history, the great arena filled to the uppermost iron beam but not a sound to be heard. Outside, in the bright bitter cold, tens of thousands of people stood with heads bared as the cortege passed, block after block after block of them.

Eighteen years later, the enlarged Forum seethed as a new hero, Maurice (Rocket) Richard, suffered an indignity so enormous in the eyes of the Montreal multitudes as to incite them to riot. This was St. Patrick's night, a week before the schedule ended, and Clarence Campbell had announced that Richard was suspended for the rest of the season, including the forthcoming playoffs. Fans threw garbage and smoke bombs at the league president as he sat in his box during the first period of a game between Detroit and the Canadiens, a bizarre piece of scheduling in that the teams were tied for first place with two games left to play. By the end of the first period smoke was curling ominously across the ice and the atmosphere was electrically tense. A nut leaped at Campbell and struck him twice. The police chief got Campbell safely out of the building. Then the city fire director ordered the Forum evacuated because there was a menace of panic. The game was forfeited to Detroit, driving the crazies crazier. As they milled into the streets, storefront windows were broken, looters streamed through them, cars were upturned and fires started. Damage mounted into the hundreds of thousands of dollars, thirty-seven people were arrested, and more than a hundred rampaging juveniles were picked up by the gendarmes.

Precipitating these scenes was the suspension of Richard. They, in turn, followed the most explosive season of the Rocket's career. Late in December he'd fought with Bob Bailey, a bellicose Toronto forward. When linesman George Hayes got them stopped Richard whipped an empty hockey glove across the official's face. The referee Red Storey handed Richard two misconduct penalties and Campbell tacked on a $200 fine. A few months later, in Boston, Richard made all of his earlier exploits seem pale. He was highsticked and cut by Hal Laycoe. He stood for a moment, touching the cut, then examining a trace of blood on his bare hand. He was immobile except for the flashing black eyes searing his tormentor, an indecisive bull studying a toreador. Then everything burst.

He charged at Laycoe, raising his stick high. He brought it down with both hands across the Boston player's shoulder, grazing his cheek.

Linesmen clutched Richard, tearing away his stick. He broke free, found another stick lying on the ice, attacked Laycoe with two one-handed swings across his back, breaking the stick. A linesman, Cliff Thompson, flung his arms around Richard's heaving chest but the insatiable Rocket broke free again, grasped yet another stick from the ice, and assailed Laycoe a third time across the back as the Boston player ducked and back-tracked. Thompson, who'd already earned the Croix de Guerre with several oak-leaf clusters, once more entered the breach. He tackled Richard this time, got him to the ice and struggled to hold him. But another Canadien player pushed him away, and Richard leaped to his feet and punched Thompson twice in the face. Finally he was dragged away by less militant teammates, and the referee assessed him a match misconduct. And it was after this that President Campbell suspended the Rocket for the season.

He was something, that Richard. He was a quiet enough fellow most of the time, a dark brooder, but his coach, the rasp-tongued Dick Irvin, had a way of winding up his passions. When the dam burst it damned nearly disintegrated everything within reach. Indeed, it was after the Boston incident and the resultant Forum riot that Selke told Irvin he had to go. On that St. Patrick's night Irvin observed in some amusement, "I've often seen the Rocket fill this place, but this is the first time I've seen him empty it." Selke was not amused, particularly when Irvin launched a tirade at Campbell after the Rocketless Canadiens lost their last game of the season in Detroit and finished second to the Wings by a two-point margin.

"Look, Dick," Selke quotes himself in his memoirs, "you can't coach this team any longer. It's all very well to keep the team full of fight. But there's a limit to that, too. And I don't think you know that limit. Now, Dick, you can stay with us or you can go to Chicago. That's up to you. But if you stay with us, you can't be coach. There will be another job for you at your full salary as long as you wish."

Oddly enough, Irvin went to Chicago, whose owner, Jim Norris, had already publicly expressed an interest in his services and had asked Selke's permission to discuss a proposition with Irvin a few weeks earlier. In professional sports it's considered ungentlemanly to tamper with another club's chattel, although it is considered gentlemanly to fire people.

Anyway, Selke brought in Toe Blake as Irvin's replacement, and Blake kept the Frenchmen flying through the next thirteen years, working for Selke and, later, Sam Pollock. He coached eight Stanley Cup winners in that remarkable run, as blunt, determined and uncomplicated behind the bench as he'd been in thirteen years as a leftwinger overshadowed by linemate Richard. No one ever overshadowed him as a coach. His goaltender through many of his tall triumphs, Gump Worsley, once undertook to explain Blake's *modus operandi*.

"This man loved to win, eh?" Worsley said. "He could communicate this . . . this . . . *pride*. Some guys can communicate, some guys can't. Toe could. He had a way, like an earnestness, of making you feel that since the idea of this game is to win, you've got to give it your best shot—every game. He blew his stack, sure, but if he had something to say to you he'd call you in, and it'd be private. To be a coach, you've got to be a psychologist, eh? You've got twenty different personalities in that room. Toe knew his twenty guys. He'd draw you aside and he'd say, 'You're not goin' so good. You're goin' down too much and when you go down you're not gettin' up quick enough. Is there anything on your mind? Things okay at home?' Now, me, I responded to this. I figured here's a guy concerned about me. I dunno how he handled the others, but that's how he handled me."

One way and another, after Blake left, claiming the need to win in Montreal carried too much pressure for a man to carry endlessly, the Flying Frenchmen went right on winning. They won for Claude Ruel and Al MacNeil and Scotty Bowman, and perhaps none of their victories better reflected the essence of the Montreal Canadiens than a first-round turnaround in the playoffs of 1971. It had been a season in which the Boston Bruins broke scores of scoring records all year long and finished in first place by a full twenty-four points ahead of the labouring Habitants. The Bruins won the first playoff game against them, too, and were leading the second by 5-1 in what looked like a runaway. Suddenly the Canadiens were touched by an unseen hand; they scored six straight goals to win that game, and went on to win the series and then another Stanley Cup. Gerry Cheevers, the Boston goaltender, wearily looked back on the disaster:

"God knows, it wasn't something new for the Bruins to pile into a big lead that season and then let up a little. The trouble is, though, that letting up against the Oakland Seals or the Buffalo Sabres is not quite the same thing as letting up against the Montreal Canadiens. The Flying Frenchmen go slightly glassy-eyed when they get to thinking of their tradition and their pride and the rest of that bullshit; they suddenly acquire adrenalin not available to other teams."

It's been that way for generations.

CHAPTER SIX: The Clan Conacher

For millions of people in Canada, hockey is a sanctuary from life's harassments, an alternative world in a land of numbing winters. For decades the most popular radio program was Foster Hewitt's Saturday-night network hockey broadcasts from Maple Leaf Gardens in Toronto, a kind of common denominator that brought the people of the whole vast disparate snowswept country together and gave them memories not of men but of figures in a bright and glittering bowl where everything was warm and glamorous.

Once, it seemed that every corner lot in every town and hamlet had its hockey rink where kids aspired to play, some day, in the NHL, and there were also the big hard-working families in the cities who raised big self-reliant kids, families who lived and grew up on the curbstones and achieved their own earthy kind of distinction starting from scratch, and finally making it, in the face of tough sweaty competition, through hockey. Such a family was the Conachers of Davenport Road, one of Toronto's higher-class slums in the 1920s.

There were ten Conachers, five boys and five girls, and they didn't have a pretzel. But, in one way and another, the Conachers gained a place in the sun. Lionel got to be a great hockey player, greater lacrosse player and even greater football player, and he was called the Big Train because he could do anything and do it hard and tough and surpassingly well. He coached the Americans and the Maroons (they won the Stanley Cup in 1935) and was officially named Canada's greatest athlete of the half-century in a poll taken back in 1950. He became a Member of Parliament and even owned a long black Cadillac. Charlie Conacher became the Big Bomber of the Toronto Maple Leafs with the legendary Kid Line, was on the NHL's first all-star team three times as the best rightwinger in the game and won the scoring championship twice. He coached the Chicago Black Hawks for the better part of three nerve-racking seasons.

Roy Conacher could put the puck in the net as well as any hockey player who ever played. He won the NHL scoring championship and was the all-star leftwinger in the 1948-49 season. Roy's twin brother Bert was an outstanding young player, too, but a hockey stick blinded his left eye when he was sixteen and prevented him from taking up a pro career. Dermott Conacher was a fine football player in the early 1920s but Derm, who was two years younger than Lionel, didn't have Lionel's zeal and gave up sports to start working. The five girls, Dolly, Mary, Queenie (she was christened Queen Victoria May Conacher), Nora and Kay, were all good skaters and softball players throughout their adolescence.

Hockey made the Conacher name one of the most famous in Canada and in the big eastern U.S. cities where the game was played. It was Lionel's third or fourth best sport but in the late 1920s and early 1930s it was the only game where he could make money. He liked the game and the family needed the money, so he turned himself to hockey. And Charlie did, too. When Charlie started playing he was terrible. He was so bad a skater that the other kids made him the goaltender to keep him out of the way.

The family lived a few doors from a school where there were two hockey rinks and a pleasure-skating rink. Chuck just about lived on those rinks. He practised shooting the puck against the boards for hours. He skated until he thought his legs would drop off. Even when he made the Leafs he kept at it. There was no Sunday hockey in the NHL then so he used to go down to the old Mutual Street Arena which pre-dated Maple Leaf Gardens and practice with Lorne Chabot, the Leaf goaltender, and he'd black-and-blue him. He'd spend an hour just shooting for spots. Then another hour skating in on Chabot, not shooting but trying to outguess him, to fake him out of position before tucking the puck in the net. Chabot would tell him where his fakes weren't fooling him, or how he was tipping his moves, and he showed Chabot where the goaltender was vulnerable. They'd have side bets for a drink or a sandwich; Charlie would bet he could outguess him six times out of ten, and it got to the point where he could always do it.

Almost everything came the hard way with the Conachers. Their father, Ben Conacher, was a teamster, and it was a good week when he made twenty dollars. One winter he made $7.50 a week cutting ice in lagoons. He used to leave the house at 5 a.m. to be at work by seven. He'd walk a good five miles to the foot of Toronto Bay, then hike across the frozen bay to an island where he'd cut ice in the lagoons until six o'clock at night and pile the blocks in the ice houses on the island for summer use. Then he'd walk home, getting there about eight. He'd eat his supper and then go to the stable and hitch up his horse to a snowscraper and clean off the rinks on the school grounds. He got a dollar a night for keeping the ice clear.

Christmas was something. The family always got Christmas hampers through the church from one of the newspapers' Santa Claus funds. Each hamper contained a pair of woollen stockings, a toque, a sweater, a pair of mitts, an apple, an orange and a bag of candy. In later years Charlie often recalled a particular Christmas morning when he'd be eleven or twelve, charging through the snow to a nearby ravine. He was wearing the new toque and sweater and mitts and when he got to the crest of the ravine he could see the kids below; they were wearing the same red toques and the same grey sweaters and the same blue woollen mitts that he was wearing. A lot of people on Davenport Road knew about those Christmas hampers.

It wouldn't be accurate to say the Conacher boys played hockey twelve months of the year because there were times when they used to sleep and eat. But trifling things like June breezes or Indian summer never deterred them. Every day, right after school, they'd go out on the street to play hockey if the weather was too mild to permit them to play on the school ice. They'd use a sponge ball or an old tennis ball for a puck and burlap coal sacks for nets. They played with a kid named Bill Hunter, who could play a mouth organ, and they'd line up on the street while he played "God Save the King", just like they did at the pro games in Mutual Street Arena and later in Maple Leaf Gardens, and then they'd start, racing up and down the street in their boots. They stuffed magazines inside their socks to serve as shin pads.

Even after Chuck turned pro with the Leafs in the fall of 1929 he continued to play shinny with his brothers, although Frank Selke, who was the assistant manager of the Leafs under Connie Smythe, used to tell him he was crazy because he might get hurt. Once, he was almost right. Charlie was starting down the front steps to join Roy and Bert, smoking a big cigar. Bert fired the sponge ball at him. He didn't see it coming and it whacked him in the balls. He felt like he'd been kicked there. He refused, however, to reveal his pain to his young brothers. "This cigar," he gasped, "must be made of rope. I don't feel so good. I'll just sit here awhile."

Those cigars of his made as great an impression on the kids as the fact he'd made the NHL. He bought his first one the day after his first game in the big leagues, the opener of the 1929-30 season. The Gardens hadn't been built then, and the Leafs opened against Chicago in Mutual Arena. In later years, millions of fans retained the notion the famed Kid Line of Conacher, Joe Primeau and Busher Jackson started right off together but that wasn't so. Actually, Conacher went out on right wing beside Eric Pettinger and Baldy Cotton. Early in the game he got a pass from Pettinger near the right boards. He faked to his left as though to split the Chicago defence, and when Taffy Abel moved to block him he skated wide around Abel's left, broke clear on the great goaltender Charlie Gardiner, and scored his first NHL goal. Two nights later, against Boston, he scored two more. The next day he bought two more cigars to impress the kids on Davenport Road.

Charlie and Roy honed their shooting and stickhandling skills in those street sessions, but there was a tragedy there, too. Once when Chuck and Bert were jostling for the ball Charlie's stick cracked Bert at the side of his left eye for a seemingly meaningless two-stitch cut. But about eight months later Bert went blind in that eye. He was sixteen then. He played junior afterwards, but he couldn't move on to the pros.

It was a marvellous day for Charlie when he signed his first contract. It was for $20,000 for two years, with an advance of five thousand. Lionel steered him in his negotiations with Connie Smythe, the Leaf boss. Lionel was coaching and playing for the Americans then. He could have signed young Chuck, but he was living high in New York and he didn't think Bill Dwyer's club the right environment for his kid brother. But he knew the Leafs needed big strong boys like Chuck, so he helped him put the squeeze on Smythe. Ten thousand dollars a year in 1929 was a great deal of money for anybody; to a family like the Conachers it seemed like all the money in the world. Charlie was a couple of months shy of twenty then; one of the first things he did was to buy a yellow Buick coupe with a rumble seat. Then he headed for the house on Davenport Road, picking up a dozen sandwiches and some soda pop at a delicatessen along the way.

Five kids were home, the twin girls Kay and Nora, the twin boys Roy and Bert, and older sister Mary. The four oldest, Dolly and Lionel and Derm and Queenie, had all married and were gone. When Charlie stopped at the curb in his yellow menace the five kids charged from the porch followed by their mother and Ben, and they piled into Charlie's car. He circled the block a couple of times, then stopped in the big ravine back of their house. They had a sandwich picnic.

In Charlie's first season he crashed into a goal post and as the year wore on he began to get pains in his back. It got so that he could barely bend to tie his skates, and finally he was hospitalized. One of his kidneys was badly damaged and had to be removed. He hated the loneliness of the hospital room. In later years he became a sophisticated man, a ladies' man of awesome repute, spectacularly endowed, a tough businessman, finally a millionaire. But when he was twenty in this hospital room he was a lonesome boy away from home. He asked Bert and Roy and Derm to stay with him. When visiting hours expired they left the hospital, then circled across a parking lot back of the building to a fire-door, tip-toeing along the corridor to Charlie's room, keeping him company until he fell asleep. On one of these visits Charlie heard someone approach the door, and his brothers squeezed into the tiny bathroom, standing in the bathtub behind the shower curtain until a nurse, who had come to check on the noise, was persuaded by Charlie she had the wrong address.

There was a particular bond between Roy and Bert. When Detroit traded Roy to Chicago in 1947 he refused to join the Black Hawks unless Bert moved in with him in Chicago. Bert said he didn't mind a winter in Chicago as long as Roy looked after the rent, so the two roomed together in Chicago. Roy's wife Fran always accepted the bond philosophically. "When I married Roy," she'd say. "I married them both." When Bert married, his wife Grace felt the same way.

Even in moments of high triumph there was that bond. In the spring of 1939 when Roy was popping in goals for Boston, the Bruins gained the Stanley Cup final against Toronto. The teams split the first two games in Boston and then moved to Toronto for the next two. The Bruins surprised by winning the third game and then closing in on the championship in the fourth game with a 2-0 shutout in which Roy scored both goals. The Boston management was so jubilant that although the team still needed one more victory to sew up the series, the players were given a party at the Silver Slipper club. Of course, Roy was the toast of the gay affair. Except that Roy didn't show.

Right after the game, Roy and Bert and Nora and a friend of Nora's named May Brown went back to the Conacher house and sat around the big kitchen table playing penny ante. Barely a dollar changed hands all night. They'd argue over whether a flush beat a straight or a straight beat a pair when there were all of a dozen pennies in the pot. Roy would always rather be with Bert and Nora than any of the guys he played with, and he was in the big league for ten seasons.

The Bruins caught a train to Boston the next afternoon and finished off their Stanley Cup triumph a night later. Roy got the winning goal in a game that ended 3-1, and turned part of his playoff money into a family pool, as all of them did as soon as they were old enough to work.

Lionel was the man who led the Conachers up from the curbstones, a truly astonishing athlete who later became a rich man in business. There was scarcely a dissenting voice back in 1950 when Lionel was voted Canada's outstanding athlete of the half-century, and by then he'd been retired for fifteen years. The *New York Times* columnist John Kieran once was asked to name the best athlete he'd ever seen in Madison Square Garden, and in part here's what he wrote:

> Naturally I saw Joe Louis perform in the Garden. Babe Ruth too—in a softball game, but it was still Babe Ruth. Bill Tilden, who whacked a tennis ball under that roof, was a great man to watch. It would be hard to pick from such a glittering galaxy the one who put on the greatest show . But for me, if it's the best athlete up for selection, one vote for Large Lionel Conacher.

In 1940 a Toronto columnist reprinted a letter from one of America's foremost football coaches, Carl Snavely of Cornell, who said that Lionel "was probably the greaterst athlete that I have ever coached in football or in any other form of athletics, and it has been my good fortune to have on my teams some of the greatest football players who ever played American football, All-Americans who will be remembered for generations because of their outstanding performances."

Lamenting that Lionel had decided to play professional hockey instead of continuing his football under Snavely at Bellafonte Academy, a prep school in Pittsburgh, the coach added: "I don't believe I have ever had a fullback who was a better runner in the open field, or who was a better punter, or who so fully possessed all of the qualities of speed, skill, dexterity, aggressiveness, self-control and the various attributes that are required for superiority in the American game of football. He was far superior to many boys on the same team who later won All-American honours in several universities."

For all of his aggressiveness and determination, Lionel played sensibly. The great little leftwinger of the Canadiens, Aurel Joliat, once remarked of Lionel, "He never tried to hurt a small player like myself." When he got hot, though, Lionel was a terror, tossing aside his stick and gloves and taking on all the policemen the other teams sent out. Hockey was the one game he found difficult, largely because he didn't skate until he was sixteen, and he always was an awkward man on the ice. But he approached hockey intelligently and figured out angles at which it was difficult for even a fast-skating forward to break clear on the net. Playing those angles, he'd force forwards wide, keeping them between him and the boards. He developed a sliding, puck-stopping method of smothering shots, dropping with uncanny timing to one knee, a style that prompted the Toronto sportswriter Ted Reeve to call him the Travelling Netminder. And because he had put more thought, of necessity, into actually manufacturing his hockey ability, he became a wily ice general. His perfect frame for contact sports helped him in his early years, and God knows he needed it for as a kid who'd had nothing he sampled the social side of big-league living, too. Sampled? When Lionel was with the Amerks and, later, the unrestrained Maroons, nobody travelled faster than he did. But he quit drinking, cold turkey, when he was thirty. At one point he'd been a two-bottle-a-day man, but just after his daughter was born he developed pneumonia, and then he had an operation and on top of all this the Maroons were ready to drop him. In this predicament he made an about-face; he had two good seasons with the Maroons and when he was purchased by Chicago, a comparatively old athlete, he led the Hawks to the Stanley Cup in 1934 and then, remarkably, was the defensive mainstay of the Maroons when they brought him back from the Hawks and won the Cup in 1935.

He took a terrific physical battering in becoming a big-league hockey star—when he was closing in on thirty-four with the Hawks he was named over Eddie Shore and Ching Johnson, the perennial all-star defence selections, on the 1933-34 team—and carried something like six hundred stitches. He had a hundred and fifty in his face and head alone, and had had his nose broken eight times. It carried a permanent curve that resembled a road detour. He tangled with Eddie Shore almost every time his team played the Bruins. Bob Gracie once told of his dilemma as a player with the Maroons when Lionel was his teammate. "When I'd skate past that bastard Shore in the Bruins' end he'd snarl at me that he'd cut my legs off if I came near his net, and big Connie would growl that if I didn't get the hell up to the other end of the ice and *do* something he'd cut my ears off."

He had his droll side. Once, the Americans were crossing the border for a game in Montreal, and a customs official told Conacher, who was the coach then, that he'd checked the players' car but couldn't find little Roy Worters.

"He's in his berth," Conacher said.

"I've looked there," the customs guy said testily.

"Well, look again," smiled Conacher. "He's in there some place."

Conacher won the Ontario 125-pound wrestling championship when he was sixteen, and the first time he ever boxed competitively he won the Canadian light-heavyweight championship at twenty. It wasn't unusual for him to compete in two championship games in a day. In 1922 he was playing baseball for the Toronto Hillcrests and lacrosse for the Toronto Maitlands. Hillcrests played for the Ontario championship one Saturday afternoon and got their last look at the rival pitcher trailing by two runs. The bases were filled with two out when Conacher drilled a triple into the right-centrefield alley to win it. He kept right on running when he reached third base to a waiting car in which he changed into his lacrosse togs while moving across town to a park where the Maitlands were playing for the Ontario lacrosse championship. When Con arrived they were trailing by three goals. He scored four, assisted on another, and the Maitlands won the game 5-3.

His best game, and the one he liked best, was football. People who saw the Grey Cup final of 1921 long cherished the memory of a raw-boned steer of a man who in the days before the forward pass grabbed a ball from scrimmage and barrelled over the turf all afternoon, scoring three touchdowns as his Toronto Argonauts whipped the Edmonton Eskimos 23-0. Once when Conacher was thirty-seven, two years retired from all sports and watching an Argonaut practice, he noticed the kicking of Bob Isbister, one of the best in the country in an era when the big punt was a vital part of the game. "Maybe I can show you how to get more distance, Bob," Conacher offered. "Try putting your foot into it this way." Wearing business clothes and ordinary shoes he lofted a punt eighty-five yards in the air.

If there was one pro game at which he didn't excel it was baseball. Still, he *did* make the Toronto Maple Leafs of the old Triple-A International League as a sometime outfielder about whom the manager, Dan Howley, once remarked, "When he's in right field he ought to wear a mask, but I'll say this, he can hit some." Conacher hadn't played ball for two years when the Leafs signed him in 1926. That year, with Carl Hubbell as one of their pitchers, they won the Little World Series.

Sports got Conacher interested in politics. The idea of government aid to community parks in the poorer districts of Toronto prompted him to run for the Ontario Legislature in 1937 when he was elected in Toronto Bracondale riding. In 1949 he went into federal politics and was elected again. He sat in the House of Commons for five years, was a Member of Parliament playing in the annual softball game between the Members and the Parliamentary Press Gallery two days after his fifty-fourth birthday on May 26, 1954. He played second base on a politically distinguished infield. The third baseman was Lester B. Pearson, who became Prime Minister of Canada, and the shortstop was Donald Fleming, a former candidate for leadership of the Conservative Party. In the second inning Conacher hit a double, which he stretched into a triple, knowing from his long years in the game that the inexperienced Press Gallery outfielder would throw to the wrong base. As he raced from second to third, a belated throw struck him on the head, but he slid safely into the bag.

In the sixth, he lofted a fly into left field, and again made it all the way to third base. Breathing heavily, he stood on the bag. Suddenly, he toppled to the ground, bleeding from the mouth. Twenty minutes later he was dead.

Charlie Conacher developed the hardest shot in hockey the hardest possible way. When he was seventeen he tried out for the St. Mary's junior hockey team, which later became the Marlboros, a feeding ground for the Maple Leafs. They played downtown in the Mutual Arena where the pros played. But he didn't make the club, so he tried out with the Toronto juniors, who played away out in the west end in the Ravina rink. He made that team and spent the winter going six miles by streetcar and then walking a mile from the carline stop to the rink, carrying all his equipment. Naturally, when the game ended he had seven miles to walk and travel by tram. The team played every Saturday afternoon and practised two or three times a week.

The fortitude of kids determined to become hockey players in that era was astonishing. Also seeking a place on the West Toronto club was Bill Hollett, who later emerged as a spectacular bandy-legged rushing defenceman with the Leafs, Detroit and Boston. One cold winter afternoon Flash Hollett, all of seventeen, set out for practice. He didn't know where Ravina rink was but he slung his skates and stick over his shoulder and set out on foot, following vague directions for four miles. At length he found the rink but when he jogged down a cinder path leading to the door he found the door was locked. Patiently he settled down by the closed door while the cold powdery snow swirled about him, believing he'd arrived early.

What Hollett didn't know was that he'd been given the wrong date of the practice. He crouched in the wintery doorway waiting for a team that never showed up. Slowly the minutes dragged past, and the dull winter afternoon closed into a freezing evening. Then, reluctantly and cramped and shivering, Hollett began the long trek back to his home. There, he developed pleurisy, followed by pneumonia, so ill that he could play no more hockey that winter. But in the following summer he was back playing lacrosse, back in full health, walking five miles from his home to the field and five miles back home when the game ended.

Long uncomplaining hikes, it seemed, were part of the process required to get a boy enough game time. One night after Charlie

Conacher had made the West Toronto juniors he headed for Varsity Arena in midtown where the West Toronto seniors were to play the famous Olympic champions, the Varsity Grads, who'd won the gold medal for Canada in 1924. It turned out that the seniors didn't have enough players so he ran all the way to his home, about a mile away on Davenport, and all the way back with his hockey stuff, and got into the game. Afterwards, Frank Selke, the manager of the St. Mary's juniors, spoke to him in the dressing room, telling him he'd improved since he'd tried out; he asked him to try out again. He made the grade in the fall of 1927 when the team's name was changed to the Marlboros, and the next year, when he was nineteen, the Marlboros beat the Winnipeg Elmwoods in the national junior final. That was the spring of 1929; that fall he turned pro.

In the 1930s every top hockey club had a top line in the NHL. The Rangers prospered with Cook-Boucher-Cook; the Maroons had the big S line—Stewart, Smith and Siebert. In Detroit it was Barry-Aurie-Lewis, in Chicago Thompson-March-Gottselig. The Canadiens had Morenz, Joliat and Black Cat Johnny Gagnon. And in most of Canada, largely because Foster Hewitt's Saturday-night broadcasts boomed the Leafs across the country week after week, the most famous line was Toronto's Conacher-Primeau-Jackson who gained a fame damned nearly everlasting as the Kid Line. Their names became a familiar part of the language, coast to coast, and in time people thought of them as triplets—that they'd played together as juniors, that none had ever played with any other NHL club but the Leafs, and that they were the same age. One thing everybody seemed to know was that Charlie Conacher played right wing, Joe Primeau was the centre, and Harvey Jackson the leftwinger, and in this, at least, the fans had it right.

When Conacher joined the Leafs in the fall of 1929, Primeau was with the team but Jackson wasn't. Primeau had been to two previous training camps, in fact, and had been farmed out each time. One night the Leafs played an exhibition at Buffalo where the Pittsburgh Pirates, then in the NHL and managed by Frank Fredrickson, were training. Before the game Fredrickson expressed an interest in Primeau to Connie Smythe.

"How much?" Smythe said instantly.

Surprised by his eagerness, Fredrickson hedged. "Well, wait until the end of the first period," he stalled, "and then I'll tell you."

Primeau twice beat the defence and scored. When Fredrickson reached the Leaf room at the end of the period Smythe told him coldly, "Primeau's not for sale." Nobody had any doubt, including Primeau himself, that his two goals stood between him and Pittsburgh.

Jackson, meanwhile, was playing junior hockey with the Marlboros. Between times he was an ice-scraper, cleaning the ice surface between periods of games at Ravina Gardens. When he'd finish scraping he'd grab a stick and a puck and fire at the empty net. One night Frank Selke took his junior team to Ravina for a game, and watched Jackson, who'd be about sixteen, glide up and down the ice between periods. Jackson fired a shot that nailed another scraper over the eye, and Selke helped Jackson carry the man from the ice.

"A kid who can skate like you ought to be playing with my club," Selke said to Jackson, and the next year Busher was. He was injured early but limped back into action in Niagara Falls and managed to score six goals in his weakened condition. He was eighteen by then, and the Leafs figured he was old enough to help them. That was just before Christmas 1929 and soon afterwards the line of Primeau, Jackson and Conacher was formed—quite by accident.

The Leafs were going badly; they'd won five of their first sixteen games, and Smythe was experimenting. He moved Eric Pettinger out of the slot between Conacher and Cotton and replaced him with Primeau. When an injury kept Cotton in Toronto for a Chicago game on December 29, 1929, Smythe told the players in the Stadium dressing room he was going to try the kid Jackson in Cotton's place with Primeau and Conacher. The Leafs beat the Hawks 4-3. Primeau fed Conacher a goal and passed off for another one by Jackson, but the Toronto writers took no particular notice of the change in lines. Three nights later when the Leafs beat the Maroons, Lou Marsh in the *Toronto Star* said that "the kid line showed well". A couple of mornings later in the *Toronto Globe* Mike Rodden referred to them as "the youthful triumvirate". Smythe kept the line intact and any reference to the "kid line" was normal sports-page procedure because that's precisely what they were by NHL standards. Primeau was twenty-two, Conacher had turned twenty in December, and Jackson was eighteen. So by a gradual process they became the Kid Line, capitals and all, and stayed together for seven years, until Primeau retired after the 1935-36 season, and Conacher and Jackson moved along to the Americans, and Jackson subsequently to Boston. But those intervening years represented the most successful in Toronto hockey history. Some say the Kid Line paid the mortgage on Maple Leaf Gardens, the rink built in 1931 that succeeded in spite of the Despression.

The Leafs finished fourth that first year, but in the six succeeding ones they were first in three and second in the other three. They won Toronto its first Stanley Cup in 1932. Jackson was the league's all-star leftwinger four times, and Conacher the rightwinger three times.

Primeau, who made Jackson and Conacher tick, never made it, although he made the second team once and also won the Lady Byng trophy as the player who best combined achievement and clean play. Primeau missed top rating for two principal reasons: Morenz and Boucher. They were two of the best centres who ever played this demanding game. Nevertheless, Joe made the Hall of Fame. The Kid Line piled up 863 points in those seven years, an even twenty more than the New York Rangers' great line of Bill Cook, Frank Boucher and Bun Cook over the same span.

The line's leftwinger, Busher Jackson, had marvellous natural ability. He could take a pass in full flight on one of his skates and somehow flick the puck up onto his stick without breaking stride. He was one of the great rushers largely because of the most unusual of athletic gifts, a natural shift. He'd take a stride on his left skate, say, and then, instead of taking his next stride on the right skate he'd somehow take another with the left. Jackson was called Busher because of an incident involving trainer Tim Daly. Right after he turned pro he made a trip with the club to New York. He'd hurt his leg in his final junior game and he wasn't dressed. As the club headed out of the dressing room, Daly grunted past his dead cigar, "Awright, kid, pick up them sticks. You can be my stick-boy."

Jackson, brash, handsome, cocky, beamed at Daly. "Pick 'em up yourself, you old fart," he laughed. "I'm a National Leaguer."

"Well, sir," Daly sputtered, "if you ain't the freshest bloody busher I ever seen."

Primeau was a completely different fellow than Jackson. He had a quiet twinkle in his eyes and was soft voiced, with a nice wry turn of humour. Under the rules and the pattern of offence of the Thirties the centreman had to be a man of courage, and Gentleman Joe had lots of that. He'd take the puck up the middle and try to draw the defencemen together to stop him so that he could then make a play to one of his wingers cutting in from the side. Attacking units didn't shoot the puck, willy nilly, into the end zone and rush after it like chickens pursuing grain as they did in the 1970s; no, they tried to finesse an opening while keeping control of the puck. With defencemen like Ching Johnson and Earl Seibert of the Rangers, and Eddie Shore and Lionel Hitchman of the Bruins, this could keep a centre black and blue all season, but Primeau, a slender fellow of 160 pounds, took everything they handed out to make his plays.

For that matter, Primeau had enough trouble with Jackson and Conacher. They both loved to get that puck. If Primeau gave it to Busher when Conacher was flying down the right boards looking for it, Conacher would curse him. Similarly, when he gave it to Chuck, Jackson would get hot because he didn't get it.

"You guys'll drive me nuts," the mild Primeau used to complain. "Whadda you want me to do with the damned puck, cut it in half?"

But Primeau was the perfect pivot for the two big single-minded wingers, and he did all right by them both. Jackson won the scoring championship in the 1931-32 season and after Bill Cook won it in '33 Conacher put together back-to-back titles, with Primeau the runner-up in 1934.

And besides the Kid Line through those seven years, there were some great hockey players, particularly a yeasty little pepperpot named King Clancy who was always starting fights on the ice but who was a man who never won one. In Montreal one night, Clancy got involved with Harold Starr, a rugged Maroon, and in short order, as usual, he was on the bottom. Jackson, grinning, hollered to Conacher, "C'mon, Chuck, let's make this one fight Clancy wins." They pulled Starr off Clancy and set King down on *top* of him and skated away. They'd gone only a few strides when Jackson looked back over his shoulder and shook his head. "It's no use, Chaz," he said. "Clancy's on the bottom again."

Clancy's spirit, shaped and sharpened by nine years with the proud old Ottawa Senators, was what the Leafs needed to produce their first Stanley Cup in the spring of 1932 when they hammered the Rangers in a tennis-like finale, 6-4, 6-2, 6-4, a series, incidentally, in which Ranger goaltender John Ross Roach was sulking over a promised pay raise that didn't materialize. A few years later the Leafs engaged in one of the most bizarre playoffs of all time, and Conacher and Clancy were central figures. Toronto had finished second in the Canadian Division to qualify to play Boston, the American Division's second-place team, in a two-game, total-goals series. Boston won the opener 3-0 at home, and got a first-period goal—to go ahead 4-0 on the round—in the concluding game in Toronto.

During the intermission, since Smythe didn't permit smoking in the dressing room, Conacher sneaked into the lavatory to grab a few puffs. Clancy had beaten him there, and was sitting on the throne, having a smoke.

"Get up," Conacher grunted.

"Get up? Whadda yuh mean, get up?" cried Clancy in his high-pitched voice. "Why should I be getting up for a bum like you? I'll not be getting up."

He'd hit Conacher where he was hurting. He was the Leafs' Big Bomber and he'd scarcely caused a draft around Boston goaltender Tiny

Thompson in four full periods; Bruin leftwinger Red Beattie was shadowing him like a gumshoe. He reminded Clancy of this. "It's a wonder the son of a bitch isn't sitting in here with us now," Conacher whined.

"Well now, sit down," Clancy said, getting to his feet and handing Conacher the cigarette for a few puffs. "Sit down and I'll tell you what to do."

Conacher sat, and the little man climbed onto his lap, put his hand on his shoulder and started to talk.

"What you do, you belt him once and for all and be rid of him. You just knock the livin' Jesus right out of him."

"Dammit, King, I can't take a penalty trailing four-nothing. Smythe'd have my ass."

"How? At four-nothin' we're dead anyway. Look, I'll get the puck and I'll wait till Beattie's right with you. Then I'll give you the puck and when he's reachin' for it let the son of a bitch have it hip an' thigh."

And that's what happened. Conacher jammed an elbow into Beattie's face in a short vicious jab, disregarding the puck as Beattie reached for it, and the referee missed it. Moments later Clancy tripped Shore, and the referee, who was Odie Cleghorn, missed that one, too. Shore was livid, screaming into Cleghorn's face. Clancy skated by and needled Shore to make things worse. "The man's blind, Eddie. You're bein' robbed, surer than hell. And he blew that one on Beattie, too."

Enraged, Shore fired the puck at the referee in disgust. That got him a two-minute penalty. Driven to distraction Shore picked up the puck and threw it into the crowd. Cleghorn tacked a ten-minute misconduct onto Shore's sentence. That kept the Bruin star off the ice for twelve minutes, and the Leafs ran in four goals to tie the series. The Bruins were so demoralized by this turn of events, and the Leafs were in such a flow of momentum, that they kept right on flying. They beat the Bruins 8-3—Conacher got three goals and two assists—and eliminated them by eight goals to six on the round.

Smythe was ecstatic, a fiery imaginative leader in those days, waving his arms at the referees, stomping around the rinks on the road shouting at the fans. At home, he once manufactured a feud between the Conachers when Lionel was nearing the end of his hockey days with the Hawks. He dreamed up a half-page newspaper advertisement showing a train billowing smoke. A picture of Lionel, the Big Train, was superimposed under the smokestack, and there was a shot of Charlie skating past the train, showing up his brother. There never was any real rivalry on the ice between the two. They'd had one hell of a fight back of the bench the night Lionel, then with the Americans, took on Red Horner and young

Charlie felt constrained to take up Horner's sinking banner, but usually they left each other alone. This night, though, they were sent off for high-sticking and as they neared the penalty box Lionel stuck his face against Charlie's chin and started yammering at him, gesticulating broadly. Charlie snarled back, bobbing his head emphatically.

"I didn't get around to the house today," is what Lionel said. "Are Mom and Dad okay?"

"Sure, they're fine," Chuck scowled darkly, "but they wondered why you didn't come."

As they left the penalty box after serving their two minutes Lionel grabbed Charlie's sweater, and Charlie retaliated by shaking his stick under Lionel's nose.

"Tell Mom I'll make it next trip," Lionel said. The crowd screamed.

After the 1936 season when Joe Primeau retired, Charlie was beginning to feel the weight of injuries. He'd had the kidney taken out, and this was followed in succeeding seasons by blood-poisoning in the hand, a broken wrist, two broken bones in his hand, a broken collarbone, a shoulder separation and even a violent attack of boils that was more painful than most of the other injuries. He decided to retire a year after Primeau made the break and stayed out of hockey during the 1937-38 season. But then he went back for two more years, the first with Detroit and the second with the Amerks where the boys logged more ice-cube time than ice time, and Charlie was right in there with both hands. The Amerks mailed him a contract for another season but after eleven years he knew he'd had enough. He left the ice cubes that year, too, and like Lionel before him he became a life-long teetotaler. He turned to coaching. His junior club, the Oshawa Generals, won the national championship, and midway through the 1947-48 season he agreed to take over the Chicago Black Hawks at a dreadful moment in their history, a period during which they rarely emerged from the cellar, and when he walked away from that in the spring of 1950 he wound up his part of the Conacher family's connection with the NHL that had started in 1925 with Lionel and was to end the following spring when Roy closed out his career. The three of them logged thirty-six years as players or coaches and each became an all-star.

In truth, those thirty-six years were really a means to an end for the Conacher family. Unlike the thousands of Canadian kids who are delighted to accept money for playing a game they'd play for nothing, the Conachers played *because* of the money, because of what it represented in terms of their lives. Charlie once said he doubted that any of them —father, mother or the ten kids—had any deep-rooted love for the game itself. To the parents it meant that their boys had made good; to the girls it meant nothing. Of course, they were aware that their brothers were playing in the biggest league of the biggest game and thereby were creating a certain amount of interest among the fans, and that they were getting their pictures in the newspapers, but they didn't get puffed up about it. Their favourite player was Roy, because he was the youngest. Once when Roy was playing for the Bruins Charlie asked Nora who she would cheer for at the Gardens that night.

"The Bruins," she replied. And then she added quickly, "But I hope you score three goals."

Hockey, curiously enough, meant misery to Roy. Before Roy turned pro with Boston he was driving a truck for a men's wear shop in Toronto for ten dollars a week. Roy loved the shinny sessions he and Bert and Chuck used to have on the street, but when he got into organized hockey he hated the game. Once when he and Bert were playing for the West Toronto juniors, Roy purposely left his skates at home, hoping he wouldn't have to play. Charlie was with the Leafs then, and had gone to the rink to see the game. He knew what Roy was up to; he sent him galloping home for his skates. When he got back he scored three goals, a magician with the puck.

He could always put it in the net, even without relish. He played hockey in the NHL for eleven seasons and his career was interrupted for a stretch of four years while he was in the RCAF, but in spite of this fine record he did his job with no enthusiasm. Each year he felt the tension growing tighter, and he found that the more goals he scored each season the more he was expected to produce the following season. It got so that Roy even refused to go to training camp or to play another year unless Bert went with him. So what hockey meant to Bert was that he could be with Roy and help him.

Roy was with Charlie at Chicago when Charlie coached there and, because they were brothers, he knew of the tensions of a losing coach. Charlie maintained for years that the most frustrating experience in hockey was to coach a losing club. He elaborated on this theme once: "You try everything you can think of to make the change that will spell the difference between victory and defeat—juggle the forward lines, switch the tactics, cajole the players, praise them, snarl at them—and all you can do once the game starts is watch helplessly."

Coaches of losing clubs can't digest their food properly and their mood is usually dark. One-goal defeats gnaw at their guts, and their tempers are always short. Charlie was of the wrong temperament to be a coach; he loved winning too much to fulfil the public-relations role thrust on most coaches. He was one of the few in the NHL who ever punched a sportswriter, perhaps the only one. The writer was Lew Walter, a Detroit newspaperman who wrote that three Chicago players were high in the scoring list because they were picking up phony assists from a lenient Chicago official scorer. A couple of nights later the Hawks went into Detroit and got whipped. Conacher figured the referee, Bill Chadwick, had been overly kind to the Red Wings, who were a winning hockey club in those days, and he was steaming. When Walter, the newsman, went into the Hawk room Conacher didn't want to look at him. He told him to get out. Walter swore at him and he knocked Walter down.

Walter was going to sue for assault, and Clarence Campbell, the league president, was going to fine Conacher, but nothing came of it, probably because a couple of days later, back in Chicago, the publicity man, Joe Farrell, told Conacher he was gaining nothing going around putting the slug on writers. He looked at Farrell's white hair and figured he was probably right, so he followed his suggestion and wired an apology to Walter.

When Charlie and Roy called it a career in the spring of 1951, all the Conachers pretty well lost their interest in hockey. It was significant of what the game really meant to the family that they rarely went to see a game again. For a time they went down when the Hawks came to town to see Charlie's son Peter play, but when the Hawks sent Pete to their Buffalo farm in the AHL they stopped going to hockey. Charlie concentrated on business; he and Roy Worters were partners in two hotels in Toronto, and Charlie made a bundle in Alberta oil. In 1967 he got cancer of the throat. In 1968 he died. By 1974 there were six Conachers left of the dozen who'd found their way up from the sidewalks of Davenport Road, Nora and Kay and Mary and Queenie and Roy and Bert. They didn't go to hockey games. In Canada, that damned nearly made them unique.

CHAPTER SEVEN: Speaking of Cashews, Meet
Major McLaughlin

Many strange birds have owned and operated hockey's major teams in the last half-century but none has been burdened with less knowledge of the game than the elegant and eccentric Major Frederic McLaughlin who introduced the Black Hawks to Chicago in November of 1926 and ran them in his weird and wondrous way until he died eighteen years later at the age of sixty-seven.

The Major was a brisk erect man of military background and bearing who wore a bow tie, a clipped mustache and kept his thin hair combed smoothly back. His face was lean, with a long narrow nose and haughty eyes. He was rich enough to consider himself infallible. McLaughlin was the Chicago-born son of a wealthy coffee importer; he graduated from Harvard in 1901 and entered his father's firm which he inherited when the old man died. He was a six-goal polo player in his more vigorous days, a prominent figure in Chicago's social life later on when, at forty-five, he married Irene Castle. She was the widow of Vernon Castle, her former partner in their internationally-known dance team.

Irene was twenty-nine when she married the Major. She adored dogs. Her favourite charity was her Orphans of the Storm animal shelter for which she gave Pooch Balls to raise funds. These dances were the highlight of each social season. A sign on the wall said, Risk a Burp to Save a Purp. This was an illustration of Irene's hearty slang, which in turn was an example of her emancipation.

While Irene was a dog fancier, Frederic liked cats. Their marriage was something like that. In 1937 she sued for divorce, a suit that went on for two years before she withdrew it and signed a separation agreement. Irene complained it was so cold in her suburban Lake Forest home that even her three dogs had to wear sweaters. She charged in a separate legal dispute in 1938 that her estranged husband had taken her name from the pass list of Black Hawk games. She could get along without the passes, she said, but she must have a new furnace.

The Major had problems with his hockey coaches, too. It was a continuing source of dismay to him that when he instructed his coaches to pursue and destroy the enemy, the coaches more often than not disobeyed. So the Major fired them. In the first ten years of his yeasty regime as resident crackpot in Chicago he hired and fired eleven coaches, dismissing one of them immediately after he had won Chicago its first Stanley Cup. On evidence, the Major often had justification for firing some of his little thinkers but no one was ever able to fathom why he hired them.

In 1932, for instance, travelling on a train between Minneapolis and Chicago, the Major and a man named Godfrey Matheson struck up a casual conversation. Matheson, it turned out, was from Winnipeg, the home town of Charlie Gardiner, Chicago's great goaltender. That, apparently, was recommendation enough; McLaughlin was delighted to hire Matheson as coach of the Black Hawks. A short time after, when the players arrived at Pittsburgh for fall training, their coach was on the ice to greet them. He was wearing a tassel cap and carrying two pails of pucks. He had pulled elbow pads over his suitcoat and knee pads over his trousers. He wore no skates. He carried the pails of pucks to a corner of the rink and settled there on all fours. As the players skated one by one from the blueline towards the goal he skidded a puck to each to be shot at the net. The goaltender Gardiner was not in the net however. Matheson reasoned that he might be hurt fending pucks so had taken the precaution of suspending a stuffed dummy in full goaltending equipment from the crossbar. Occasionally, to sharpen the players' shooting, Matheson rigged crossed planks to the goalposts and directed the players to shoot for the openings between the planks.

Similarly, Matheson's ideas of offence were, well, unusual. The bulky and jovial Taffy Abel played defence for the Hawks then, 230 pounds of sunshine who used to bunt incoming forwards with his belly. The team's star rightwinger was Harold (Mush) March, five foot five, solidly constructed, a jack-rabbit on skates. It was Matheson's scheme that little March would fling his 139 pounds at rival defencemen and drop the puck for the trailing Abel who would then move unimpeded upon the goaltender. It was a stroke of genius that unfortunately had nothing in its favour: Abel was slow moving toward the net and was usually caught before he got there. He was a poor shot on the occasions when he did get there, and March provided rival defencemen with untold merriment ricocheting off them like the ball in a pin-ball machine. Before this ploy was abandoned, March had called Matheson everything but Tilt.

Not surprisingly, Matheson was replaced. Surprisingly, he was replaced by a man named Emil Iverson, who'd never been heard from before and hasn't been heard from since, and he in turn was replaced that same season by Tommy Gorman. Gorman won the Stanley Cup the following year for the Hawks and of course was fired. He went to the Montreal Maroons and immediately won the Stanley Cup again. Since Major McLaughlin had no influence in Montreal Gorman was retained in Montreal.

A few years later McLaughlin hired Bill Stewart as his coach. Stewart was a baseball umpire—naturally—who had worked in the American League. He had also been an NHL referee. Stewart piloted Chicago's second Stanley Cup team in the spring of 1938, and shortly before Christmas that year he was looking forward to baseball: McLaughlin had fired him.

"Listen to this," Stewart wailed to a Boston newspaperman soon after his dismissal. "With a minute and twenty seconds to go in the third period against the Canadiens last week, Toe Blake let one fly at Mike Karakas, my goaltender. But one of my defencemen, Earl Seibert, I guess it was, skated in front of Mike, blocking Mike's view. The puck went in and McLaughlin blamed me. He suggested I run the club from the balcony, for God's sake. Maybe he wanted me to put strings on the guys so I could twist them around like marionettes."

McLaughlin's penchant for firing his coaches produced one of the more hilarious chapters in hockey's history, an incident that became known as the Curse of the Muldoon. It haunted the Chicago Stadium for years. Although they twice won the Stanley Cup in the spring playoffs, the Hawks never finished a season's schedule in first place, not in the Major's life-time, not for years after his death, and not, indeed, until they were guided there in the spring of 1967 by Billy Reay, the twenty-second Chicago coach.

According to the legend there was a curse upon the Hawks, put there by the aristocratic hand of the Major after his team's first season.

He had spent a great deal of money assembling that first team and when they concluded the season in third place he could not believe they had been properly handled by the first of the Major's long string of coaches, a man named Pete Muldoon. So he fired Muldoon. The coach, embittered by his novel reward for bringing a first-year team into the playoffs, raised his hands and intoned a proclamation: "This team will never finish in first place."

Curiously, all through the Thirties while the Hawks were avoiding first place, no one ever mentioned the Curse of the Muldoon. But in the 1940s and 1950s and into the 1960s it was a spring perennial, solemnly raised every season by Chicago columnists and even whispered about uneasily in the Hawk dressing quarters.

The reason for this is that the Curse of the Muldoon was not invented until 1941, the work of a Toronto columnist, Jim Coleman, desperate for an idea late one afternoon as the deadline for his morning newspaper, the *Globe and Mail,* approached implacably and a topic to write about perversely evaded him. Puffing furiously on a cigar, pacing stoop-shouldered from his cold typewriter to the water cooler and back, scanning papers, staring out the window, Coleman finally was over-whelmed by an idea.

"God dammit," he cackled, rushing from the water cooler for the fiftieth time, smoke from his cigar pouring past his ears, "it's the Curse of the Muldoon!" Startled ladies in the social department eyed him distastefully as he fled past them to his machine, the idea burgeoning, and began to pound rapidly, interrupting his labours from time to time to emit a whoop of delight, closing in triumphantly on his deadline.

"The Hawks are victims of a hex Pete Muldoon put on them many years ago, after he was fired as coach," he wrote. "He had a stormy session with Major Frederic McLaughlin, the strange eccentric who owned the Hawks when they were admitted to the NHL in 1926.

"Muldoon coached the Hawks to a third-place finish in their first year, but McLaughlin was not impressed. 'This team was good enough to be first,' he said.

"Muldoon was amazed at McLaughlin's criticism, but not to the point of shutting up. 'You're crazy,' he fumed.

"McLaughlin was outraged by such heresy. 'You're fired!' he roared.

"Muldoon flared back in a black Irish snit. 'Fire me, Major, and you'll never finish first! I'll put a curse on this team that will hoodoo it till the end of time!'

"And so, kiddies, that's why the Hawks always fail to grab the flag in the NHL. They cannot beat the Curse of the Muldoon."

114

It was all a figment of Coleman's imagination, of course, but he never admitted it until the early 1960s when a close friend and boon companion, Rudy Pilous, was leading the Hawks. Pilous got Chicago its third Stanley Cup in the spring of 1961, but even without the Curse of the Muldoon he was unable to fashion a first-place finish in five years as coach. McLaughlin, however, lived to learn of the Curse; he died in 1944. For three years he kept telling people that he had no recollection of a confrontation with Pete Muldoon during which the spell was supposed to have been cast, but no one paid any attention.

McLaughlin was in his forty-ninth year when one of his acquaintances in what he liked to call the sporting world, Tex Rickard, called him from New York in the spring of 1926 to suggest he seek a franchise for Chicago. Rickard noted that the Americans had drawn far better crowds than he'd anticipated the previous winter, and revealed that the Garden had acquired its own franchise for the forthcoming season. So the Major, who had been briefly exposed to college hockey in Ivy League days, formed a syndicate of about a hundred society friends and they paid $12,000 to join the burgeoning league. The franchise was granted in the name of one of the Major's friends, H.R. Hardwick, in May; at a subsequent league meeting McLaughlin was nominated as the governor to represent Chicago.

The Major chose the name Black Hawks. During World War I he'd been commander of the 333rd Machine Gun Battalion of the U.S. Army's 85th Black Hawk Division. His wife Irene designed the original black-and-white uniforms, including an Indian head on the crest and crossed hockey sticks as shoulder patches to commemorate an Indian chief of the 1880s. Chief Black Hawk had roamed the plains west of Chicago.

So the Major was all set; all he lacked was a rink in which Irene's sweaters could be flashed and hockey players to flash them. He surmounted the first obstacle by leasing the Chicago Coliseum, whose six thousand seats ordinarily were used by people basking in the earthy vapours of cattle shows, and the second was solved by the demise of the Western Canada league. McLaughlin and friends paid $150,000 for an assortment of West Coast players from the Portland Rosebuds and the Vancouver Maroons, and picked up the controversial Cecil (Babe) Dye from the Toronto St. Pats, the eighth top scorer in the NHL the previous season.

Dye was an involuntary contributor to the firing of Connie Smythe as manager of the new team in New York, the Rangers. Smythe had a chance to get the Toronto star but passed him by. When the Hawks got him, the Major couldn't resist the temptation to crow to Rickard.

Rickard, in turn, muttered darkly to the Ranger president Col. John Hammond and Hammond in *his* turn decided to dispense with Smythe's services for this and other reasons, one of which was that Lester Patrick became available. Years later, the old Amerk goaltender Jakie Forbes remembered Babe Dye as the hardest shooter he'd ever seen. "He was a terrible skater but he was foxy and he had tremendous wrists," Jakie said. "One time the son of a bitch shot from centre ice and if Lou Marsh, the referee, hadn't seen the puck go in the net a goal wouldn't have counted. Babe was at centre and he shot a low bullet that rose about two feet off the ice and just stayed there, going past the two defencemen and then into the net before you could blink."

Dye had a big season with the Hawks. He scored twenty-five goals, tied with Howie Morenz behind Bill Cook who had thirty-three in leading the league. And his Hawk teammate Dick Irvin, who had joined Chicago from the Portland Rosebuds, finished second among all the point-getters. His eighteen assists topped the league in an era when it was necessary to make a key play to earn an assist; in a later period people were getting them if they shouted "Shoot!" The Hawks had no trouble putting the puck in the net that year; their problem was keeping it out. Their goaltender was Hughie Lehman, a star for twelve years with Vancouver but forty-one years old when the Major imported him to Chicago. The defence was old too: Bob Trapp and Puss Traub from Portland and Gordon Fraser from Victoria. The coach, Pete Muldoon, was justified in thinking he'd done a good job in getting this assortment into third place, but the Major, his mind untrammeled by any real knowledge of the game, thought otherwise and brought in Barney Stanley in the fall of 1927. Stanley lasted twenty-two games, in which the Hawks soared to victory exactly three times, and was replaced by the old goaltender, Lehman. Lehman played four games to open the season and then gave way to a twenty-two-year-old curly-haired chatterbox from the Winnipeg Maroons of the American Association, Charles Robert (Chuck) Gardiner.

Gardiner was one of the great performers for the Major, colourful and agile and always smiling. He loved his work. Once, a jubilant fan tossed a derby hat onto the ice and Gardiner dashed from his cage to retrieve it and put it on his head at a jaunty angle. He wore it for the remainder of the game. He was quick and daring and talkative. One time Bill Cook of the Rangers skated around the defence and, with no checker in the vicinity, took his own good time, picking a spot and whistling a low rising shot to Gardiner's stick-side. But Gardiner whipped out his arm, stick and all, got a piece of the puck with his elbow and deflected it past the post. "Nice try, you bastard, but no cigar," he laughed as Cook circled the net, cracking his stick against the ice in chagrin.

Later, against the Canadiens, Morenz beat him after fifty-one minutes and forty-three seconds of overtime to eliminate the Hawks from the playoffs in 1930. Gardiner climbed to his feet after diving in a futile effort to stab Morenz's shot, and threw his arms around the Canadien star's shoulders. "That was one hell of a shot," he said, "but there'll come a day."

He was almost prophetic. A year later the teams met again, this time in the Cup final, and Gardiner was a marvellous dervish in the Chicago goal. He outwitted Morenz time after time in this best-of-five final, blanking him as the teams split the first four games. But in the deciding game the Canadiens nursed a 1-0 lead into the final minute, and then Morenz exploded from a Chicago attack and rushed in alone on Gardiner. He fairly blew the puck by him. "Dammit, How, you fooled me," Gardiner said, the grin returning. "I didn't think you had any of them kind left."

Gardiner's good nature was lost on the Major, however—or maybe the kindly old Maj merely tried to take advantage of it. In any event, after Gardiner won the Vezina Trophy in 1932 McLaughlin cut his pay by $500. However, when the story got into the papers the Major, grumbling at the "meddlesome press", restored Gardiner to the $5000 level, the highest salary he ever made.

By the spring of 1934 the goaltender was at the absolute top of his game, winner of the Vezina again with a sensational 1.73 average and ten shutouts, and named to the No. 1 all-star team for the third time in four years. He allowed only twelve goals in eight games through the playoffs and capped everything by shutting out Detroit 1-0 in the deciding game of the Stanley Cup final after thirty minutes and five seconds of nerve-wracking sudden-death overtime. That was on April 10. Two months later, on June 13, he was dead at twenty-nine, victim of a brain hemorrhage. There was speculation for years that Gardiner died as a result of a head injury, this in spite of a statement by the Winnipeg doctor who attended him. "His illness originated in a tonsular infection," Dr. W.G. MacIntosh said. "Uraemic convulsions developed today, and from this condition the hemorrhage resulted. There was also a trace of Bright's disease."

Major Frederic McLaughlin was not a toper. At home, he and Irene enjoyed a glass of wine with dinner but the Major was not a man to abide a man who abided Demon Rum. This made it difficult for the tall, spare, gentle publicity man of the Hawks, Joe Farrell, who ran up formidable liquor bills assuaging the voracious thirst of the watchdogs of the press who covered the Hawks. The Major steadfastly refused to countenance any expense account that included alcoholic refreshment, and Farrell was hard put to cover costs after a night of revelry entertaining the newshounds during Prohibition. So he began to itemize the purchase of pucks on his expense sheet, pucks by the gross. One day, the Major became aware that Farrell had been buying up enough pucks to float the Wrigley building in a heavy sea.

"What are we doing with all these pucks?" enquired the puzzled Major.

"The hockey writers have been asking for them, Major," Farrell lied amiably. "They've been giving them to their families and friends and the grasping managing editors. They're in great demand as souvenirs."

The Major was delighted. "Splendid, splendid," he exclaimed, to Farrell's surprise and intense relief. "Nothing can beat word-of-mouth publicity. Keep up the good work."

Farrell needed all the pucks—or bootleg bottles—he could lay his hands on. In the early years of the Depression crowds often dwindled to less than five thousand, and the ticket scale had a mere two-dollar top. By then the Hawks had moved from the tiny Coliseum to the cavernous Chicago Stadium with more than sixteen thousand seats and standing room in the aisles and balconies for another four thousand, but these were luxuries that only the playoffs ever accommodated.

McLaughlin got his team into the Stadium in 1929 following a lengthy battle with another millionaire, James Norris, a Montrealer who went to Chicago in 1907 and became president of the Norris Grain Company. He also had interests in the Hilton hotel chain, West Indies Sugar Corporation, Chicago's First National Bank, the Rock Island Railroad, and Atlantic Mutual Insurance company. Eventually he controlled companies worth about $200 million, including a fleet of forty Great Lakes tankers. In the depths of the Depression, Norris bought up vast land areas in Indiana, numerous grain elevators, a Chicago furniture mart and two sports white elephants, Detroit's Olympia Stadium and the bankrupt Chicago Stadium, and put money into Madison Square Garden, too. He enlisted the aid of his son Jim in salvaging these sports investments. "We have got to find a lot of regular work for a great many boxers, skaters, wrestlers, circus hands, and athletes of all types," he told his son. "If we don't give the fans happy nights to forget their troubles, we are sunk and so is this country." James D. Norris followed his father's instructions. He became the czar of boxing as president of the

International Boxing Club in the 1950s, raced a string of expensive thoroughbreds and when his father died at seventy-three in 1952 James D. became owner of the Black Hawks and the Red Wings in the NHL and owned a major piece of the Madison Square Garden Corporation which owned the Rangers. At one point, the inventive columnist Jim Coleman suggested that NHL stood for Norris House League.

At any rate, before the senior Norris rescued the Chicago Stadium from bankruptcy in the early 1930s he had applied for an NHL franchise in 1928 but was rejected when McLaughlin refused to approve a second franchise in Chicago. Miffed, Norris founded the Chicago Shamrocks and gave support to their league, the American Association, and hired Tom Shaughnessy as coach of the Shamrocks. Shaughnessy had just been fired by McLaughlin. So a tidy little feud brewed between the two millionaires. The Shamrocks played their games in the new Stadium, even drawing fourteen thousand one night, and challenged the NHL for the Stanley Cup. The governors haughtily ignored the upstart. The American Association subsequently folded and McLaughlin moved his team into the Stadium, signing a three-year contract. But the rink lost vast amounts of money and was rescued by Norris. McLaughlin refused to play there starting the 1932 season, opening back in the Coliseum. Norris insisted he honour his contract and the Major, though his team was playing virtually in private in the small rink, refused until the league stepped in and ordered him to return to the Stadium. In 1933 Norris finally bought his way into a governorship by salvaging the Detroit franchise, which had gone into receivership, but that only increased the animosity that existed between him and McLaughlin. Seated in the same room at league meetings, they wrangled frequently.

Norris was not the only governor who argued with McLaughlin; Connie Smythe, Lester Patrick and Art Ross found him distasteful upon occasion, never more so than in the waning nights of the 1937 season when the Major instituted a plan he'd long been nurturing. On January 26 that year he told a reporter from the New York Times that his team soon would become the Chicago Yankees. "I intend to throw off the traditional Canadian influence over this game," the Major said. "If American boys can be developed into star football and baseball players, why can't they be made into hockey players? If they are equipped with the necessary physique, possess a modicum of ability, and are willing to submit themselves to the proper theories of skating, I think there is a place in hockey for our own Americans."

With five games remaining on the Chicago schedule that year, the Major instructed his coach—Clem Loughlin at that time—to dress an all-American line-up. The Hawks already had a core of native-born players. Goaler Mike Karakas was born in Aurora, Minnesota, Alex Levinsky was from Syracuse, Doc Romnes from White Bear, Minnesota, and Louie Trudel from Salem, Massachusetts. All of them, except Karakas, had remained in the United States scarcely long enough for their parents to pay the hospital bill and had grown up in Canada but, still, they *were* American-born. Loughlin, following his employer's orders, added five youngsters the Hawks had scouted at towns in border states: defencemen Ernie Klingbeil of Hancock, Michigan, and Paul Schaefer of Eleveth, Minnesota, centre Milt Brink of Eleveth, and wingmen Al Suomi of Eleveth and Bun Laprairie of Sault Ste. Marie, Michigan.

None of the American rookies figured in the Hawk scoring when Boston beat Chicago 6-2 on March 11 and the Major launched his experiment, though defencemen Klingbeil and Shaefer were on the ice for all of the *Bruin* goals. Two nights later the Hawks invaded Toronto with their stars and stripes intact. The Leafs were lucky to pull out a 3-2 victory, and Klingbeil got one of the goals.

Nevertheless, Ross and Patrick and Smythe were in full bray, insisting the Major's excessive nationalism was unfair to teams not fortunate enough to be on the Hawk schedule. When the Hawks went into New York and beat the Rangers 4-3 Patrick was unusually silent, noting only that the attendance had dropped. In their last two games the American line-up was lathered 9-4 by the lowly Amerks and 6-1 by the Bruins. However, the Major had the last hurrah, a totally unexpected one a year later when the Hawks sneaked into the playoffs by a two-point margin over Detroit and a full twenty-three points back of the second-place Rangers. Chicago was beaten 6-4 in the first playoff game against the Canadiens but surprised by coming back to win the next two games and eliminate the Habitants. Then they met the Amazing Amerks in the semi-final, and again lost the first game and again won the next two to enter the Stanley Cup final against heavily favoured Toronto. This was a series which spawned yet another Black Hawk myth. In the legend, beer-soaked goaltender Alfie Moore is dragged from a pub a few hours before the first game, drenched in a shower and spooned hot coffee until his double vision dissipates, and finally emerges as a star in the Chicago goal.

"I suspect it was Joe Farrell who started the story that I was primed with beer," Alfie Moore remembered years later. Moore had played eighteen games for the Amerks the previous season, and then had been shipped to the AHL where he toiled for Pittsburgh all through the 1937-38 season. "I was living in Toronto in the off-season and had gone home when Pittsburgh's season ended," he recalled. "I didn't intend to go near the Gardens for that Stanley Cup series, but some friends wanted tickets so I went down to see Bill Stewart, who was coaching the Hawks then, and he got me eight. When I got home there was a message that I'd better go down to the Gardens because I might be needed."

What had happened was that Karakas, the regular Hawk goaltender, was unable to play. He'd injured his toe in the wrap-up game with the Americans, and what had been regarded merely as a bruise turned out to be a broken bone. The Hawks had a spare goalkeeper, Paul Goodman, but in the mysterious ways of the times he'd been sent home to Winnipeg before the playoffs started. Chicago was holding out for Davey Kerr, the regular Ranger netminder, as the replacement for Karakas, but Smythe wouldn't stand for it. When he and Stewart met in a corridor leading to the rival dressing rooms, they exchanged insults and piled into one another. Cooler heads, as they say, intervened.

Moore got a warm welcome in the Hawk room.

"Christ Almighty," grunted Louie Trudel. "You. Why didn't you break your leg in Pittsburgh?" But, with nobody else, the Hawks rallied around Moore. In the first minute of play Gordie Drillon banged the first shot at Moore and Alfie missed it. One shot, one goal. But that was all. Moore played an inspired game and the Hawks won it 3-1. Aided by the yeasty brain of Joe Farrell, Moore became a legend, the only man ever to be dragged, kicking and screaming, from a beer hall to become a Stanley Cup hero.

The Hawks got Goodman onto a train out of Winnipeg in time for the second game in Toronto, and Karakas was ready to wear the tools when the series switched to Chicago. The Hawks won it, three games to one, and Major Frederic McLaughlin was overjoyed in clasping the Stanley Cup to his bosom, pointing out inevitably in his acceptance speech that eight of his boys were American-born—Karakas, Levinsky, Carl Voss, Roger Jenkins, Romnes, Trudel, Virgil Johnson and Cully Dahlstrom.

The Major was so delighted that he didn't fire Bill Stewart until almost Christmas.

CHAPTER EIGHT: Jolly Jawn

The lowly writer rarely has a hand in history. Usually he stands around with his notebook and his ballpoint, watching the great men make it or listening to them recount how they climbed unaided from obscurity to richly deserved fame and, in the cases of hockey players in recent years, fortune. Impecunious I am, God knows, but nonetheless I was history's man in the dumbest trade ever made by one of the all-time great traders, Jack (Jolly Jawn) Adams, who ran the Detroit Red Wings for thirty-five years.

Nobody was tougher than Adams, who spent fifty years of his life in pro hockey, first as a player in 1918 when the game was crude and cruel, and last as president of the Central Professional Hockey League in which capacity he died at his desk of a heart attack on May 1, 1968, at the age of seventy-two. Between times, his Red Wings topped the NHL standings twelve times, won the Stanley Cup seven times, and set an astonishing record between 1949 and 1955 when the NHL was a compact six-team unit: seven straight first-place finishes, five Stanley Cup finals, four Stanley Cups.

Adams ran the Wings with a fist of iron until 1962 when the team's owner Bruce Norris shoved him aside and turned the team over to Sid Abel. He built up a far-reaching and productive farm system, and engineered numerous trades in sending off his veterans and bringing in kids in Detroit's long run of success. He was a fat voluble man, a confident after-dinner speaker with a sudden expansive grin that completely illuminated his red beefy face. Still, the sobriquet Jolly Jawn was misplaced; it was more an accommodation of alliteration than an expression of personality. He laughed a lot but he didn't have much humour; the grin was a muscular reflex, like forehead wrinkles, and the sound of his laughter was not joyful but mechanical. He could be a peevish man. For two years he refused to speak to Ted Lindsay, the best leftwinger in Detroit history who when he became a thirteen-year veteran began to question the autocracy of management. He traded Lindsay off to Chicago when Lindsay helped found the original, and as it turned out short-lived, players' association. He stopped talking to Glenn Hall, too, a brilliant young goaltender, and shuffled him off to Chicago, as well. Hall and Lindsay went in a package in exchange for Johnny Wilson, Forbes Kennedy, Hank Bassen and Bill Preston. This was a bad trade, all right, but it wasn't dumb because Adams had already traded with Boston to get back the demon goaltender Terry Sawchuk. No, the dumbest one of all was the one I had a hand in.

What happened was that in the fall of 1959 I went to Detroit to undertake a long magazine piece under Adams's name, the life and times of the game's most successful general manager. I spent several days following him around with the notebook and ballpoint, talking in his office in the Olympia, listening to a luncheon speech of his to some automotive executives, watching the Tigers play the Yankees. Then I went home and started organizing the notes. Just before Christmas the Red Wings came to town and I went down to their hotel to see Red Kelly, their all-star defenceman who'd been having a slow season. Also, a year earlier, the Wings had missed the playoffs for the first time in twenty-one years and I thought there might be a piece there somewhere.

Kelly and I talked in his hotel room and not much developed that looked promising. "Of course," Red remarked casually as I was about to leave, "it didn't help that I broke my ankle."

"How's that again?" I said. "Broke what ankle?"

"Well, there was nothing in the papers," Red said. "The club wanted to keep it quiet. But a year ago I broke my ankle. Six days afterwards Mr. Adams asked me to play. So I played. I wore a plaster cast. It's just beginning to feel good again now."

And then he told the whole story. Thirteen months earlier, the Wings were staggering as they set off on a four-game road trip. They lost three in a row and were scheduled to play in Chicago before returning home. Kelly was in Detroit, his leg in a cast, when the goaltender

Sawchuk was hurt in the third game of the trip, unable to play in the Chicago game. Desperate, Adams asked Kelly if he could help out in the emergency, and brought in the veteran Bob Perreault from Hershey to play goal for Sawchuk. Red said he'd give it a try. A doctor removed the cast and taped the ankle from the instep almost to the knee. Kelly played, and though he could stand little pressure on the ankle and had no power in his skating he helped the Wings to a 3-2 win. Moreover, he finished out the schedule. The fans got on him some as the dismal season petered out and the papers hinted he was over the hill. Even the coach Sid Abel damned him indirectly. "Our trouble is that our veterans aren't producing," Abel told the newspapermen. He fined his players a hundred dollars each for lack of effort. Through all of this Kelly kept quiet.

"The club announced I had a sprain when I first got hurt," he said this day in his hotel room, rubbing his hand over an area just below and in front of the main ankle bone. "I guess they didn't want other teams to know it was broken and maybe start taking whacks at it. Hang, I didn't figure it was up to me to say anything, though I must admit I was surprised when I got fined the hundred."

Well, I went home and wrote that piece for a magazine and then got back to the Adams memoirs, a much longer undertaking. In mid-January I finished the series under Adams's name, got his approval of the manuscript, turned it in to the magazine, and was waiting for the cheque when a telegram arrived, signed by Adams: UNDER NO CIRCUM-STANCES WILL MY NAME APPEAR OVER YOUR STORY STOP PERMISSION TO USE MY NAME HEREBY WITHDRAWN STOP DETROIT HOCKEY CLUB IS AN HONORABLE ORGANIZATION STOP AM CONFERRING WITH MY LAWYERS STOP SUIT MAY FOLLOW.

What bothered me most was that word suit. What also bothered me was the prospect of losing $1,500 from the magazine for the Adams series. And what also bothered me was what the hell he was mad at. I phoned him and he refused to take the call. And then I got a call from Marshall Dann, a hockey writer for the *Detroit Free Press.*

"Hey, you really stirred up the pea-patch," Dann cackled. "I hear Adams may sue."

"What's it all about?" I said. "The magazine hasn't even bought the damn series, yet."

"What series?"

"The series under Adams's name. The crazy bastard okayed it, and now he's hollering suit."

Dann laughed. "Look, what he's hot about's the piece on Kelly. I picked up the magazine in Windsor and when I saw it I phoned Adams for comment. He blew his stack. He said the club's never forced injured players to play. I don't know if he's even *seen* the piece; he just knows what I told him. Oh, we *did* run a little item on it in the *Free Press* this morning, like an eight-column line on the section page."

"My God," I said.

One thing about it, Adams didn't take long to strike back. He sent me the wire and got on the phone to trade Kelly. The next day he sent him and a youngster, Billy McNeill, to the Rangers for Bill Gadsby and Eddie Shack. But Kelly refused to go to the Rangers; he said he'd retire. When McNeill, whose wife had died that summer, said he too was retiring, the deal was cancelled. But Adams wasn't through with Kelly. Before the week was out as his pique continued, he traded him to Toronto for Marc Reaume, a journeyman defenceman. In the previous two seasons Reaume had recorded a total of two goals and twelve assists for the Leafs; *that* season, in thirty-six games to that point, his record showed no goals and one assist. After the trade Reaume played forty-seven games for the Wings with no goals and two assists, and then drifted off to Hershey, never to return. Kelly, meanwhile, played the next seven and a half years with Toronto. He was switched from defence to centre by Punch Imlach. He contributed 119 goals and 232 assists, and helped the club to four Stanley Cup victories before finally calling it a career in the spring of 1967 after the Leafs beat the Canadiens in six games in the Cup finals.

For his part, Adams cooled in time, dropped his threat of a suit, and after a couple of telephone calls from the magazine editor gave him permission to run the series. He hardly relented on Kelly, though. "When Toronto offered me Marc Reaume for Kelly I was ready to do business because Reaume is seven years younger," he said of the trade.

Adams was never a man to admit a mistake. He didn't have to; he was the boss. The players had no voice. Their feeble attempt to organize had been quickly squelched—by Adams in Detroit and by Connie Smythe in Toronto. With those two out, the union fell apart. Players were fearful for their jobs. The NHL was a six-team monopoly and players who didn't toe the line went to the minors or were suspended or were shipped to what passed for purgatory then—the fumbling Chicago Black Hawks (in one twelve-year stretch in the 1940s and '50s the Hawks finished last or second-last eleven times).

Adams was the product of a time when hockey was a crude and well nigh barbarous pursuit, and he rarely forgot it. When he was a player salaries were so low that no one could make the game a year-round endeavour. He signed in 1918 with Charlie Querrie who owned and ran the Toronto Arenas who later became the St. Pats and in turn became the

Maple Leafs. He was twenty-three and got eight hundred dollars; the payroll for the nine-player roster for the entire season was $5,350. Even as late as 1935 the collective salary limit for NHL teams was, by league decree, $62,500, with a limit of $7,000 to any one player. Five years later when the New York Rangers won the Stanley Cup with a team described in 1973 by its coach, Frank Boucher, as the finest hockey club he'd ever seen, the total payroll for sixteen players was $76,500, an average of less than $4,800 per man. Still, that was six times greater than the salary Adams started with.

When he broke in, most of the players were easy-going undisciplined men who liked the bodily contact. Mostly, they were a hard-drinking crowd, and it wasn't unusual for Querrie to make the rounds of the better-known bootleggers on the afternoon of a game to round up his players. They didn't have to be in shape; they'd play only eighteen or twenty games a winter. Pre-season training was a matter of three or four days of skating in mid-December and they were ready to go. Rinks were small and dingy, and the ice grew heavy with snow as the games wore on. The players were sixty-minute men who came off the ice only if they were badly injured. The spares sat out game after game, rarely logging even a few minutes of ice time. Crowds were small and boisterous. The old Jubilee rink in Montreal had to run a netting along the end of the rink to catch the empty gin bottles hurled by the steamed-up fans. In this atmosphere tempers soon frayed as the regulars slogged up and down the scarred heavy ice, and fights were inevitable. A team would keep a pail of cold water and a sponge on its bench; when a player was cut he skated to the boards where the trainer sloshed off the blood, put some sticking-plaster over the cut, patted him on the shoulder, and sent him out for more lumps.

Once, in a game between the Arenas and the Canadiens in that old Jubilee rink, Adams was cut over the eye, down the cheek, and under the chin. He was water-sloshed and plaster-stuck from his hairline to his Adam's apple. When the game ended, a couple of his teammates accompanied him on the tram to the Montreal General Hospital for stitching. The cuts were dripping blood when he was led into the emergency ward. His sister Alma was nursing there then, and by coincidence was on duty when he arrived. He was so beat up his sister didn't recognize him until he was registered and she heard his name. Of that game, the *Toronto Mail* reported:

> The Arenas refused to quit and that tells the whole story. For the entire first period, the Canadiens hammered and battered these game youngsters. They put Ken Randall out of the game for keeps, cut Jack

Adams's head to ribbons, battered Rusty Crawford from head to foot, sent Harry Mummery hobbling off halfway through the period with one leg limp from a sweeping slash, broke the teeth of goalkeeper Harry Holmes, knocked out Harry Meeking and Alf Skinner, and bumped every other opposing player on the ice—but the Arenas didn't quit. It was the most punishing game ever played in an NHL final, and Canadiens made punishing play the main issue. An unforgettable picture was chunky Jack Adams dashing up and down the boards with blood streaming from cuts over his eyes and ears.

Adams closed out his playing career in 1927 with the Ottawa Senators who beat Boston in the Stanley Cup final that spring. The final game ended in a wild brawl on the ice that continued in a corridor leading to the dressing rooms. There, Bruin defenceman Billy Coutu attacked a referee and was barred from hockey for life for the assault. Coutu, who also played under the name Couture, led a surge of Boston players toward referee Jerry Laflamme, engulging the referee and knocking him to the floor with cuts and bruises on his face. The league president Frank Calder fined or suspended five players for the fight and for the assault on Laflamme. Hooley Smith of the Senators was fined a hundred dollars and suspended for the first month of the following season. And as though a life suspension were not enough, Coutu was nailed for a hundred-dollar fine, as well. Five years later the suspension was lifted, but by then Coutu was through; he'd played ten years for the Canadiens going back to 1916 before they'd traded him to Boston.

It was a time of small money, big fights and larger appetites. Massive Harry Mummery's was prodigious. Mummery was a locomotive fireman who took a few months off each winter to play hockey, weighed all of two-sixty, and was a gruff hard-eyed plain-spoken man. As a child I knew him in Brandon, Manitoba, where he and my father both worked for the Canadian Pacific Railway, drank beer together and talked hockey. Mummery had a very tiny wife and they raised twelve kids, all of whom were good athletes, boys and girls alike. I remember once he turned out for an old-timers' hockey game in the Brandon Arena, which was really the local cow palace for the annual winter fair; the display ring was flooded every winter for hockey until the spring thaw turned the ice to slush and water. Mummery must have been well over three hundred pounds by then, cruising slowly across the ice like a ship manoeuvring to dock. No hockey pants could be found to fit him so he—or, more likely, his wife—had cut the legs from a pair of his work pants just above the knees. He had a good time bumping into anybody he could reach. He'd had a long career with the St. Pats, the Hamilton Tigers, the Canadiens and the Quebec Bulldogs, and it was obvious that night in the Brandon Arena that he still knew what to do on a hockey rink. But by then he was just too ponderous to do it.

Jack Adams told me once of a night when he and Mummery were playing for the Toronto St. Pats. On his way to the dressing room Adams could detect the most wonderful aroma of frying beef. He looked around the room and noted that Mummery was missing. He went prowling through the dark corridors looking for him, and found him in the furnace room. The door of the furnace was open and Big Mum was crouched in front of it, wearing his hockey stockings and his longjohns. He was holding a shovel over the flames on which a steak was sizzling. This was late in the first war and steaks were hard to come by.

"Hello Bo," Mummery grunted. He called everybody Bo.

"Where'd you get that?" Adams asked him.

"I got a friend, a butcher," he said. "I gave him a couple of tickets and he let me have it."

"But the game starts in about fifteen minutes," Adams said. "Couldn't you have waited?"

"Oh, I got a little hungry, Bo," said Big Mum.

John James Adams grew up on the western tip of Lake Superior in the twin-cities area of Fort William and Port Arthur which were amalgamated in 1970 to become the city of Thunder Bay. Thirty below zero was not an uncommon temperature for hockey games and there was nothing uncommon about kids freezing their feet, their hands, their faces and, sometimes, their crotches. Toes turn absolutely white when they're frozen and they're no trouble as long as they stay frozen. But it's when they thaw out that the pain can be excruciating as the blood returns to the veins. That doesn't happen much these days; heated artificial-ice rinks in even the tiniest communities have taken the agonizing charm out of this aspect of the game. In an earlier time it wasn't unusual to see the tip of a kid's ear or the end of his nose suddenly turn white as it froze while he was playing. It was possible to watch the colour leave the flesh as the blood receded. If somebody told a kid his nose was frozen he'd grab a handful of snow and rub it on until the frost came out and the circulation returned.

Adams and the kids he played with would go into the bush and whack down an ash tree to make their own hockey sticks. They'd cut the end from a piece of cordwood to make a puck. In larger towns where a stand of trees was not close by, kids never wanted for pucks as long as horses were drawing the milk rigs and bakery wagons. People who regard the word horseshit merely as an uncouth expletive have led sheltered lives; horses drop round balls when they raise their tails for their morning smile. Frozen, these horse balls serve ideally as pucks. They're quite as effective as old tennis balls; they are, indeed, quite couth.

Fort William had two newspapers in Adams's time and he worked for both. He got up at five to deliver the *Morning Herald*, and he sold the *Times-Journal* on the streets after school. His best customers were the miners and woodsmen in the bars. One evening a man offered him a drink as a tip. He didn't drink; he was in his mid-teens, a stocky kid with fair curly hair and light blue eyes and a pink complexion. He said no thanks.

"C'mon, kid," the man said. "One drink won't hurt you. Time you were a man." He was a dark smirking guy, half in the bag, talking loudly past the butt of a cigar. Little Jack was getting nervous.

"Naw, I don't want a drink, mister," he said, seized by an inspiration, "but I'll tell you what: I'd like a cigar."

He'd remembered that an old gent who looked after the town rink smoked cigars, and he figured if he took him one he'd let him skate free. The drunk seemed placated, gave Adams a cigar, and when he took it to the rink the old gent there handed him a scraper and said he might as well clean off the ice, seeing he was going to be skating free. After that, whenever Jack was offered a tip in the saloon he asked for a cigar. He got in a lot of extra ice-time that way.

Eventually he joined Charlie Querrie's Toronto Arenas for his eight-hundred-dollar salary, and he played nine seasons with the pros, in Toronto, in Vancouver, and in Ottawa. He was thirty-two and hopeful of getting a coaching job by then. During the Ottawa-Boston Stanley Cup final he learned that the Detroit club, then called the Cougars, was looking for a coach. They'd finished dead last among the ten teams in the NHL's two divisions, and had lost $84,000 operating across the river in Windsor in their first season after their franchise had been transferred from Victoria when the Western Canada league folded. The owners were building a new rink in Detroit, the Olympia, which would be finished by the fall of 1927.

Frank Calder, the NHL president, was in Boston for the Cup final in the spring, and Adams went to his hotel room to say he'd heard Detroit was looking for a new man. Calder apparently liked Adams as a candidate; he put in a call to the Detroit president, Charlie Hughes, and set up an interview for Adams after the playoffs. The Ottawa victory in the Cup final helped him in that interview; the Senators had owned a hallowed name in hockey for years and it was never taller than after the Boston series. Adams said in later years that when he walked into his interview with Hughes he realized he had a psychological advantage; he said he sensed that the Cougars were grateful to him, that they'd have felt that way about *any* Senator player applying for the job. At any rate, he got it, though he didn't get much. For the next five years the Cougars staggered around near the bottom of the American Division, and even holding a contest to rename the club, a contest Adams hoped would stimulate fan interest, didn't help a great deal. As the Falcons, they sneaked into the playoffs in the spring of 1932 but the Montreal Maroons knocked them off in the first round, and when they made it again in 1933 the Rangers took care of them.

The turning point came one morning late in the spring of '33 as Adams walked without enthusiasm to the Olympia. The rink had gone into receivership, and there were rumours the club would fold. But the girl on the office switchboard greeted his glum face with a smile.

"There's a long distance call for you from Chicago," she said. "The new owner wants to talk to you."

"New owner," cried Adams. "Who?"

"Mr. James Norris, the grain millionaire," the girl replied.

Norris told him he'd meet him the next morning at the trust company in Detroit that had taken over the rink. When he arrived he was shown into an office where a big bald blunt man with heavy black eyebrows, round features and a wide nose was sitting behind a desk.

This was the senior Norris, who'd once played hockey for the Montreal Amateur Athletic Association, a men's club to this day steeped in a tradition of amateurism its members tend to dote on. It's usually called the M.A.A. in conversation; columnist Ted Reeve was once unkind enough to refer to the A.A. as Almost Amateur. At any rate, the M.A.A.'s clubs are called the Winged Wheelers, and apparently Norris hadn't forgotten his association with them. "We'll call this team the Wings," he told Adams. "In fact, we'll call it the *Red* Wings. Our emblem will be a winged wheel; that's appropriate here in Detroit. And I'll give you a year in your job—on probation."

He also gave Adams a bankroll and one boss, instead of several, a welcome change from the multiple ownership that used to debate team policy in the broad lounge of the Detroit Athletic Club, worrying about costs, going deep into debt, and finally failing.

In the early years of the Depression before Norris came to the rescue, the team rarely attracted even 80,000 people a season. They travelled in day coaches and munched sandwiches on the trains. In that bleak period they were literally giving their tickets away. People simply had no money. Once, the club played an exhibition game to help a fund being conducted by Detroit's mayor, Frank Murphy. There was no admission charge, as such; people delivered food or clothing to the firehalls and got tickets in exchange. The game attracted a capacity crowd of some fourteen thousand. Just before it started Adams heard there was a guy driving up and down Woodward Avenue outside the rink. He had five bags of potatoes and wanted in. Adams took his potatoes and gave him standing room.

In that atmosphere it was hard to build a hockey club. If Howie Morenz had been available for $1.98 Adams couldn't have afforded him. He had a chance to get a fine centre, Bill Thoms, for $600 but didn't have the money. After Norris arrived, there was money, all right, but even so Adams made one of his best trades without it. One cold March morning in Montreal he was standing on the steps of the Windsor Hotel with Frank Patrick, then Boston's general manager. They were in Montreal to watch the Maroons play the Leafs in the Stanley Cup final. The wind was howling up the Windsor Street hill from the station below the hotel, but they were oblivious to it. Oddly enough, they were talking hockey.

"If I had Cooney Weiland," Patrick said of Detroit's slick little centre, "my club would be here."

"If I had Marty Barry," Adams said of Boston's big solemn centre, "we'd win the Cup."

They exchanged glances, laughed, and shook hands on the deal. Adams put Barry with Herbie Lewis and Larry Aurie to form a line that soon made a prophet out of Adams. Norris's money played its part, too. Adams paid $35,000, a fortune then, to get Syd Howe from the St. Louis Flyers, and about half that amount to pry Hec Kilrea loose from Toronto. With those additions they won their division and qualified to meet the Maroons, who'd won the Canadian Division, in the most stupefying game ever played. The series opened in the Forum where tidy work by the two netminders, Detroit's small acrobat Normie Smith and Montreal's peripatetic stoic Lorne Chabot, kept the game scoreless through regulation time. Then things settled into a sort of six-day bike race on skates, fans yawning, getting up and leaving, coming back, going to the bathroom, dozing, finally drifting off home. Still the players moiled in their goal-less grind, hour after hour. One o'clock came and then two o'clock and by then the ice was slashed and chipped and brutal on the players. At 2:25 a.m. Adams looked along his bench for the strongest legs—or even to see who was awake—and broke up lines to send out Syd Howe, Hec Kilrea and young Mud Bruneteau. They slogged around for awhile, and then, like everyone else, became listless automatons.

Well, it *did* end, of course, or else they'd be playing yet. Bruneteau picked up an ounce of energy someplace and got the goal that ended the longest game ever played, after sixteen minutes and thirty seconds of the *sixth* twenty-minute overtime period, just three and a half minutes short of three full *games*. The teams played 176 minutes and thirty seconds in six hours in the Forum. The goaltenders were remarkable, of course; just standing there that long was a feat, but Adams later confessed that poor ice conditions contributed most of all to the record. It was two years before anyone came up with a solution to this sort of sopor, and it turned out to be Adams who did so. He got his inspiration in Paris, of all places, in the spring of 1938 when the Red Wings and the Canadiens took an exhibition tour of France. One night he dined in a restaurant where the tables lined a sheet of ice on which part of a floor show was a curling demonstration. Now watching a curling demonstration is not every man's notion of a night out in Paris, but it turned out to have its advantages for Adams. When the curling act ended, attendants swept the ice with sheepskin brushes and flooded it for the next show. That turned on the light. Adams discussed the ice-flooding procedure with NHL governors when he returned from France, and by the 1940-41 season, moving with the speed of sound, the govs had passed legislation incorporating ice-flooding into the rules.

The next season Adams got his biggest jolt until the one Bruce Norris delivered in directing him to the exit twenty years later. Playing Toronto in the Stanley Cup final in 1942, the Wings were well on their way to another championship. They won the first three games and were leading in the fourth with fifteen minutes to play, but lost it by a goal after what Adams called the most irresponsible refereeing he'd ever witnessed, a succession of penalty calls that confounded him. The Wings weren't a particularly rough club that season; in the forty-eight game schedule they'd drawn 440 minutes, a fraction more than nine minutes a game. But in the first four playoff games against the Leafs they picked up 135 minutes, nearly thirty-four a game.

When that fourth game ended, Toronto staying alive with a 4-3 win, Wing players Sid Abel, Don Grosso and Eddie Wares rushed the referee Mel Harwood at the exit gate and were thoughtfully discussing his ancestry when Adams steamed across the ice and joined the group. He was later charged with belting the referee although he claimed he didn't get within ten feet of him, and was suspended for the balance of the series by the league president Calder. Wares and Grosso were fined a hundred dollars each, and the Toronto papers stormed that it wasn't enough, that lynching might not be enough. The Leafs won the last three games, the only time a team ever won the Stanley Cup in a series in which it had lost the first three, and Adams said the whole thing was a farce. "The Toronto newspapers and that little son of a bitch Smythe controlled the whole thing," he said. "Their influence on Calder provided me with the darkest moment I ever knew in this game." At the next governors' meeting, in Toronto a month later, he still hadn't cooled. He turned to Calder. "You're through persecuting me, my boy," he said. "I'm through being your patsy."

After that, it seemed to him, his teams started getting an even break. To others it seemed they did better than that, although perhaps that was only because they grew to be so formidable, dominating, pugnacious, even arrogant, especially in the Olympia. Latter-day fans, whose hair stood on end in the 1970s when the Philadelphia Flyers brought the word intimidation back to the language, would have *adored* those Red Wing teams. They carried their sticks like lances, and they plastered visiting players against the boards as though they were advertisements. Adams was not much for Lady Byng winners; he could accommodate Red Kelly, who played hard but clean, because he had guys with bones of iron like Leo Reise, Marcel Pronovost, Benny Woit, Tony Leswick, Marty Pavelich and Vic Stasiuk hewing the wood and carrying the water while Howe and Lindsay and Abel were ripping defences to shreds. Lindsay was a bulldog turned loose in a pit, an eruptive smirking infuriating leftwinger beside two tall though inflexible linemates. Howe was an impossible man to contain for long. I remember one night coming out of Detroit sitting in a Pullman smoker with Joe Primeau, then the Toronto coach. Leo Boivin, a Leaf defenceman in that period, a fireplug of about five-eight, came into the room wearing fresh stitches over both eyebrows and a gash on his chin. His nose was swollen, his cheekbones were red and his forehead carried a dark purple welt. He washed his face tenderly and returned to his berth. Primeau could not contain a soft chuckle of understanding. "Poor Leo," he smiled wanly. "He's just the right height for Gordie in the corners." Yet there'd been no fight that night, no overt violence between him and Howe; Boivin's head merely reflected the night's work of a man trying to check the old master face-painter.

Adams said many times that Howe was the best all-round player he ever saw. He was an admirer of Rocket Richard's truculence and eerie scoring skill, but for pure versatility, high purpose and team contribution Howe was Adams's boy. He had such uncommon reflexes and a faculty of anticipation that he'd likely have been a leader in any sport. He occasionally worked out at the ball park with the Tigers and looked right at home, he became a scratch-handicap golfer of immense distance off the tee, a fine bowler, and he could fight. When Lindsay and Abel departed and he was teamed with any number of linemates he maintained his high productivity through twenty-five years as a player at Detroit. After he retired in 1971 he turned bitter toward the Red Wing organization and took two of his kids and himself to the World Hockey Association for roughly half of all the money in Houston in the fall of 1973. The three Howes, Gordie, Mark and Marty, all excelled with the Aeros, the old man forty-five by then.

Howe had been made a Wing vice-president in Detroit but his nose got out of joint when the management neglected to take him into its consultations. He was reported to be getting $50,000 a year, a nice round number to be retired on, but he wanted something more. "I'd think I was going into an executive-training program, and I'd wait for someone to make good on all those promises I'd been hearing," he whimpered once to writer Jack Ludwig after he'd gone to Houston. "They wouldn't get in touch with me for days. I expected to get into the insurance business—the number of things I thought were going to happen. And—nothing."

This was a switch. Howe had never been concerned about how management ran things at Detroit while he was a player. He was a real company man, commensurately paid for the times. He wasn't interested in Lindsay's early efforts to form a player association, was silent when Adams began to cut up Lindsay, didn't complain when Kelly was harpooned by Adams. No, Howe only began to bitch when circumstances affected *him*. Then he got lucky; the WHA wheeled up hundreds of thousands of dollars and Howe jumped at the chance to ride with his teen-aged sons back into the limelight.

Still, he did everything a man could do in the NHL. Including playoffs, he played 1,841 games, scored 853 goals, was credited with 1,114 assists for 1,967 points, made the No. 1 all-star team twelve times and the No. 2 team nine times, was among the league's top five scorers through nineteen consecutive seasons, was the scoring champion six times and was the league's most valuable player another half-dozen times. He accomplished so many things as a player over so long a period of time that it's almost forgotten how fortunate he was to have played at all after 1950.

That year, the Wings played the Leafs in the semi-finals, a blood-curdling series in which the sticks were carried so high they turned the arena into a tiny moving forest. Near the end of the first game in the Olympia, Toronto's Ted Kennedy was carrying the puck near the boards. Howe sped toward him, cutting diagonally across the ice. A fraction of a second before the impact Kennedy drew himself up and Howe crashed headlong into the boards. He lay limp on the ice, bleeding from the nose and one eye. Later, in hospital, there was every indication he was dying. He was unconscious, vomiting, had a broken cheekbone and nose, and a brain specialist operated, boring a hole into his skull to remove fluid pressing on the brain. Even the next day his condition was critical. Then he rallied and twelve days later when the Wings played the New York Rangers in the final after disposing of the Leafs, he was able to watch the decisive seventh game in the Olympia. And when Pete Babando scored an overtime goal to turn the Wings into champions the cheers from the multitudes were for Howe. The fans wanted him on the ice for the Cup presentation and Howe, head swathed in bandages, moved carefully across the ice, a tall lean kid just turned twenty-two, a farm boy in a rumpled suit, awkward, shy, not knowing what to do with his hands.

In those days, and for years afterwards, Adams always insisted Howe was one player who'd be at Detroit as long as he wanted to stay. But Jolly Jawn was like that, expansive and beaming when things were going well. He said the same thing about Lindsay and Kelly, too, but time took care of them. Time even took care of Adams; by 1962 he was gone from the office in the Olympia from which he ran everything for thirty-five years.

CHAPTER NINE: Who Do You Think You Are, Sprague Cleghorn?

No matter what's done to cool the fights and reduce the injuries, hockey is still the hardest game. Expansion continues to water down an already watered-down product but it remains a game of pain. Scars appear and teeth disappear faster in hockey than in any major sport. It has the dislocations and separations and fractures of pro football, the other tough contact game, and, in addition, it has three unique lethal weapons: sticks, skates and a flying puck.

Scientific research has not eliminated the pain of hockey. Manufacturers keep producing better equipment to protect against injuries but they can't prevent the injuries. Trainers keep devising sophisticated devices for protecting injuries already inflicted but they can't find anything to stop them. Doctors have come up with better ways of treating the casualties of the game's havoc, but they can't eliminate the havoc.

Still, crusty old iconoclasts hardly recognize the modern game for the blood-and-thunder thing it once was. They insist it has been sanitized: by the third-man rule which levies an automatic match penalty and fine on any player who enters a fight already in progress; by the fraternal affection incubated by the Players' Association; by a stricter interpretation by referees of what constitutes a felony; and of course by expansion itself, bringing in boys to mix with men. Once, every team had a herd of bad men, not merely a lonely roughneck employed as a policeman to protect the little fellows; little fellows protected themselves or they didn't survive.

In the memory of people who have watched the game or been part of it for five decades, such as Frank Boucher, King Clancy, Red Dutton, Conn Smythe and Jack Adams, among others, the roughest era by far was the early 1920s when free-swinging hit men like Bad Joe Hall, Minnie McGiffin, Newsy Lalonde, Billy Coutu, Ken Randall and Sprague Cleghorn carved stitches in rival hides like Stuttgart duellists.

"Hockey is a tough game nowadays, but it's a picnic compared to what it used to be," Adams said as long ago as 1960 when his Red Wings were a pretty thunderous bunch themselves. "The Halls and Coutus and Cleghorns of forty years ago have no counterpart in the game now. If you were lucky enough to skate by them in one piece they'd turn and hook their sticks at your face or crack you over the head. That Cleghorn, why, that son of a bitch was an unwashed surgeon."

Cleghorn's is a name that always comes up.

"One time soon after we got Clancy from Ottawa he sailed straight into Cleghorn," Conn Smythe said in 1974. "When he dropped off, he dropped unconscious. I remember back with the St. Pats, Bill Brydge was gonna give us some muscle, he was gonna be our bad man. And when Cleghorn came down, he did give it to him, the knee, the elbow, the stick. But Cleghorn paid no attention; he just waited. Then the time came and, my, he did straighten out Mr. Brydge. He just made a mess of him. Fifty stitches."

Red Dutton played against Cleghorn in the Stanley Cup final of 1924, Dutton with Calgary and Cleghorn with the Canadiens. "If some of the longhairs I see on the ice these days met Sprague Cleghorn," Dutton glowered late in 1973, "he'd shave them to the skull. Jesus, he was mean. If you fell in front of Cleg he'd kick your balls off."

Ace Bailey, who led the NHL in scoring in his third season with Toronto in 1929, played against Cleghorn in his rookie year. "Sprague was an old man of thirty-six or thirty-seven by then, and he'd gone to Boston," Bailey laughed in recollection in 1974. "We were ahead by 5-1 or so, and Boston scored. But the referee, Ag Smith as I recall, wouldn't allow the goal; he said it was offside. Sprague started arguing with him, and I skated up to listen. 'That goal wasn't offside,' I heard Sprague say. So I butted in. 'Your asshole wasn't offside,' I said. Sprague didn't even turn to look at me, he didn't know me from a load of coal. Pop! His fist came from nowhere, caught me right on the nose, and knocked me down. I struggled to get up. 'Stay down, you crazy bastard,' Bill Brydge said, grabbing me. 'Do you want to get killed?' ".

King Clancy: "When I turned pro in 1921 I was seventeen. It was in Ottawa, where Sprague played for the Senators. But they'd traded him to the Canadiens by the time I got there, and the trade infuriated him. He was just a terrible man to have to play against, a terrific stick-handler, a master with the butt-end, and tough, holy Jesus he was tough. One night he broke loose with the puck and sped towards our goal. There was just one man between him and it. I came rushing back and as Sprague neared the last man I tapped my stick on the ice a couple of times like you do when you want the puck, and I yelled, 'Over here, Sprague.' Well, he naturally thought it was a teammate and he slid me the puck without looking, and I sped the other way with it. So when the period was over I was feeling pretty good as I walked to our dressing room and the fans were applauding me and just as I was going in the room I heard this friendly voice, 'King,' and I turned to see who it was. Well, I want to tell you, my friend, did I ever get a sweet wallop in the kisser. It was Sprague, all right, just quietly turning off my lights. Jesus, did he hit me a beauty."

Sprague Cleghorn was born in Montreal in 1890, and he died there sixty-six years later. He did not look the part of the assassin described by his peers. Pictures showed him to be a handsome man, strong featured with light brown curly hair, tall and slender at six-foot-one and 185 pounds, a dapper dresser. Frank Boucher remembered him and his brother Odie as Beau Brummels. They wore derby hats, spats and yellow chamois gloves, often preening in front of the dressing-room mirror before a game.

"For all that," Frank said, "Sprague was one of the most aggressive players the game has ever known. To get by him you had to face up to body-checks, charging, cross-checks, elbows, butt-ends and fists. He was quite a guy."

Ah, yes. On January 5, 1918, recuperating from a broken leg, Sprague Cleghorn was arrested on a warrant sworn out by his wife on a charge of assault. The lady said he'd belted her with his crutch. The charge was dismissed in court on January 22.

Cleghorn was productive of more than mayhem. In 1922, Newsy Lalonde was playing coach of the Canadiens and quit in a pique claiming the owner Leo Dandurand had accused him of not giving his best. Lalonde was gone for four games before the breach was healed, and in that period Cleghorn handled the club. He and his brother Odie scored four goals each against Hamilton and a few nights later they scored six more between them against Ottawa. When Lalonde returned, Sprague reverted to his feud with the Ottawa team that had sent him packing to the Canadiens. He attacked Eddie Gerard, his old Ottawa defence partner, for five stitches over the eye. He butt-ended Cy Denneny for eight stitches in the forehead and nose. He charged Frank Nighbor and smashed him to the ice. Referee Lou Marsh gave him a match misconduct penalty and wrote in a report that he considered him a disgrace to the game. Ottawa police offered to arrest Cleghorn but the referee said he didn't think that was necessary.

A year later, Ottawa and the Canadiens met in the playoffs. From the start, the defence pair of Cleghorn and Billy Coutu assaulted whatever Ottawa players they could reach. Cy Denneny scored for Ottawa and as he circled the net Coutu caught him from behind and crowned him with his stick. Denneny suffered a concussion and required several stitches. Meantime, Cleghorn and Lionel Hitchman were carving up one another. Near the end of the game, Cleghorn charged Hitchman, caught him in the face head-on with a cross-check that knocked him unconscious. Cleghorn was banished for this attack. "Even the Canadiens' manager Leo Dandurand was shocked by the antics of his two defencemen," historian Charles L. Coleman wrote in his two-volume *The Trail of the Stanley Cup*. "Without waiting for league action he suspended both players, and they did not appear in the return match in Ottawa."

And a year after that, Cleghorn was still rampaging. He got a match penalty for hooking Red Stuart across the face in a game in Toronto, and was fined fifty dollars by league president Calder. A special NHL meeting was called in Toronto on January 26, 1924, to consider charges laid by the Ottawa club that Cleghorn was deliberately injuring rivals. Specifically, he was charged with spearing Cy Denneny on the point of his stick, almost puncturing his spleen. However, the meeting rejected this charge. In the next Ottawa-Canadiens game, Cleghorn didn't lay a glove on poor Denneny; he got a one-game suspension for slamming Lionel Hitchman into the boards instead.

But this was no one-way street Cleghorn was on; he took his share of abuse, too, although he noted in 1935, six years after he retired as a player at thirty-nine, that he'd been lucky. "I have only half a dozen permanent scars on my head and face," he said. "Lots of old timers have twice that many." He was still an amateur when Norman Mowatt of the Montreal Victorias smashed his nose with a stick and broke it for the first time. While Cleg was with the Montreal Wanderers, Bad Joe Hall, then with the Quebec Bulldogs, twice split his scalp with wood-chopping stick jobs for long stitching sessions. Ottawa's Marty Walsh once sliced

140

his left ear in two and left it flapping beside his jaw, requiring another lengthy stitching operation. His Wanderers were playing the Canadiens one evening when Jack Laviolette gave him about four inches of stick in a butt-end stab in the chest that tore loose two ribs. The first time he broke his leg, Toronto's Ken Randall piled into him with a body-check that sent both of them sliding into the boards. He emerged on a stretcher from that pile-up with a shattered leg, and Randall's skate had carved a neatly scalloped design down his left cheek.

"You'd need a battery of adding machines to tabulate all the minor cuts, bone bruises, torn ligaments and pulled tendons my quarter century of hockey gave me," Cleghorn said once, dismissing the trivial incidentals.

Nineteen of those twenty-five years in hockey were spent with the pros with six different teams. Then he coached for four more years, concluding with the Montreal Maroons after a short stint with the Bruins in Boston.

Cleghorn appears to have followed no unusual pattern as a boy that might have explained why he turned into one of the most violent men in this violent game. No gross deprivation is apparent in his childhood, no history of being bullied. Like thousands of Canadian kids the brothers Cleghorn got their first skates almost as infants. Sprague was five and Odie four when their father, Bill Cleghorn, gave them skates for Christmas. Bill had been an athlete; in 1885, in fact, he toured Europe with a Canadian lacrosse team made up partly of Indian players. They called him Big Horse and it was his job to look after them.

"That must have been a lot of fun," Sprague said in later years with a touch of the bigotry common to the times. "Especially when the noble red man got tanked on white man's liquor and wrecked a couple of swanky European hotels."

Bill was a competitive man who encouraged the boys to play competitive games and to play them hard; perhaps it was from him that Sprague, being the oldest of five children, acquired his bellicose turn. Once, when he was ill and Odie was playing a game in Montreal, Odie was cut down by a rival and Bill Cleghorn, a spectator, leaped over the boards and started for Odie's assailant, swinging a heavy walking stick. The rink owner, a friend of Bill's, climbed over the fence after him, caught him by the coattails and calmed him down.

Or perhaps the Cleghorns were merely clannish. Sprague and Odie were always close. They played hockey on the same school teams and the same amateur teams. They began as pros together in 1910 in Renfrew in a partnership that lasted for seven seasons, then was resumed in 1921 with the Canadiens until 1925 when Odie went to Pittsburgh as coach of the Pirates in their NHL inaugural, and Sprague went to Boston to play out his career with the Bruins. Between 1918 and 1921 they were on rival NHL teams, Odie with the Canadiens and Sprague with the Senators in Ottawa. Their mother did not share their zeal for the game, even when they were headliners. She went to only one hockey game in her life, an exhibition for old timers after both boys had retired. Her only comment was: "Well, if that's for fun, I'm glad I never saw you play in earnest."

In the autumn of 1909 Sprague was working behind a counter in a sporting goods store in Montreal owned by Art Ross, the same Ross who later ran the Bruins for nearly four decades. Cleg was nineteen then, long and lanky. One afternoon Ross was visited by Ernie Dufresne, a Montrealer who lived in New York and worked for a wealthy promoter, Cornelius Fellowes. Fellowes was involved in a five-team amateur hockey league in New York, owner of a team called the Wanderers. Dufresne talked to Ross in a little office at the back of the store. Then Ross called Cleg and introduced him to Dufresne. Dufresne gave him "the sort of careful once-over a man gives a horse somebody is trying to sell him," Cleghorn remembered in later years.

"Young fellow, how would you like to play hockey in New York?" Dufresne asked.

Cleg was delighted but said he'd have to have a job. Dufresne said that would be no problem. Then Sprague had an impulsive thought.

"Wait a minute, Mr. Dufresne," he said. "I'll be glad to go. But only if Odie can go, too."

Dufresne turned to Ross.

"What is this? Who's Odie?"

Ross laughed. "It's all right," he said. "Odie's his brother. You can use them both."

So it was settled. The Cleghorns were to play for the New York Wanderers and were each to get $50 a week. Odie was given a job in a brokerage office, adding figures on a blackboard. Sprague was no man for figures; he was taken to a Spalding retail store to sell sporting goods. But when the store manager took him to an upstairs room he knew he wouldn't be selling. The room was stacked to the ceiling with footballs.

"There you are," said the boss. "Get to work on those footballs."

"What do you want me to do with 'em? Count 'em?"

"No, I don't want you to count 'em. Blow them up and lace them."

"Not me, mister," said Cleg. "I don't aim to blow myself blue in the face or cut my fingers to ribbons lacing up a million footballs."

That was the end of that job; Dufresne found him another with the New York and New Jersey Telephone Company where his assignment was to show up every Friday and collect a $25 cheque. The other twenty-five kept turning up regularly at the rink in the toes of his hockey boots.

All five clubs of the New York Hockey League—St. Nicholas, Crescents of Brooklyn, the Wanderers, the New York Athletic Club and the Hockey Club of New York—played their games in the old St. Nicholas Arena at Broadway and Sixty-second Street. The playing surface was artificial ice, a full fifteen years before Tex Rickard installed an ice-making plant in the new Madison Square Garden at Forty-ninth Street and Eighth Avenue for the introduction of the Amazing Amerks. The rink had been made over from a riding academy, the ice floor built above the old tanbark surface where the heady aroma of tanbark and horse manure still persisted. The rink was owned by Sam Austin, publisher of the *Police Gazette,* and Fellowes, who travelled with a sporting and theatrical crowd, people the era was pleased to call Broadwayites. The teams had one or two imports from Canada, the balance composed of local New Yorkers or Canadians who'd moved to New York to work. Most of them swiped at the puck as though sweeping a rug and laughed wildly as they fell on their asses.

The brothers Cleghorn shared a room on Sixty-fourth Street, and put in their spare time with Fellowes and his Broadway friends. Fellowes was a generous boss then courting a raven-haired dancer who called herself Mademoiselle Dazie, whom he later married. Each night he sent Odie and Sprague to the theatre with huge boxes of flowers and candy. As Dazie finished her act the Cleghorns would march down the aisle and hand Cornelius Fellowes's gifts over the floodlights.

One day at the rink Fellowes called Sprague to the bench and introduced him to the most stunning woman he had ever met. "Sprague," he said, "I want you to meet Miss Lillian Lorraine. She wants to learn to skate. Do you think you can teach her?" Lillian Lorraine was a musical comedy star, the toast, as they used to say, of Broadway. Cleg laced her boots, threw an arm around her, and began teaching her to skate. It took weeks; indeed, it took until the arrival of spring when his $50-a-week ended with the last of the hockey season. He returned to his job in Art Ross's Montreal store for the summer, and then the whole hockey picture changed for the Cleghorns.

In truth, it had changed drastically for scores of hockey players five years earlier when silver was discovered in northern Ontario in 1905, a hectic period when millionaires were made overnight. By the winter of 1908-09 the little towns of Cobalt and Haileybury and Renfrew were filled with rich men looking for excitement, expense no object. In the spring of 1909 the silver magnates brought the Ottawa Senators and the

Montreal Wanderers to the north country for an exhibition series. When the teams returned home, half the players stayed behind to cash in on the bonanza. The whole area was hockey crazy. Tens of thousands of dollars were bet on each game; often thousands changed hands on a single goal. Miners in the crowds fought in the rinks during the games and up and down the streets after them, and during that wild period the best hockey players in the world were performing in this backwoods league formed to take advantage of the silver discovery. Some of the players lived there, others commuted. It got so that no team in the Eastern Canada Hockey Association, the world's only admitted professional league, could be sure of the services of its players from game to game. Once, the management of the Montreal Wanderers offered to send up the whole team to play in Cobalt uniforms if the league would promise to lay off its players. Cobalt thought it was a marvellous idea, but the other teams only laughed.

The Renfrew Millionaires played a one-one tie in a post-season exhibition in Brockville against the Wanderers, a result that should have satisfied Renfrew's fans, since the Wanderers had won the Stanley Cup in 1908. But it did not. The fans posted a $5,000 bet that Renfrew could beat the Wanderers in a return match. Montreal fans covered the bet. Renfrew won, 3-1.

Later, Renfrew went into Haileybury for a game for which the Millionaires' goaltender Bert Lindsay was unable to dress. Lindsay, father of Ted Lindsay, the Detroit star who became NBC television's hockey analyst in the 1970s, had been hit in the eye by a high stick in a game in Cobalt and couldn't see properly. To replace him the Renfrew owner, M.J. O'Brien, offered $500 for that one game to Chief Jones, the Cobalt goaltender. Jones was more than willing but Haileybury's crazy fans had other ideas; they raised $700 and gave it to Jones to stay the hell in Cobalt.

The games were wild. In one, Frank Patrick of Renfrew battled Bad Joe Hall. He carved Hall's forehead with his stick. Bleeding over both eyes, Hall knocked down Patrick and slugged the referee over the head with his stick. The referee, one Tom Hodge, gave Hall a game-misconduct penalty but when a tie score sent play into overtime Hall felt he should be allowed to return; he pointed out, civilly, that blinded by blood from the cuts over his eyes he'd combed Referee Hodge thinking he was Patrick.

It was into this milieu, then, that the brothers Cleghorn stepped in 1910, becoming professionals above as well as beneath the table when they signed with Renfrew for $1,200 each. By then, the Eastern Canada pro league had had enough of the mining league's raiding, and the two leagues amalgamated to form the National Hockey Association, the forerunner to the NHL. Odie reported first to Renfrew while Sprague went to New York for a farewell visit with his skating pupil, Lillian Lorraine. He headed north in December and arrived in Renfrew on a bitterly cold night wearing a light topcoat. Odie met him piled to the eyes in sweaters and scarves and a fur collar on his overcoat. Renfrew had two railroad stations, both placed for the convenience of milk shippers on the far outskirts of the town. There wasn't a light to be seen.

"Where in hell are we?" Sprague asked. "What *is* this?"

"This," laughed his brother, "is Renfrew."

They walked from the station to a horse and cutter Odie had borrowed from Larry Gilmour, who ran a livery stable. There wasn't a house, only the vast expanse of snow gleaming in the clear cold midnight. But Renfrew fans soon won them over. Their enthusiasm for hockey was astonishing. They came for miles across the frozen countryside. A twenty-mile ride in an open sleigh behind a steaming horse in below-zero weather was no hardship whatever. Guys squeezed their girls under fur robes in the cutters and belted their booze back neat from icy bottles as their horses, wearing bells, jogged across the snow.

Fred (Cyclone) Taylor was Renfrew's idol then, a big defenceman and lightning fast. He was the first man in hockey to use pads on his shoulders; when the Cleghorns broke in as pros they pulled on long underwear and their hockey stockings, climbed into short pants and a sweater bearing the team's crest, grabbed a pair of light gauntlets and went out looking for a fight. But one day Cyclone Taylor picked up a couple of pieces of felt at Larry Gilmour's livery stable, cut them to fit, and sewed them to the shoulders of his underwear. That's how shoulder pads were born.

Taylor never took a drink of hard liquor and he didn't believe in dressing up; not in Renfrew, anyway. He'd climb into his underwear and trousers, pull on a couple of sweaters and he'd be dressed for anything from church to a card game. Taylor had arrived in Renfrew from the Ottawa Senators and he lined his pockets with silver during the process. Bill Jamieson, one of M.J. O'Brien's associates at Renfrew, went to Ottawa to lure Taylor north. He paid him $5,000 to show his good faith. Taylor banked it and went to Renfrew to show *his* good faith. But then the Ottawa club sent a delegation to Renfrew to seek the return of the talented Taylor. Showing there were no hard feelings on his part, Cyclone returned to Ottawa with them. Whereupon Jamieson rushed back to Ottawa from Renfrew and returned home with Taylor.

Tommy Gorman, later the hockey boss of the Amerks, the Maroons and the Black Hawks, was the sports editor of the *Ottawa Citizen* then, and he tore Taylor to shreds in print, calling him among other things a yellow pup. This annoyed Taylor, oddly enough, and he wired a $100 bet to Gorman that when Renfrew and Ottawa played he would score a goal against his old team skating backwards. Gorman accepted.

The teams met in Ottawa on February 11, and Dey's Arena was filled to capacity. The crowd threw everything that wasn't nailed down at Taylor, including chairs, lemons, eggs and even stale buns tied with long yellow ribbons. If nothing else, it proved Gorman had readers.

One of hockey's undying legends is that Taylor confounded the Ottawa team and seven thousand fans in the crowded rink by skating backwards and scoring not once, but twice, the second time to prove it was no fluke, and for generations the legend persisted across Canada that Cyclone Taylor was the fastest man who ever lived, so fast that he could skate backwards through an *entire team* and score whenever he felt like it.

But the facts seem at variance with what will likely remain the deathless version. Hockey historian Charles Coleman relates in *The Trail of the Stanley Cup* that "although Taylor scintillated with his rushes," the Ottawa defence stood impregnable and "he never got a clear shot" on the Ottawa goaltender Percy Lesueur. On March 8 the teams met again in Renfrew where the Millionaires drubbed the Silver Seven scandalously, 17-2, and with the issue far beyond doubt Taylor did indeed skate backwards after taking a pass from Lester Patrick. He travelled about five yards and "climaxed the act by hoisting a swift one into the corner of the Ottawa nets," writes Coleman.

Some forty years later Lester Patrick reminiscing in Victoria called Taylor the greatest performer in history, and remembered an incident taking place in Ottawa, not Renfrew. "On one of his rushes the Ottawa defence stopped Taylor cold and turned him around with his back to the Ottawa goal," Patrick said. "He flipped the puck, back-handed. It nosed past the goaltender. I was on the ice and saw the whole thing, and we went on playing. But by the time the sportswriters had finished with it you'd have thought the Cyclone had deliberately won a bet, and you'd have thought he repeated this performance just about every night afterward. The Cyclone didn't make the legend. The public did."

By 1912 the silver boom was over and little towns like Cobalt and Haileybury and Renfrew went back to being little towns, no longer blessed by a magic silver wand. The Cleghorns joined the Montreal Wanderers for five years where Sprague, emulating the rushing style of Cyclone Taylor, became a high-scoring defenceman and a terror on the backline, which he remained through the rest of his playing days with Ottawa, the Canadiens and the Bruins. He said once he'd "probably been in fifty stretcher-case fights and collisions." He was arrested once in

Toronto for assaulting Newsy Lalonde after Newsy had laid out Odie. Some spectators believed Lalonde had been killed as he lay unmoving on the ice bleeding from the nose and several head cuts. Still, it was Lalonde who showed up in court, his head encased in bandages, to note that Cleghorn "was probably provoked" into the attack, and Sprague escaped with a $200 fine.

A half dozen tumultuous years later he was closing out his playing career at Boston when the Edmonton Express, Eddie Shore, joined the Bruins. "I broke Shore into the big time and I claim some credit for making him the standout defenceman he became," Sprague said later. "He had a lot of stuff when he joined us, but there were still things he needed to learn and I taught him those things."

Late in the 1928 season Art Ross, Sprague's old employer in the Montreal sporting goods store, was laid low by intestinal trouble and Sprague took charge of Ross's Bruins for the final eleven games. They won nine, tied one and lost one and topped their division. They beat the Rangers and Chicago in the playoffs, then lost to Ottawa in the Stanley Cup final that produced the seething confrontation between Billy Coutu and referee Jerry Laflamme and out of which Cleghorn's old defence mate Coutu received his life suspension.

Ross set up an arrangement whereby Cleghorn was to manage and coach a new club in Newark in 1929 but a promised new arena never grew higher than its foundation. Cleg moved on to coach at Providence in the old Canadian-American League after that, and then owner Jimmy Strachan took him to Montreal in 1931 to handle the unrestrained Maroons. Cleghorn proved as unrestrained as his players, and didn't appear particularly interested in his new job. He frequently didn't turn up at practice at the Forum, and sometimes took women friends with him on road trips, locking the door behind him as they stepped into his drawing room for the overnight train journeys. Once, owner Strachan made a trip with the team but his presence didn't faze Cleghorn.

"Sprague, get her out of there," Strachan whispered hoarsely, tapping on the door as the players watched covertly from their Pullman seats. "What will the players think?" The door stayed closed.

Occasionally the shoe was on the other foot. Strachan implored his coach to crack down on the players and Cleghorn imposed an 11:30 curfew. That night the players piled off an afternoon train from Montreal and checked into the Royal York Hotel in Toronto. At 11:30 the coach began checking the rooms, tapping on the doors and counting noses. He stopped at a room shared by Nels Stewart and Hooley Smith and tapped gently. Then he knocked louder.

"Hooler, Hooler, it's me, Sprague. Let me in." He was talking conspiratorially in a stage whisper but players down the corridor could hear him. Finally, he thumped heavily on the door and getting no response he cried, "Listen, you sons of bitches; I know you've got broads in there. Let me in, God dammit, *let me in.*" The door stayed closed.

Lorne Duguid, a rookie defenceman on that club, remembered that Cleghorn was a great one for practical jokes. "One time in New York when we weren't going too well everybody was ordered to Jimmy Strachan's suite for a lecture from the owner," he recalled. "Strachan was a nice man, very mild mannered, and he told us he'd like to see us bear down and try a little harder. In the middle of his talk there was a sudden *b-a-a-a* sound, just like a sheep. It turned out that Sprague had this toy sheep in his pocket that gave off the sound, but Strachan was undismayed. 'Sprague, please put that away,' was all he said. We had a good time when Sprague ran the club. Most coaches frown on cards and gambling, you know, but the first road trip we took with Sprague he brought along a game of crown-and-anchor and a miniature roulette wheel."

Cleghorn lasted one season with the Maroons. Through his latter years he drifted mostly, doing a little of this, a little of that, and drinking a good deal. When he died in 1956 he was flat broke.

CHAPTER TEN: Connie Smythe and How He Grew—and Blew

> The difference between a hockey
> player and a football player or a
> baseball player is this: hockey guys
> play if they can breathe.
> —*Conn Smythe*
> *October 1973*

There you hear the voice of a man who adjusted the style and social patterns of the country to his own tastes, who dressed the roughneck game of hockey in black tie and mink and for a time reshaped the Saturday-night habits of millions of people from one coast to the other. It's now more than a dozen years since he quit running hockey, and that's a long time to be out of the hot news and still be an authority. But by 1974 and pushing eighty, he remained a living force in the game he built as much as any man and more than most, a man still talked about with awe and wonder. Late in 1973 the *Toronto Star*, with a circulation of more than 700,000 weekend newspapers, undertook a five-part series under a six-column colour picture of him on its front page, and the whole *raison d'etre* for this lavish display of his views on everything from politics to welfare to the state of his health was that the views—acerbic, compassionate, vitriolic, sentimental; the whole gamut of emotion—were coming from *him*, a bombastic, romantic, bigoted, inventive, intimidating, quixotic, terrible-tempered paradox of outlandish proportions.

Constantine Falkland Cary Smythe, a self-made millionaire, believed there was no substitute for hard work, though a friend of his once described him as "a practical mystic". "He believed in playing hunches and he believed in luck; mix his superstitions with his practical ability and you had him, a belligerent Irishman." At the height of the Depression, in 1931, he built Maple Leaf Gardens and for thirty years it was the finest, cleanest, brightest arena on the continent. He made hockey so respectable in Toronto that it was right up there with ballet and opera (which he also brought to the Gardens) in the town's social scale, yet many people blamed him for turning the game into a burlesque of what it once was, and others regarded him as an ogre and a dictator. He condoned players who drew penalties and preached fire and brimstone to them before games ("If you can't beat 'em outside in the alley," he'd say in his most enduring philosphy of hockey, "you can't beat 'em inside on the ice."), yet he neither smoked nor drank nor had patience with those who did. He twice introduced his team's retired captain on national broadcasts as "Syl Apps, our captain, who does not smoke or drink." He fought like an alleycat to get into World War II at age forty-seven and then spent weeks and months fighting army policy; just before his discharge he helped precipitate a national political crisis by risking a court-martial to denounce the army's recruiting methods and the uproar led to the resignation of the minister of national defence.

One way and another—as coach, general manager, managing director, president, board chairman, in person or in absentia—he led the Maple Leafs from 1927 when he and two brokers bought the franchise of the old St. Pats for $160,000 until November 23, 1961, when he resigned as president and sold majority control of Maple Leaf Gardens to his son and two others for two million dollars. Queen and country always ranked high with him; thus, on March 9, 1966, he resigned from the board of directors by telegram from Florida because his successors, including his son, agreed to stage the heavyweight championship fight between Muhammad Ali and Ernie Terrell in Maple Leaf Gardens after it had been rejected by many other cities on the grounds that Ali was not a patriotic American.

"You fellows know what it is to be traded," rasped Smythe to newsmen calling him in Florida. "Well, I was traded for a Black Muslim minister and $35,000." (The figure was the Gardens' fee for staging the fight.) He said he was resigning because the Gardens' owners "are putting cash ahead of class."

He abhorred hockey's wholesale expansion which came six years after he sold out his interest in the Leafs. "I'm for perfection," he said. "We had the best players in the world split between six teams and hockey was always worth the money. In the old days there were just as many players could handle Howe as he could handle. In his last few years, before he went to that Texas team, they couldn't get near him. Hockey today is like everything else; what are the cars like, what are the shoes like, what are the shirts like compared with before when the rule was the customer is always right? They are not made as tough and they haven't the same class. Maybe more people see hockey than before and more players get employed but nobody will ever see again the brand of hockey we produced, and I would have to say the big mistake is that everybody's after the fast buck.

"That's what I think is the matter today in the whole world; everybody is after the fast buck. It was the long-term view that built England and all the good institutions we have here now in this country. It's not like the army; of a hundred men in the army, you could trust maybe ninety-five. Today in civilian life from a hundred people you would be lucky to get five you can trust. They're after your buck and sometimes they're after your woman and sometimes they're after your job. Today it's grab it while you can and defend it against all people. I would be a failure running the Gardens today."

When Smythe was running the Gardens and was a kingpin in the tight little six-team monopoly that was the NHL, the owners had all the answers and the players were puppets to be dropped and lifted onto a conveyor belt leading to the minors. Smythe called Jimmy Thomson, a thoughtful defenceman who had a hand in the early abortive attempts to form a players' union, "a Quisling", and dumped him. The Gardens was his manor and he was the lord of it and the people who worked there, including the players, were serfs literally afraid of him and of his volatile moods. He could be an utterly charming man, funny, expansive, warm and outgoing, with a sudden sunny smile, a merry twinkle in his pale blue eyes, and a powerful quality of personality that drew people to bask in his favour. He was a leader, a man who never doubted his own *rightness,* and he had a way of imparting this conviction to others. Or he could shred people at a whim, the blue eyes round dimes of ice; it wasn't so much that he didn't speak to them, it was that they weren't even *there.*

But his business was hockey and he knew his business. He was among the first to conceive of the NHL as "a splendid, capitalistic, money-making enterprise," in writer Jack Batten's neat phrase, and he saw winning championships and earning profits as equal visions. From 1931, when he opened the Gardens with its marvellous sightlines and not a post in the place, until he retired in 1961, his teams finished first five times, won seven Stanley Cups, lost out in the Cup final eight times, and missed the playoffs only three times. Their most successful period, the one in which they really sold themselves to the city and, more particularly, to all of Canada was the decade of the 1930s when they were their most colourful. The Kid Line of Primeau, Jackson and Conacher was at its peak then, Clancy was at his most flamboyant, Flash Hollett was flying from one end of the rink to the other, Baldy Cotton was patrolling his beat under a shining pate, Red Horner was smashing incoming puck-carriers with terrifying zest, Andy Blair was a serene and mustached centre, and George Hainsworth was a calm and superbly graceful goaltender before giving way late in the decade to Smythe's favourite whipping boy, the phlegmatic Turk Broda, who always excelled in the playoffs. "It's the excitement," Smythe once said of Broda's springtime successes. "It moves him all the way up to normal."

But perhaps more important than any of these glittering figures was Smythe's inspired idea to turn Saturday night into hockey night and to put his team's Saturday games on radio coast to coast. The broadcasts became a national ritual, a favourite program in which the players became as familiar to millions of Canadians as movie heroes, and people grew almost as emotionally involved with them as if they were members of the family. This was due in large part to the voice of the broadcaster, a young newspaper reporter named Foster Hewitt who fell into broadcasting; in the late 1920s his paper owned a radio station and assigned him to sports events for the splendid reason that none of the older reporters would touch them.

When Smythe hired him for Leaf games in 1931 Hewitt had a natural style. As a self-effacing man he never intruded himself into his descriptions; he was simply the medium that transported the marvellous gladiators into millions of homes. In his captivating way, he attracted hundreds of thousands of people whose initial interest in hockey was, at best, cursory. His weekly broadcast became the most popular radio program in Canada, and his unique style turned bath-night listening into an institution from the Atlantic to the Pacific. Indelibly established in the 1930s, Hewitt's broadcasts became a tradition that carried into the television age, and he himself never lost his touch. His son Bill eventually succeeded him as the regular play-by-play man but Foster kept his hand in, and it was he who was selected from a big field to handle the epic Team Canada-Russia series in 1972. Johnny Esaw, the executive producer of those telecasts in the two countries, was surprised when asked once how he'd happened to pick Foster, then nudging seventy, for the assignment. "Jesus, for a thing like this," said Esaw, his eyebrows arching, "who *else* would you go to?" Forty years before, when the national broadcast of sports events was in its infancy on the continent, Hewitt made heroes of the players toiling beneath his booth, and he turned his standard phrase, "He shoots! . . . He scores!" into household words.

In building this team which Hewitt damned nearly immortalized, Smythe combined a mania for detail with a passion for gambling. Building the Gardens in the Depression years was gamble enough, but only a beginning. He bought the fireball King Clancy on the proceeds of a big day at the race track. Later, after he got back from the war carrying a wound that slowed him, physically, for life, he gambled with a group of fresh-faced rookies who had been gathered by Frank Selke, disposing of all but three holdover players and winning the Stanley Cup with his beardless wonders three times in a row. Much earlier, in 1926, he got into pro hockey by parlaying a modest windfall he'd been paid for assembling the New York Rangers into nearly $20,000 on two bets on hockey games; then, so buoyed up by the experience, so determined to get back at the Rangers who'd fired him and brought in Lester Patrick to run the team he'd put together, he was able to talk two Toronto brokers into joining him in the purchase of the St. Pats.

Unlike many gamblers, he was not a creature of impulse, although he often pretended to be. Behind everything he did was a meticulous and calculating mind, and away from the public view he was as fussily efficient as a bookkeeper. In his Gardens office he kept charts on every conceivable aspect of his players' performances long before charts became the vogue in pro sports: how many minutes each player was on the ice, whether he was on when the opposing team scored, how many goals he scored against inferior opposition as opposed to his record against the top teams, his every move, check, shot and pratfall. Smythe once astonished fans by trading Gaye Stewart, who had scored thirty-seven goals the preceding season; the charts revealed the large majority had been scored against inferior teams and that very few had been winning goals in one-goal victories. Smythe's was the first team to keep a movie record of every home game and he and his top assistant, Hap Day, spent hours studying the films to get a better line on the merits and deficiencies of every player in the league. Even away from the rink he constantly set his mind to hockey. After a Stanley Cup playoff game in Detroit in the late 1940s he got a midnight train for Toronto and spent the night dicating notes on his observations and reactions to his secretary, Madeleine

McDonald. With Smythe still dictating at breakfast, a waiter spilled a cup of hot coffee on her and Smythe was so absorbed he failed to notice. She had to stop him for five minutes while she got herself cleaned up.

Once, late in 1947, Smythe called to Day on the ice during a Leaf practice. The coach skated to the bench where Smythe was standing.

"Who's the best centre in the league, Hap?" Smythe asked.

Day pondered the question.

"Max Bentley, I guess," he replied.

A few mornings later Smythe sat watching the Canadiens working out at the Gardens the day before a game with the Leafs. When they'd finished he stepped up to Bill Durnan as the Montreal goaltender left the ice and clumped toward the dressing room.

"Hey, Bill, tell me something," Smythe beamed at the big dark-haired Durnan. "Who's the best centre in this league?"

"Hell, they all give me fits," smiled Durnan.

"No, Bill, I'm serious."

"Well, you'd have trouble beating Max Bentley."

"Thanks, Bill."

That afternoon Smythe called in Day. He told him he was thinking of making a trade. It turned out to be one of the biggest trades of the decade. Smythe sent five excellent youngsters, two defencemen and a complete forward line, to the Black Hawks to acquire Bentley. He traded Bob Goldham and Ernie Dickens, the defencemen, and Gus Bodnar, Bud Poile and Gaye Stewart, the forward line, for Bentley and a rookie named Cy Thomas who proved of little consequence. It could have been an absolutely disastrous trade and for weeks it was enormously controversial, but Smythe had done his homework; the Leafs won the Stanley Cup that season and Bentley was a highly productive Toronto star for five more years.

Before shrapnel grazed his spine a month after D-Day in France where Smythe was an artillery major in command of the 30th Battery, he used to use the aisle in front of the box seats at the Gardens as a one-man race track; he'd charge around shouting at players and officials from behind both goals and from the sides of the rink. One of his favourite forms of self-expression was to ride the referee from his own bench, leaning across the boards and shouting at the poor devil, then galloping around to the other side of the ice to shout at him from there. Things often happened in these forays that made good newspaper copy, too, and Smythe was always aware of the advantage of keeping his team in the public eye. He was hockey's most publicized figure for thirty-five years, partly because he discovered early that feuds with rival teams made good copy, both at home and on the road. Sometimes his ploys started out in a premeditated fashion, but sometimes they grew serious. For instance, in one stretch he and Boston's Art Ross didn't speak to one another for *twelve* years, and he launched the silent treatment on Jack Adams for five years on another occasion.

One of the first deals he made when he bought the St. Pats was with Ross. He paid $18,000, a princely sum, for Jimmy (Sailor) Herberts whom Ross recommended highly, and Herberts turned out to be a liability in Toronto. That soured Smythe and in later years he claimed Ross seemed to have devoted his life to making a fool out of him. "He stationed two longshoremen near our bench in the Boston Garden and their instructions were to goad me into a fight," Smythe said. "Ross wanted to have me put in jail." One night as he was making his way toward the Toronto dressing room after a game the longshoremen began pushing him and insulting him. Smythe shouted back at them and then he saw Ross nearby, obviously angry. "He started after me but little Frank Selke saw him coming and dove at him with a flying block that knocked him down," Smythe said. "We got out of there fast, but not before I yelled at the longshoremen, 'When your boss gets up tell him I can't waste my time with anybody that a man as small as Selke can lick.' "

One night Ross did succeed in getting Smythe behind bars, but that turned out to be a tiny incident in a night of near fatality. It was the December night in 1933 in Boston when Ace Bailey was almost killed by Eddie Shore. Bailey had been ragging the puck while the Leafs were two men short through penalties. He held it for almost a minute, frustrating the Bruins, before there was a play stoppage. In the lull, Ross called Shore to the Boston bench and they conferred briefly. When play resumed Shore got the puck and undertook one of his whirlwind dashes. Inside the Leaf zone he was tripped by King Clancy who dashed away with the puck as Shore slid on his hands and knees harmlessly toward the Leaf net. As Clancy sped away, Bailey dropped back to fill his defence position beside Horner, crouching with his stick across both knees and resting on it. Shore got slowly to his feet. Some viewers in the pressbox thought he'd stayed down on purpose hoping to induce a penalty on Clancy. None was called, and Shore started slowly up the ice. All of a sudden he picked up momentum heading for the wide space between Bailey and Horner who had their backs to him, and his lowered shoulder rammed into Bailey's kidneys. Bailey went into the air and his head struck first as he came down on the ice; his skull was split at both temples. While he lay unconscious, the burly Horner sought out Shore.

"You son of a bitch, you can't do that," Horner cried. And he walloped Shore on the chin, knocking him down. Shore's head hit the ice and he, too, lay unconscious, a widening pool of blood forming around his head from a cut that later required sixteen stitches.

Now Horner became the villain; for the moment, at least, the Bailey collision seemed an accident whereas Horner's act was patently deliberate. Bruin players charged toward Horner but before they got to him Charlie Conacher came off the Leaf bench and stood back-to-back with Horner, waiting. By this time, however, it had become apparent that Bailey was seriously injured. He appeared to be in convulsion and players who were on the ice turned their attention to him.

Meanwhile Smythe, leading the way when players gently carried Bailey to a dressing room, heard a fan shriek, "Fake, fake! The bum's actin'." Smythe wheeled and swung. He struck a bespectacled spectator whom he believed had shouted. Blood spurted from the fan's face and Boston policemen took charge of Smythe and escorted him to jail. The fan charged assault and battery but, according to Smythe, Ross, who originally had instructed the fan to lay the charge, demanded he withdraw it when the seriousness of Bailey's injury became apparent. He was realeased from the jail at two a.m.

When a doctor examined Bailey it was soon obvious he realized the player was in critical condition. "If this boy is a Roman Catholic," he said, "we should call a priest right away." Then Bailey opened his eyes and, seeing Selke, said to him, "Put me back in the game, Frank. They need me." Meantime the Boston club doctor was hurriedly making telephone calls, trying to reach surgeons whose specialty was cranial medicine. Then Ross, Shore and a flurry of reporters crowded into the room. Shore apologized and Bailey, apparently lucid, sat up and smiled. "It's okay, Eddie," he said. "I guess it's all part of the game." But suddenly his colouring changed to a sick evil grey, and Selke hurriedly pushed him onto his back again and ordered Shore and Ross from the room. Bailey was taken to a Boston hospital where an immediate operation was performed on his skull.

Through the next week the drama of Bailey's fight for survival filled headlines in two countries. It developed that he had sustained a double concussion, that he would die without a second operation, but that in his weakened condition he would not survive another immediate one. So his life hung suspended for a week during which his condition slowly worsened. His grieving father became so distraught that he bought a gun, took a train to Boston and went looking for Shore. Somehow word of his mission reached Selke who phoned an acquaintance in the Boston police department, and the cop rounded up the senior Bailey. They went to a bar where the cop slipped a Mickey Finn into

Bailey's glass, and while he was thus rendered helpless the policeman got him into a berth on the overnight train to Toronto. And while Smythe stayed with Bailey in Boston Selke was compelled to deal with Frank Patrick, then the league's managing director, who arrived in Toronto with depositions naming Horner as the villain of the affair, and labelling Bailey's injury an accident. Patrick sought signatures from Leaf players saying as much but Selke refused to sit still for that.

After Bailey's second operation his condition showed no immediate improvement, and Smythe called Selke from Boston to tell him to start preparing for the funeral, to clear up any legal border-crossing problems that might develop as the body was transported to Toronto. Selke later wrote in his memoirs that he was "bewildered and shocked" by Smythe's callousness and that, instead of preparing for a funeral he contacted the radio stations and asked them to urge their listeners to unite their prayers for Bailey's recovery. Inside the hospital room, nurses sat by his bed, imploring him to fight, even after doctors had given up hope. Bailey was in a semi-coma one morning at 2:30 when quite suddenly he settled into a peaceful sleep, the first since the injury. Two weeks later he walked out of the hospital and took a train home.

By then Frank Patrick had completed his inquiry; he'd interviewed fifty-one witnesses and had abandoned his early notion that Shore was blameless. The Boston defenceman was absolved of an intent to injure Bailey but Patrick concluded the collision was intentional. He suspended Shore for sixteen games, a third of the season, and the Boston management sent him to Bermuda to get away from it all. He was back in the line-up five weeks later against the Rangers in New York where a throng of sixteen thousand bell-ringing, whistling fans trooped noisily into the Garden. Ordinarily, he was the target of boos and catcalls in the Garden; on the night of January 28, the orchestra leader and movie star Buddy Rogers faced-off the puck and asked the referee Mike Rodden to introduce him to Shore. When the pair shook hands the fans roared their acclaim. "I was nervous as a kitten," Shore said. "I thought they might be hostile."

Horner's reception was less cordial. Patrick had set him down for six games, and his first game back was in Chicago. A newspaper story said an anonymous caller had threatened to shoot Horner if he played. Nonetheless, he played, booed at every turn by an antagonistic crowd. Early in the second period a sudden sharp report ricocheted through the rink and smoke curled up from a dark object on the ice.

"It scared the hell out of me," Horner remembered years later. "I began feeling around for blood."

But it wasn't a bullet or even a crude bomb; a light bulb, unprotected by a wire cage in the Stadium roof, had somehow come loose and its faulty wiring sizzled and smoked when it fell and hit the ice.

"There were no easy games," Horner said of the era. "Red Dutton charged me from behind once in Madison Square Garden. He hit me with his stick, the back of my head hit the ice, and I fractured my skull. I came back before I should have in an improvised helmet, my head still very tender. We played the Maroons and they gave me a bad time. Hooley Smith got his arms around me against the boards and began massaging the back of my head with the handle of his stick. That started the bleeding again, but I got loose and kept playing."

Horner and Shore and Bailey met again in February when the Leafs played an NHL all-star team in Toronto to raise money for Bailey. Bailey, a slim figure in a dark topcoat and wearing glasses, was approached by Shore, who was lined up with the all-stars. They shook hands at centre ice before Bailey dropped the ceremonial first puck, and all acrimony vanished in that moment. Bailey never played again but he stayed in hockey, as a coach at University of Toronto and later as a timekeeper at Maple Leaf Gardens, a role he was still filling in the mid-1970s.

But peace didn't break out between Smythe and Ross. Once, when the Bruins were going particularly poorly, Smythe infuriated Ross and packed the Boston Garden by inserting a signed four-column advertisement in a Boston newspaper addressed to the fans: "If you're tired of what you've been looking at, come out tonight and see a decent team, the Toronto Maple Leafs, play hockey." Ross, referring to Smythe as "the big wind from Lake Ontario", wanted the league to fine Smythe a thousand dollars for his impertinence and claimed the stunt had no class. So the next time Toronto visited Boston, Smythe decked himself in top hat, white tie and tails and strode gaily around the corridors, tipping his hat and bowing every few steps. Smythe and Ross finally made up after a dozen years of this sort of thing, following World War II, for a reason entirely typical of Smythe. "His two sons both served overseas with excellent records," said the lifelong imperialist. "I figured anybody who could rear two boys like that must be all right."

Smythe was born a hundred yards from the future site of Maple Leaf Gardens and a lot of things happened to him, he once said, because he was Irish: "I was sired by an Irishman and dammed by an Englishwoman. I've got my father's fight and my mother's common sense." He was pale and puny, the only son of Albert Ernest Stafford Smythe, a newspaperman who though less than wealthy sent the boy to boarding schools after his mother died when he was seven. One of the first things he did was to shorten his imposing collection of Christian names to just plain Conn. His father hoped he'd become a lawyer and because he was a student himself he surrounded the boy with volumes of Dickens and Tennyson. But the confinement drove him outdoors and the fact he did not have the proper changes of clothes in school and was compelled to pay his tuition in driblets often made him furious. He was blondish, always short in stature (about five foot seven when his growth ended) but wide set and strong. He discovered an outlet, an evening-up place, in sports, in which he excelled. When he threw his weight around violently enough he discovered he got what he wanted.

"I was taught when I was a kid that when you went into a fight you should be cool, calm and collected but I found that all you did when you were cool and calm was do the collecting; you got licked every time. We were playing football in school one time and were getting licked when one of the other team's best men got knocked out. As they carried him off, our school's coach made us line up and shout that old chorus, you know the one, 'What's the matter with so-and-so, he's all right.' I refused to join the chorus; I was glad he was knocked out because I figured now we had a better chance of winning. The school principal took me upstairs in the school and licked me but I didn't mind and we certainly did a hell of a lot better in the second half without that other fellow out there."

Smythe was a nineteen-year-old undergraduate at the University of Toronto when war was declared in 1914; he went overseas as an artilleryman. He was commissioned in battle, and won the Military Cross in 1916 and then transferred to the Royal Flying Corps where as a reconnaissance pilot he was mentioned in dispatches. He was cocksure and dogmatic, a squirt of scarcely a hundred and twenty pounds who argued constantly with his observer, a big tough Irish Catholic, over religion. The day their plane got hit behind enemy lines Smythe, a Protestant, looked at the earth spinning up to meet them and then shouted to his observer, "In about one minute we're gonna find out which one of us is right." There was no such painful resolution; they both walked away from the crash. Smythe was captured and when he began to argue with a German soldier he was shot at from close range. The guy must have missed purposely; the bullet ripped through Smythe's flying jacket without hitting him. He spent fourteen months in prison camp, occasionally trying to escape (he was recaptured twice) and playing bridge. "We played so damned much bridge that I never played the game again," he said a generation later.

After the armistice he got back to England late in December but there were no officers to arrange leave and transportation for his group when it reached London.

"I had a date in Manchester," Smythe related, eyes twinkling, "and I wasn't about to miss it. Then I got an idea as we wandered aimlessly around the train station. 'Hey, anybody here ever work for the railroad?' I asked. There was a guy from the prairies who said he could drive a locomotive engine. We ducked into the yards and found one steamed up, and we jumped into the cab. We swiped this engine and reached Manchester at two-thirty in the morning. I had one fine Christmas dinner that year."

Back in Canada at twenty-four, he felt like an old man. He figured he'd lost four years out of his life. He wanted to make money, to be independent, so he went back to university and finished his civil-engineering course. He got a job in Toronto's public works department but didn't stay long. "I was the worst engineer who ever graduated," he reflected years later, "and when the City of Toronto found its sewers running uphill they agreed with me." Misdirection wasn't alone responsible for his decision to leave engineering. On every project he undertook he found difficulty obtaining sand and gravel. So he bought into a small firm in that business, got control of it in time, and it eventually made him wealthy. While it was growing, Smythe became coach of the University of Toronto hockey team which won Canada's senior championship in 1927 and, as the Varsity Grads, represented Canada at the 1928 Olympic Games in St. Moritz and won a gold medal. Earlier, the team's showing in inter-collegiate games with Boston College, Harvard and Princeton in games in Boston, and Smythe's handling of the players, had impressed the Bruin owner Charles W. Adams. When in 1926 the NHL moved into Chicago and Detroit and gave New York its second entry, the Rangers, Adams recommended Smythe to Ranger president Col. John Hammond as the man to assemble and coach his club. Smythe agreed to a $10,000 salary but before the team played a game Hammond decided to replace him with the more experienced Lester Patrick. He offered Smythe $7,500 in settlement, which Smythe reluctantly accepted. He stomped from Hammond's office; on the night of the opening game against the Maroons, then the world's champions, Smythe ran into Tex Rickard, the Garden president.

"Well, do you think we'll hold them down to ten goals?" Rickard asked genially.

"Hold them down?" snorted Smythe, his mood unleavened by Rickard's amiable salutation. "You'll beat them."

Smythe had assembled a fine line-up, the Cook brothers, Boucher,

Ching Johnson, Taffy Abel. They fulfilled his promise, beating the Maroons 1-0 and delighting Rickard who praised Smythe's acumen. "You should be a vice-president in charge of hockey around here," he laughed.

"I wouldn't *work* around here," growled Smythe. "You don't treat people right."

He told Rickard he was owed money by Hammond. Rickard led him to Hammond's office, listened to details of the agreement, and instructed Hammond to pay Smythe the twenty-five hundred. He took that to Montreal where his old Varsity team was playing McGill and bet the bundle on Toronto. When they won he parlayed his winnings on the underdog Toronto St. Pats to beat the Ottawa Senators. Which they did. That money launched his subsequent purchase of the St. Pats, and the rest, as they say, was history. But not unblemished history.

When Smythe sold his interest in the Gardens in 1961 to his son Stafford, and to two of Stafford's friends, Harold Ballard and John Bassett, he still had a way of reappearing in events. One night in 1962, Ballard, a beefy robust uninhibited man, sat drinking with Jim Norris in a suite in the Royal York Hotel in Toronto. Young Jim, as Norris was called to differentiate him and his powerful father, owned the Black Hawks then, and had poured hundreds of thousands of dollars into the club to make it at long last respectable. Although the Hawks had won the Stanley Cup in 1961 Norris still detected weaknesses in the line-up. One drink led to another and the name of Toronto's skilled and moody leftwinger Frank Mahovlich entered the conversation. Several drinks later the men agreed to a deal: Mahovlich would go to Chicago and one million dollars would go to Toronto. They shook hands on it. Norris peeled a thousand dollars from his folding money as a deposit.

Some time after Ballard had tottered off into the night, Bruce Norris, Jim's brother who ran the Red Wings, got word of the deal. He phoned Conn Smythe. He asked him to intercede. Smythe called his son Stafford at three a.m., said he shared Bruce Norris's concern that the deal wasn't good for hockey, and advised him to cancel it. In the morning, Tommy Ivan, the Hawk general manager, arrived at Maple Leaf Gardens bearing a First National Bank of Chicago cheque made payable to Toronto Maple Leaf Hockey Club in the amount of one million dollars. The words "for payment in full for player Frank Mahovlich" were typed on the upper left-hand corner opposite the date, October 6, 1962. The cheque even included the zeros for pennies so that it read, $1,000,000.00. They were tantalizing zeros. But Conn Smythe's words of admonition were strong on Stafford. He called a meeting of board members and followed it with a terse announcement: "The sale is not in hockey's best interests. The cheque is going back."

Jim Norris had two kind words for the decision: "They welched."

But money maintained its powerful attraction around Maple Leaf Gardens. The new owners streamlined the operation to bring money in by the bucketful. They enlarged the rink's seating capacity by four thousand seats, raising it to 16,314, steadily increased the price of tickets, sold advertising space inside the arena where none had ever appeared in old Connie's time, opened a bar and restaurant called the Hot Stove League charging a thousand dollars for a life membership or a hundred-dollar initiation fee plus fifty-dollar annual membership dues. In 1965 they sold broadcast rights for six years for nine million dollars to a Toronto advertising agency. Then they completely depleted their player reserve by selling two farm clubs, Victoria of the Pacific Coast League and Rochester of the American Hockey League, for $900,000.

They grew ever richer; in November 1965, shares were split, five for one, when the stock hit $93. Profits for six months ending February 1969 were $810,000 or $1.10 a share. By then, anyone who had invested a thousand dollars in Gardens stock in 1935 would have realized thirty thousand dollars.

But there were growing signs that this was not Nirvana, after all. The Royal Canadian Mounted Police on instructions from the Department of National Revenue suddenly seized the financial records in the Gardens. The board, uneasy about the investigation, decided by eight votes to seven to depose Harold Ballard and Stafford Smythe who temporarily lost their jobs as president and executive vice-president of the empire. The deciding vote belonged to the chairman of the board, their old buddy John Bassett. In an ensuing struggle for control, Smythe and Ballard acquired enough stock and proxies to hold the whip-hand over Bassett. Beaten, Bassett sold out his interest, leaving his former pair of partners in full command.

But not for long. On July 9, 1969, an investigator for the Department of National Revenue swore out two informations against them, each charging five criminal counts under the Income Tax Act. The information against Stafford Smythe charged that he had evaded taxes totalling $278,920 which he had received from the Gardens between April 1965 and March 1968. The investigator's statement alleged Smythe had used $208,166, all of it undeclared on his tax returns, to finance construction and improvements on his marble-floored home. Half of the remaining money, $35,178, was appropriated from the Gardens for personal and family expenses, the statement said, adding that another $35,575 had come from the Toronto Marlboros junior hockey club, owned by the Gardens, for unspecified use. Equally damning was the information sworn out against Ballard; it claimed tax evasions of $134,685.

Within three years, Stafford Smythe was dead at fifty and Ballard in jail at sixty-nine. Smythe died in hospital following an ulcer attack; Ballard was sentenced to two concurrent three-year prison terms on counts of theft and fraud from the Gardens involving about $205,000. By then he controlled eighty-five percent of Gardens stock. When he came out of jail late in 1973 after serving slightly more than a year he returned to his lavish Gardens office filled with vim and vigorous plans for the future.

When it was all over, old Conn, nearing eighty, was still filled with fire. "Ballard's been a life-time friend of mine but I wouldn't give him a job at ten cents a week because I don't like his way of doing business," he told the *Toronto Star*'s Bob Pennington. "I've always known him as a brave, dashing buccaneer. To me, he was like one of those old pirates who would go to sea and battle and board each other and take whatever was there. If they had to walk the gangplank they didn't holler. That's his way of living."

He was reflective on the foreshortened life of his son: "Stafford was a very successful young man. He figured wrongly in thinking that he could beat the tax people, but a great number of people have also figured this wrongly. Because of his name, he was cruelly treated by all the publicity. Hundreds of fellows got more out of taxes or were caught with more in that position and got off with paying a fine. But they were going to make an example of Stafford and Harold and, well, maybe they should have because they had positions of trust."

CHAPTER ELEVEN: The Patricks Were Crazy Like Foxes

The best way to run a railroad, of course, is to own it, a concept the Patrick brothers, Frank and Lester, applied to hockey in conceiving of the most remarkable operation in the game's history. Over the years, the Patricks revolutionized hockey on a massive scale, and it's conceivable that if they hadn't poked their long bony fingers into the pie it never would have grown national in scope nor eventually climbed to the international status it knows today.

For forty years one or the other or both of them were dominant in this game, and for more than sixty years there was *always* a Patrick somewhere in the big leagues. Lester's sons, Lynn and Muzz, were outstanding players for the Rangers in the 1940s and became coaches and general managers of the Bruins and the Rangers, respectively, in the 1950s. And even as the 1974-75 season was launched, Lynn was the senior vice-president of the St. Louis Blues and his son Craig was undertaking his fourth year with the California Golden Seals.

Frank and Lester lived a unique and well nigh Utopian existence for fifteen years; they organized and ran their own league, built and owned their own rinks, raided rival leagues and signed their own players, drew up their own schedules, made up their own rules, and owned, managed, coached and played on their own teams. They almost went broke doing it, it's true, but then like ranchers selling cattle they recouped most of their losses by selling their players for $300,000 to the burgeoning NHL, took jobs there themselves, became powerful figures in the league's structure, and in the end were elected to hockey's hall of fame. They died exactly four weeks apart in June of 1960, Lester at seventy-six and reasonably well heeled, Frank at seventy-four and broke.

These days, Lester is the better remembered but that is only because he made his mark later than Frank and did it within easy range of the New York publicity mills. From 1926 he ran the Rangers from behind the bench for thirteen seasons; was general manager for seven more, and then was vice-president in charge of hockey at the Garden until 1950 when he retired to Victoria. Frank made most of his contribution prior to 1930 and did it in relatively remote Vancouver. He was more inventive than Lester, was a dreamer where Lester was practical, was a big drinker and sociable where Lester, though highly vocal and demonstrative, was wary of strong drink and reactionary. Frank contributed far more to the development of the game itself. To this day, the NHL rulebook carries twenty-two pieces of legislation introduced by Frank Patrick; it was he who originated artificial-ice rinks in Canada, post-schedule playoffs, and even the Stanley Cup final itself. He introduced the penalty shot, the forward pass, assists for players helping on a goal, and the bluelines that divide the ice surface into thirds. He legalized kicking the puck, and he was the man who recognized the folly of compelling goaltenders to stand on their feet; he told 'em to go ahead and stop the puck any way they knew how, even standing on their hard heads if they thought it would help.

The brothers were born in eastern Canada—Lester in Drummondville, Quebec, in 1883 and Frank in Ottawa in 1885—where their father Joseph was in the lumber business. In 1908 the old man moved his wife Grace and the family of eight to the interior of British Columbia amid the lush virgin forests around Nelson, and within three years he sold his properties and became relatively wealthy. In the meantime his sons, both of whom had already established themselves as amateur hockey players, were lured back east by the *nouveau riche* silver magnates in northern Ontario. One November day in 1909 Lester received three offers in telegrams from the east—from Ottawa, Montreal and Renfrew. The old man advised him to stay in the lumber business with him in B.C. but the lumber Lester liked best was in hockey sticks so he fired off three telegrams asking big money for the twelve-game schedule in the new NHA: he asked the Montreal Wanderers for $1,200 because he'd played amateur for them; he asked the Ottawa Silver Seven for $1,500 because he was less attracted to Ottawa; and he asked the Renfrew

Millionaires for an unheard of $3,000 because the idea of a winter in tiny icebound Renfrew struck him as preposterous. Within an hour he had a reply—from Renfrew, naturally: catch the next train. Lester tried one more ploy to escape the frozen north: he'd go there if he could bring brother Frank at $2,000. The men maddened by silver strikes replied instantly: run, do not walk, to the nearest train station.

And so the brothers played the two-month season from January 15 to March 15 for Renfrew; the Millionaires finished third in the seven-team league with an 8-3-1 record behind the Wanderers and Ottawa. The Montrealers' record of eleven wins and one loss earned them the Stanley Cup. Lester was fifth-highest scorer with twenty-two goals, including one five-goal spree against Cobalt.

In 1911 when Joseph Patrick disposed of his holdings in Nelson, Frank paid a visit to Vancouver. There, he met many former Eastern residents lamenting the fact they never saw a hockey game and had no place to skate during the balmy winters. Frank grew thoughtful; then he presented a plan to his father and Lester: why not build three rinks on the west coast and start a hockey league? Joseph was the first to approve, then Lester came around when Frank said he'd heard of people in the east who manufactured a machine that could freeze water indoors and keep it frozen. They launched plans to build a $350,000 arena in Vancouver, the largest of its kind on the continent, seating ten thousand people; and two smaller rinks at about a third the size and cost in Victoria, across the Georgia Strait on Vancouver Island, and in New Westminster, outside Vancouver. Frank tried to sell stock but people were unreceptive. After disposing of $5,000 worth the Patricks abandoned their plan to share their project with the public and bought back the stock Frank had sold. They curtailed expenses by eliminating the New Westminster rink from their plan and putting that team's games into the Vancouver building. While Lester went east to consult with the artificial-ice manufacturer, Frank and his father designed and supervised construction of the two arenas, and when Lester returned with specifications for the ice plants they ordered two, the first artificial-ice rinks in the country.

The next problem was playing talent, enough for three teams. Ontario and Quebec were the only large sources of supply so Frank went east to dicker for players. He used money as a convincer, even luring Cyclone Taylor and Newsy Lalonde from the east. Of course, the end of the silver boom meant the end of the three northern teams so that players were available but, even so, the four remaining teams in the NHA had high hopes of signing the stars. Patrick got sixteen players, and his mission caused a great stir among NHA owners and was the start of a hockey war between east and west that reached its peak in 1915.

Now the Patricks were ready. They organized the Pacific Coast Hockey Association, drew up a sixteen-game schedule for each of the three teams, and assigned eight players to each team from their pool of twenty-four men. They had the sixteen experienced players from the east and, with themselves, that meant six good players for each club. The other two on each team were grab-bag performers, former easterners living on the coast. It was like repertory theatre in a sense, but there was no alternative. Some fans, particularly those who bet on the games and lost, hurled charges of fix, but the mass of fans had faith in the Patricks. Financing was so carefully balanced in this era of seven-man hockey that the spare player on each team served as a referee. Frank was the league's president, and he also managed, coached and played for the Vancouver Millionaires; Lester, a league director, filled similar roles for the Victoria Aristocrats. The busy brothers hired Jimmy Gardner to handle the New Westminster Royals.

So the night of January 2, 1912, was a historic one in hockey's development, the opening of professional hockey in the West. The inaugural was played in Victoria, the provincial capital, where Lieutenant Governor Paterson faced off the ceremonial first puck. The visiting Royals beat the home-town Aristocrats 8-3. Three nights later the Royals helped the Millionaires open Vancouver's big new arena for some six thousand fans. In a surprising turnaround the Royals were whipped by the same score they'd beaten Victoria. Did this mean the Patricks had grossly erred in their allocation of players? No, the teams turned out to be fairly well balanced; New Westminster topped the standings when the season ended on March 19 with a 9-6 record; the other two were tied with seven victories each. Frank Patrick set a scoring record for defencemen on March 5: playing for his Vancouver team against New Westminster he scored six goals on Hughie Lehman, the league's top goaltender, and against one of hockey's fabled figures, defenceman Moose Johnson. The mark is still in the record book.

The first season indicated to the Patricks that their house league might make it. People who lacked enough faith to buy stock were willing to pay to watch the game, although two teams in one rink taxed Vancouver's interest. So Frank bustled into Oregon and promised Portland businessmen that if they built a rink he'd supply players for a coast-league entry. When they complied he transferred the ailing New Westminster franchise to Portland, adopted the name Rosebuds and introduced professional hockey to the United States on December 8, 1914. Diplomatic relations ended when the puck was dropped; Frank and his Vancouver Millionaires beat the Rosebuds 6-3.

Frank's biggest contribution to hockey's development came in this period when he introduced the bluelines and the forward pass. Until then, there were no ice markings; the teams played on a blank sheet and were permitted to pass only laterally or to a man trailing. Frank dreamed up the twin innovations one night in Victoria when his Millionaires went across to the island to play Lester's Aristocrats. The game was interrupted endlessly and annoyingly by offside calls. So Frank came up with a solution: by dividing the ice into thirds and permitting forward passing within the middle and defending zones, he eliminated at least half the offsides and speeded up play enormously. It was five years before the NHA came to its senses and adopted the changes in the east and another decade before forward passing was allowed in all three zones.

Next Frank suggested an annual Stanley Cup final between the winners in the NHL and the Coast league. He wanted the total-goals concept dropped for a three-of-five game series. The switch was undertaken in March of 1915 and, in essence, it's the method employed today. In that first east-west series, Ottawa travelled to Vancouver and to the dismay of effete easterners was swamped by the western upstarts. The Millionaires won the opener 6-2, frolicked 8-3 in the second game, and romped 12-3 in the clincher.

Harmony, however, was still only a mirage. Rumours reached Vancouver that Ottawa was sneakily negotiating Cyclone Taylor's return to the east from the Millionaires. Taylor worked for the Department of Immigration by day and Ottawa's management was arranging his transfer to the head office in the capital. Cyclone refused to move, but Frank retaliated anyway. He strapped on his money belt and lured six players west from Toronto's NHL entry. He set them down in Seattle and renamed them the Metropolitans, giving the Coast league a fourth team. However, it was soon apparent that the only people benefiting from cross-country raiding were the players; bidding shoved salaries ever higher, as it was to do fifty-odd years later when the WHA and the NHL knocked heads. So a new agreement was signed and the two leagues respected it as long as the game thrived on the Coast. Which, as it turned out, wasn't all that long.

Fortune was kind to the Patricks until World War I. Then support in Victoria dwindled and died. The club was transferred to Spokane but it survived only one season. Los Angeles was the next stop but it, too, proved a failure, pushing the Patricks to the brink of bankruptcy. The end of the war gave them hope; the Portland franchise was transferred to Victoria and a three-team league, Victoria, Vancouver and Seattle, carried on for five years. In the fall of 1921 the Western Canada Hockey League, an amateur circuit, reorganized as a pro group with four teams, the Calgary Tigers, the Edmonton Eskimos, the Saskatoon Shieks and the Regina Capitals, and their champions played off with the Coast league winner for the right to play the NHL winners for the Stanley Cup. The Coast league switched to six-man hockey in 1922, a decade after it had been introduced in the east (each spring Stanley Cup games were played alternately under eastern and western rules). The Vancouver and Victoria clubs changed their names to Maroons and Cougars; Millionaires and Aristocrats appeared too grandiose in a league struggling to survive.

In 1924 the lease held by the Patricks on the rink in Seattle expired and a renewal was denied. This left the Coast league with two teams, a hopeless position, but Patrick was equal to this new challenge: he talked Western league directors into accepting the two coast teams. The move was a life-saver for the Patricks; at no cost they were now in a revitalized six-team league. A year later when Regina had financial problems, the Patricks bought the club and moved it to Portland.

But by the fall of 1925 losses were mounting and it was obvious the western circuit could not long survive. Players were made restless by reports from the east where New York, Boston and Pittsburgh had joined the NHL along with a second Montreal team, the Maroons. Salaries were going up and the western towns, except for Vancouver, were too small to pay top-line players. But, as always, Frank Patrick had an idea. He and Lester and their father already owned three western clubs, and he arranged with the Calgary and Edmonton owners to become their agent. When the Victoria Cougars went to Montreal to meet the Maroons in the Stanley Cup final of 1926, Frank made overtures to the NHL governors: he said he had five clubs to sell; if the NHL did not meet his terms, he'd organize a rival league in the east. This may have been an idle threat but, at the same time, the NHL was preparing even broader expansion into Detroit and Chicago and a second franchise in New York, and all of them required manning.

So a deal was concluded by which Patrick provided the NHL with fifty players from the western league for $300,000. He got $100,000 from Detroit for the Victoria Cougars and $150,000 from Major McLaughlin in Chicago for the Portland Rosebuds and a few Vancouver Maroons. Those transactions, representing a quarter of a million dollars, allowed the Patricks to almost break even for their fifteen years of operation on the coast. Also, on behalf of the Edmonton and Calgary clubs, Frank got a percentage of his sales of their players, notably one $50,000 package to Boston that included Eddie Shore and Duke Keats of Edmonton, and Harry Oliver and Archie Briden of Calgary. And, of course, Lester went to New York to run the Rangers.

Frank had several offers but he didn't go; not yet. He speculated in mining stocks and gambled and lost heavily on an oil project in the Cariboo country of B.C. He went into the Peace River country of northern Alberta again looking for oil and again coming up dry. Ironically, thirty-five years later oil strikes were made in both places. So Frank joined the NHL as managing director in President Frank Calder's Montreal office, handling the Bailey-Shore incident among other assignments, and it was believed he was in line to succeed the eldering Calder as league president. But instead Frank joined Art Ross in Boston as coach of the Bruins in the fall of 1934 and stayed there for two years. Then he went to Montreal as general manager of the Canadiens. After 1940, though, Frank faded from the public gaze. He returned to the west coast, though there was nothing for him there. Both rinks had burned down, the one in Victoria in the early 1930s and the Vancouver arena a few years later. An outgoing heavy-set man with curly hair and a pink complexion, the most sociable of companions, he had never taken a drink until he was forty; after that, he began to make up for lost time. Unlike Lester, he never was one to look after his money, and the last twenty years of his life were by far the saddest ones.

Frank Boucher, a gentle perceptive man who spent twenty-five years working for Lester Patrick as a player, coach and general manager of the Rangers, once observed that Lester was by long odds the most knowledgeable hockey man he'd ever met. He also termed him "pleasant, kind, excitable, sarcastic, pompous, understanding, headstrong, warm, callous and contrite, depending upon the circumstances."

Lester could be an enigmatic fellow, all right. I remember once in the autumn of 1940, Boucher's second year as coach, when the Rangers pitched their training camp in Winnipeg. They were the world's champions; they had whipped the Maple Leafs in six games in the spring. During the first week of camp, Lester sat impassive in the old wooden Amphitheatre rink watching the workouts, keeping to himself, rarely having a word with the Winnipeg reporters, of which I was one. One day his old friend of Vancouver days, Andy Lytle, then sports editor of the *Toronto Star,* dropped into Winnipeg during a swing through NHL camps. Lester greeted him grandly and sat with him constantly at the rink, pointing to this player and that, filling him with rich stories of the Rangers which we poor Winnipeg wretches would read in the *Star* days later when the Toronto sports pages reached our offices. For young and eager Winnipeg reporters, I'll tell you, it was *humiliating.*

And then one afternoon at the rink Lester called an impromptu press gathering and turned all of his considerable charm upon us. He said a terribly important experiment was about to be launched by the world's champions. There was only one opening in the line-up, he said; third-string right wing. This was surprising because the Rangers, as Stanley Cup champions, appeared to have a pat line-up. But Lester said the man for the job would be selected in a forthcoming three-game exhibition series with the New York Americans, one game in Port Arthur where the Amerks were training, one in Winnipeg, and one in Saskatoon. A leading candidate, said the Ranger general manager, was a Winnipeg boy, and he, Lester Patrick, had decided to permit the Winnipeg boy to play in the Winnipeg game.

"There's a wonderful story for you," Lester told us. "Tell your readers to come out and watch their home-town product seek his place among the world's champions."

I trudged to my office, hardly elated. This was not the sort of copy Patrick had been feeding Andy Lytle, by God. And then I noticed on the Ranger roster that the player who would be playing right wing in Port Arthur was from Port Arthur, and the player who'd be playing in Saskatoon was from Saskatoon. So in the story of Lester's press conference I wrote that the Rangers were set with a pat team, although they were trying to drum up a little box-office action for their exhibitions by pretending local players had a chance to crack the line-up.

One thing about it, Winnipeg reporters soon gleaned new glances into Lester's personality. When we entered the dressing room at practice next day he shook a forefinger under my nose and began to shout. His face grew red; I was an insolent young pup, he said, and ordered me from the room. He bade me never to enter. The next day it was all forgotten; the only difference was that Lester suddenly had become congenial. He talked to the Winnipeg reporters as though all of us were Andy Lytle.

Lester's most famous exploit, a larger legend even than the one that grew around Cyclone Taylor, concerns the night in 1928 when as the forty-four-year-old coach of the Rangers he went in goal in a Stanley Cup final in Montreal against the Maroons. The story has been told hundreds of times: Lorne Chabot, in the Ranger goal, is felled by Nels Stewart's shot; the puck knocks his eye from its socket; he gloves it back in and tumbles to the ice; the Rangers have no spare; the Maroons refuse to allow Ottawa's Alex Connell, who is in the crowd, to replace Chabot; Frank Boucher and Bill Cook confer and decide Lester must be the man; Lester, taken aback, recovers, agrees, climbs into Chabot's sweat-drenched tools; he holds the Maroons to one goal in the ensuing forty-three minutes and triumphs when Boucher scores in overtime.

Years later Boucher remembered that Lester had been in his glory in that game. "Every time the puck came near him he'd drop to his knees and smother it," Frank recalled. "He was shouting at us, 'Make them shoot, make them shoot.' But the players were absolutely determined no Maroon would get close enough for a tough shot. On the one that beat him, Lester had plenty of time to prepare. He waited until the last moment and then decided to drop. But the puck trickled through his legs into the net. That tied the game and we won in overtime."

In the legend, Lester is next thing to a decrepit old man throwing aside his crutches and hearing aid in his team's hour of need, turning back shots that would have dropped Horatius. In truth, Lester was not long out of retirement as a player; in 1923 he was slowing down at Victoria but still was taking occasional turns on defence. In a game in Vancouver on January 9 that year he replaced his regular goaltender Norm Fowler when Fowler got a major penalty for fighting. He even outwitted Jack Adams, the league's leading scorer, on a penalty shot, though Adams scored on him in a subsequent thrust. Ten nights later in Victoria Fowler was in another scrap and drew another major; Lester replaced him again, and reporters began to refer to him as the Praying Colonel because he fell to his knees for every save (or maybe because they'd read eastern papers where Clint Benedict was called the Praying Netminder). Even in 1926, only two years before his famous reincarnation in Montreal, Patrick returned to competition in Victoria when his defence pair, Gordon Fraser and Slim Halderson, were hobbled by injuries. He played twenty-one games and scored five goals. He even played the first game of the western playoffs against Saskatoon, and it took a broken thumb to get him out of the line-up. A year later with the Rangers he played defence against the Americans in New York in March of 1927. So although he was forty-four, it was no doddering old man who faced the Maroons, a point that should detract less from the legend than add to his stature as an athlete.

Lester was theatrical in bearing and gesture. He even bore a facial resemblance to John Barrymore, and he was at his best after he went to New York. Tall and erect, with a crown of white wavy hair that earned him the sobriquet the Silver Fox, he was a didactic man who had both an audience and all the answers. When newspapermen trooped into his office in the Garden they were lambs in a verbal slaughter, stricken dumb by their unfamiliarity with hockey and almost deaf by the wordy tirade of their host. Lester loved it all. Sometimes he'd dive to the carpet to illustrate a point about goaltending; other times he'd rise from behind his desk, tilt back his head, stretch his arm and make a complete turn as he talked about the enthusiasm of the crowds piling up to the rafters in the Garden. Lester could, in Red Smith's arresting phrase, be unspeakably verbose.

But there was this about him: he spoke from authority as well as with it. With the inception of all-star teams in the 1930-31 season, his fifth as Ranger coach, he dominated the voting for the league's best coach. He was the choice in seven of the first eight all-star years; after that he became general manager, no longer on the coaching ballots. And long *before* that, he was making history. In 1903, a few months shy of his twentieth birthday, he stopped off in Brandon where he worked in a laundry and played hockey. The defenceman's job in that period was to get the puck and loft it high above the lights to safety at the other end of the rink. In his first game Lester rushed with the puck and scored. The local management hurried horrified to the dressing room and admonished him to stay where he belonged. After a few more goals, management began to realize that the lanky gangling kid might have something and allowed him to rush as he pleased. Where he rushed was to Ottawa with his Brandon teammates, challenging the Silver Seven for the Stanley Cup but proving no match for the defending champions in the era's usual two-game total-goals series. Brandon lost by 6-3 and 9-3 and Ottawa's Frank McGee was far more impressive than Lester; he scored eight goals. Lester got his revenge. His peregrinations took him to Montreal for three seasons with the Wanderers, and there he engaged in one of the most bizarre Stanley Cup engagements of all time.

It was in March of 1906 and the Wanderers astonished hockey followers by walloping the lordly Silver Seven 9-1, carrying a seemingly insurmountable eight-goal lead into the concluding game in Ottawa. Early in that game Moose Johnson boosted the score to 10-1 on the round, and the Wanderers turned to a defensive game to protect their enormous advantage. It was a mistake. Slowly Ottawa began to peck away; as the Silver Seven crept ever closer the Wanderers grew concerned, then tense, finally frantic. The home team scored nine straight goals, levelling the count at 10-10 on the round. And at this critical point, who else but young Captain Patrick came to the rescue. Forsaking the defensive shell, Lester sped down the ice not once but twice to pop the puck past the Ottawa goaltender Percy Lesueur and break the Silver Seven's four-year rein as Stanley Cup holders.

After two more years with the Wanderers and his foray with brother Frank into the silvered wilds of Renfrew, Lester settled on the west coast for fifteen years, then moved on to New York where, in time, he brought his sons Lynn and Murray into the big league. Lynn, three years older than Muzz, was signed first. It was a very difficult time for him, and for Lester; when the boss's son was put into the Ranger line-up in 1934 the fans were soon hostile, and one night hundreds of them howled at Lester to get him out of there.

"A father and son stood shoulder to shoulder yesterday against the rabid fandom of hockey," wrote George Dixon in the *New York Daily News*. "Cut to the heart over wildly bellowed demands that he yank his eldest boy Lynn from the Ranger line-up, Coach Lester Patrick declared he will stand by his son. . . .

" 'Why should I fire Lynn?' asked Lester Patrick later. 'I use him only on the third line to give the regulars a breather. He's young and he may develop. If I released him, some other club would grab him as a prospect. Wouldn't I look like a sucker if I let him go and he turned out to be a great player?' "

He stuck with him, and of course he turned out to be dead right. Lynn became a star who had ten seasons with the Rangers. Murray was a rough and rambunctious defenceman when Lester put him into the line-up three years after Lynn broke in. Then, like Lynn, Muzz made a mark in the administrative end of the game. Neither of them quite climbed to the eminence of the earlier Patrick pair, but, then, who ever did?

CHAPTER TWELVE: Super Al

In the spring when the season ends, the big hockey player loses his voice. He becomes speechless and he grows invisible. When the general manager sits down to sign his players for the next season he cannot hear the big players or see them. What he has in front of him is an expensively tailored suit and a brief case and the ungiving face of a lawyer. The lawyer does the talking, the talking that matters; the only time he listens is when the numbers get interesting. Any numbers under a hundred thousand dollars these days are very uninteresting; if lawyers hear them they allow themselves a brief soft chuckle. Then they dismiss them. One day Alan Eagleson phoned Sam Pollock to tell him he thought it was a shame that a nice kid like Yvan Cournoyer was making less than a hundred thousand dollars a year. "It's a matter of pride, Sam. Why don't you just shove Yvan over that hundred-thousand mark?"

"How much over?"

"Oh, twenty over."

"Okay," said Sam.

Some people make less than a hundred thousand dollars for playing hockey, but they are mostly the dregs. A lot of them don't even have lawyers. Lawyers are for people 'way up there, and almost everybody in Alan Eagleson's stable is 'way up there. Once, hockey players were the raggedy-assed illiterate country cousins of the big rich U.S. spectator-sports players but, because of people like Eagleson, not any more. The lawyers are the new tough guys of hockey, laying life's facts on owners on behalf of their mute clients.

One soft autumn day in 1973 Alan Eagleson is sitting in his tastefully conservative office in downtown Toronto dictating letters to a nice sunny girl named Linda Biesecke, his secretary. He is writing about his client Bobby Orr to the general managers of twelve teams in the WHA. He is advising them that Orr's five-year million-dollar contract with the Boston Bruins expires in the spring of 1976. He is requesting that they forward to him their offers for Orr's services. The Eagle looks up from his work.

"I would suspect Bobby Orr will sign for two and a half million dollars in the summer of 1976," he says. He leans back in his chair and smiles a long slow smile. "The bidding should be interesting," adds the Eagle.

Until a day in Moscow when I ran into him unexpectedly at an elevator bank during the Canada-Russia hockey series, I'd known Alan Eagleson as a guy of endless energy, always rushing off somewhere waving and grinning and ducking through traffic, one of those people not notably humorous who laughs a lot, a physical-fitness freak, flat bellied, expensively tailored, a non-stop talker delighting in his triumphs, a boy with a toy.

I'd known him since 1967, when he was propelled into prominence as Bobby Orr's lawyer negotiating a landmark contract and then as the organizer of the NHL Players' Association, another landmark. Not long after he'd become the boss of the hockey players' trade union he also became president of the Progressive Conservative Association, the ruling political party in Ontario. So he was the anti-establishment establishment man, a Bay Street lawyer in a big firm assaulting the Savile Row suits into which the panjandrums of the NHL were stuffed. In those days he looked like Clark Kent, ol' Super Al in his black hornrims and groomed hair, all lean and athletic. In the 1970s, like a lot of bushy tails, he'd moved into correctly mod suits, carefully lengthened his hair, switched to wire-rims, and had become increasingly powerful in hockey's structure, though by September of 1972, at thirty-nine, he still had all this bounce, this *glee*.

I remember meeting him by chance on a Sunday morning in the lobby of the Grand Hotel in Stockholm while Team Canada was there and he said c'mon, he'd show me some marvellous architecture in the courtyard of the Swedish parliament buildings. So we set off across one of the old city's innumerable bridges, and I told him three separate times, for God's sake, what's the hurry, we've got all day, and he laughed and slowed his pace for a few moments but soon he was into his quick relentless gait again. Afterward, we climbed into a sight-seeing launch and cruised the waters of the city with a couple of the players. Forced to sit, he chuckled softly, grinned reflexively, and said he had thought it would take him five years to make Bobby Orr a millionaire but the way things had turned out it had taken a little longer than that, five years and a few months, as I recall.

And so from these few hours on a tranquil Sunday in Stockholm I was entirely unprepared for what transpired some days later when I ran into him at this elevator bank and for the first time saw an Eagleson I'd never known before, the one everybody in Canada was to see on television from the Moscow Ice Palace a few days later. I was waiting to take the down elevator in the Intourist Hotel when the up elevator deposited Eagleson at the sixth floor. This was the day after Canada had blown a 4-1 lead in the third period of the opening game in Moscow to lose 5-4 and go two games down to the Soviets. The Russians had won twice in Canada, lost once and tied once, so now the series stood 3-1-1 for the bad guys, and this was the first game I'd seen, because I'd been at the Olympic Games in Munich for the *Toronto Star* while the teams were playing in Canada. Eagleson wanted to know what I'd thought and I told him conversationally that I'd never seen a team pass the puck as impressively as the Russians.

"Jesus," he said. "You must be a Communist." He was very intense, his face was pale and drawn, and there was no question he was serious.

"All I said was that the passing knocked me out," I said.

"We lost, you know," he said.

"Yeah, I know we lost."

"We lost, and you're telling me you like their passing."

"That's right."

"Anybody who thinks like you do has to be a bloody Communist."

"What is this?" I said. "I tell you I like their passing and you give me this ideological gobbledygook. What the hell has. . . ."

He interrupted.

"Are you calling what I have to say gobbledygook?" he demanded. "If that's what you're saying, our friendship ends right here."

I was astonished and he was seething and as we stood glaring at one another I remember thinking, what a dumb word to be arguing about, gobbledygook.

"Friendship is worth more than that," I said. We were still glaring when the elevator came and I walked into it.

Six days later, in the frenzied emotion of the eighth game, the one that meant everything, practically every human in Canada saw this other Eagleson. Until this single moment, as I've indicated, he had been Ralph Nader in a jockstrap. Six years before in forming the players' union he had stood up to—hell, he'd trampled over—the remote millionaires who'd been manipulating players for generations like cards in a gin game. Late in the summer of 1972 he'd untangled the labyrinths of red tape inherent in Canada vs. Russia, salving egos, puncturing balloons, threatening, cajoling, circumventing, *solving,* and finally bringing off, just this side of single-handedly, the impossible series—the capitalist pros and the Communist amateurs on the same ice floe.

And then in this stupefying moment his feet had turned to clay right there on the tiny screen in full view of sixteen million Canadians (a mere twelve million had watched the first man walk on the moon). When Canada scored the tying goal at 5-5 the red light back of the Russian net did not go on. Eagleson leaped to his feet, screaming, and bounded down an aisle to ice level where he was strong-armed by Russian cops. The milling commotion brought Peter Mahovlich and a wild grim band of stick-waving Canadian players to his rescue and he was escorted by them across the ice to the safety of their bench. Approaching it, face ashen, head bowed, he suddenly shook himself free and turned to the Russian fans across the rink. In a crude gesture, he jerked his arm aloft, once, twice, *four* times, his eyes hot behind the steel-rims, hair tumbling across his forehead, jaw working, a man enraged.

This was surely the moment when he fitted a word the Russians supplied for him. The word was *nekulturny* and, translated loosely, *nekulturny* means yahoo or boor or simply a pain in the ass. John Robertson summed it up in the *Montreal Star*: "I saw us as a bunch of barbarians being led by a man who qualifies as a walking diplomatic disaster." Letters to the editor in papers across the country echoed the sentiment.

But wait.

There is a benefit softball game on July 1, 1967, in the little Ontario town of MacTier up near Georgian Bay. Canada is a hundred years old this day and Eagleson, who had been the town's recreational director one summer during his undergraduate days in the 1950s, has been invited back to play in this laugher of a softball game. Also invited are his nineteen-year-old client, Bobby Orr of nearby Parry Sound, who had just completed his first NHL season, and Bobby's dad Doug, against whom Eagleson had often played ball that summer when he'd been the recreational director. All right. Down 7-6 in the ninth, Bobby Orr is the tying run at third base. Eagleson is batting. As the catcher lazily returns the ball to the pitcher, Orr breaks for the plate. The pitcher whips the ball to the catcher and Orr is clearly dead. But he barrels into the catcher, who drops the ball, and the game is tied. The first baseman, infuriated, rushes Orr and punches him from behind. Outraged, Eagleson drops his bat, tears off his glasses and hammers the first baseman to the ground. Now half a dozen opposing players rush Orr and Eagleson who, standing back to back, flail away as though it's Boston greeting the Rangers. Bobby's sister Pat, a spectator, wants in too, but in her rush down a hill she falls and suffers a shoulder separation. That breaks up the fight, but Orr and Eagleson agree it's been one hell of a fine Centennial Day celebration.

The point of all this is that there is an aspect to Eagleson's make-up that made the arena in massive Moscow no different than the ball park in tiny MacTier, a fact I began to appreciate only after we had stood eyeball to eyeball beside the elevators. Beneath that facade of geniality and garrulousness and energy he is fiercely, even blindly, partisan, and he is competitive to the point of indecency. His wife Nancy says that if he beats her five straight sets in tennis, he wants to make it six. He wants to beat every driver on the highway, every amber light on the street. One day in the summer of 1972 when a sixteen-year-old boy hit Eagleson's eight-year-old daughter, Jill, at a tennis club he told the boy to get his father. The father arrived, angry words ensued and Eagleson knocked the man down. He was charged with common assault. Then he was advised the charge would be withdrawn if he were to apologize in open court. Long since cooled out, he apologized in open court.

So here we have a partisan, competitive man; anybody who attacks his friend on a ball field, who doesn't turn on the red light when his team scores, who, indeed, admires the Russian passing plays when his team is trailing, has stripped through his facade and bared a nerve. Of *course* he's a walking diplomatic disaster; whoever charged him with being a diplomat? Of course he was a *nekulturny* in Russia; he went there to win. And maybe things weren't all that bad in Moscow, anyway. At Christmas 1972 the Canadian Ambassador to Russia, Robert A.D. Ford, enclosed these words in his Yule greetings to Eagleson:

"In retrospect I think we can consider the hockey series a great success and I have so assessed it in my report to the Government. In spite of the many snide remarks made by Soviet officials and the press about our type of hockey I think the important thing is that maybe as many as 150 million Russians saw the games (on Soviet television) and were able to appreciate the high standard of Canadian hockey.

"I don't need to say how much of the success was due to your unstinting efforts. You know it much better than I do but I got pretty angry when I began to receive the Canadian papers and saw some of the unfair comments made about your role. However I have no doubt of your ability to defend yourself. All in all, it was a great experience."

Russia is almost a year away by the summer of 1973 and there is a whole new development in professional hockey. Alan Eagleson occupies a cool pedestal where the pressures are negligible. Accordingly, he is the Mr. Smiles-and-Chuckles we knew before Canada-Russia. He sits in the catbird's seat where nobody can threaten him or his friends, the players he represents. The WHA has come on the scene, challenging the NHL's dominance. A great auction develops in which Eagleson and lawyers and agents like him deal the most skilful of their clients to the highest bidder. The owners are helpless. They are squeezed in a price war. If they don't meet salary demands of a player whose contract has expired, the player jumps to the other league. When young players graduate from junior ranks their agents offer their services to both leagues. The highest bidder wins. Thus, Eagleson is able to command $250,000 for junior graduate Rick Middleton on a three-year contract with the Rangers. Middleton, twenty years old on December 4 that year, had never been to New York and when he finally got there he was earning $83,333.33 per year. If the Rangers hadn't come up with the money, Eagleson would have got it, or very close to it, from the Minnesota Fighting Saints of the WHA. The Fighting Saints were very anxious to sign young Middleton who, as it turned out, didn't make the Rangers, though he likely will one of these days after a little seasoning.

Eagleson's power in this war boggles the mind. He and his friend and client Mike Walton decided that Walton had had enough of Boston. The Bruins changed coaches midway through the 1972-73 season. Walton liked the old coach, Tom Johnson. He didn't like the new coach, Bep Guidolin. Mike is what Eagleson describes as "a certifiable psychiatric case". He knows Mike will get understanding from an old friend, Bob Pulford, coach of the Los Angeles Kings of the NHL. He knows he'll be understood by Harry Neale, coach of the Minnesota Fighting Saints of the WHA. He gets on the phone to Boston where another old friend, Harry Sinden, coach of Team Canada and now a Bruin executive, is advised that Walton is through with Boston now that his two-year contract has expired.

"If you want to keep Mike in the NHL," he says into the phone, "make a deal with Pully in LA. If you don't, he's gone to the Fighting Saints."

182

Now he gets on the phone to Pulford in Los Angeles, tilting back in his chair, grinning into the mouthpiece.

"Pully, how are you? How's the weather out there? It is? Hell, it's wonderful here. Pully, listen: I've talked to Boston and I've told them Mike's through there. He'll either play for you or he'll play for Minnesota. But you've got to come up with the money. Listen, if he can get fifty goals for Jack Kent Cooke, Jack Kent Cooke's going to come up with a hundred and a half, right? Okay, you and Larry work on it and let me know."

Later, Pulford is back. He and Larry Regan, the general manager, have worked out an offer, a three-year package for Mike Walton —$100,000 for the first year, $115,000 for the second year and $125,000 for the third year. Also, there are incentive bonuses (*incentive*, yet) starting at twenty goals. For every five goals Walton scores above twenty each season, he receives another $5,000.

Eagleson hangs up and stares into space. "Well, now that I've got him signed at LA," he muses, "all I've got to do is get him to LA."

But he doesn't get him to LA. Regan and Sinden are unable to work out a deal. Five days later Eagleson and Walton fly to St. Paul for a press conference at which the Minnesota Fighting Saints announce they've signed Mike Walton to a three-year contract for $440,000.

"It's *around* $440,000," Eagleson says on his return to Toronto. "Actually, it's a basic $405,000, but there are incentives that could bring it to, let's see . . ." he breaks into smiles . . . "about half a million dollars."

I ask him how he managed to bump a $340,000 base offer from Los Angeles to $405,000 at Minnesota.

"Aw hell," he grins conspiratorially, "when it became apparent that Boston and LA weren't getting together I just sweetened the pot a little at Minnesota. They were glad to get Mike."

Everybody laughed when the Toronto Maple Leafs played hockey during the long *long* winter of 1972-73. To be charitable, they were lousy. But one of their rare assets was a blond, earnest, solemn young man of twenty-two named Darryl Glen Sittler, six foot, one-ninety, who after two undistinguished seasons with the Leafs scored twenty-nine goals that season. Some people these days score that many by Christmas, but don't forget this was Toronto where there hasn't been a scoring champion since 1938 when Gordie Drillon did the deed, and where even the top ten is virgin territory year after year.

Just about the time that Sittler's contract was coming up for renewal in the spring, Johnny Bassett, tall, slim, mustached, thirty-four, sat in his office at a Toronto television station which his old man owns and where he is a vice-president, and came up with this idea to buy the Ottawa Nationals of the WHA. Using a telephone, he rounded up a dozen friends who, like Bassett, have legal access to money, and, sure enough, in due course they acquired the Nationals, changed the name to the Toronto Toros, and set about the business of tearing people away from the ticket wickets at Maple Leaf Gardens. The way to do it, Bassett and friends concluded, was to hit the Maple Leafs where it hurt most: sign Sittler. To salvage at least face out of the previous season's farce, the Maple Leafs recognized they must go to the moon, or right near there, to retain him.

And so the bargaining begins. Well along in it, Eagleson and his wife Nancy, and Sittler and his wife Wendy, are dinner guests of Johnny and Sue Bassett in the Bassetts' big and expensive home in a big and expensive neighbourhood in the northern reaches of Toronto where three of Bassett's partners and their wives are assembled, too. It is very congenial. Everybody laughs a lot.

"Well," beams Johnny Bassett, at length, "let's get down to the nitty-gritty. Darryl, what will it take to sign you?"

"Ask the boss," says the shy young Sittler, indicating Eagleson, who has not had to rehearse his speech.

"Five years," he says. "A million dollars."

Nobody drops a drink.

"Okay," says Bassett.

Levity breaks out. People clink glasses, grin.

"There are a few other things," Eagleson beams.

"Like what?" chuckles Bassett.

"Like legal fees," says Eagleson.

"Yeah," says Bassett. "Legal fees."

"Plus a shopping credit at Eaton's for Darryl and Wendy at a maximum of, oh, let's say $2,000." John C. Eaton, one of the Eatons, is a Bassett partner.

"And a shopping credit for Darryl and Wendy at McDonald's hamburgers." George Cohon, president of McDonald's Restaurants of Canada, is a Bassett partner.

"Al," Bassett chortles, "I'd love to read that in the contract just to see the look on George Cohon's face."

"And a couple of watches for Darryl and Wendy at Peoples." Irving Gerstein, president of Peoples Credit Jewellers, is a Bassett partner.

"So we've got a deal," says Bassett.

Now the next step seems somewhat vague. Eagleson recalls that he told Bassett he'd have to get in touch with Jim Gregory, Leafs general manager. Bassett recalls that Eagleson picked up the telephone right then and cancelled an appointment with Gregory.

"As far as I'm concerned," Bassett declares several days later when the papers suddenly announced that Darryl Sittler had signed a five-year contract with the Maple Leafs for $750,000, "we had a deal. All that talk about hamburgers and watches was a bunch of nonsense, a lot of hilarity after we'd made a deal. It's my conviction that either Eagleson euchered us or Sittler changed his mind."

Eagleson constructs it differently. He says he was entirely in earnest in discussing the fringe benefits. And he says he *did* call Gregory the next day and told him to get his people together and figure out the best possible deal the Leafs could offer. That deal, he says, was the one for $750,000 for five years.

"I told Darryl to go home and think about the two offers, to talk them over with his wife, and then to let me know," Eagleson recalls. "He told me, finally, that he and Wendy had decided the extra money from the Toros wouldn't mean that much happiness to them, that it'd be cut by taxes anyhow, and that he'd had three happy years with the Leafs and wanted to stay with them. What he told me was this: 'Last year I made $30,000 and I was happy. If I was happy at thirty I've got to be happier at five times that.' So what the hell, it was up to him."

Alan Eagleson had no thought of becoming king of the castle or even any thought of getting himself involved in hockey when the first sod was turned on his empire in 1966. The whole thing really started that summer at MacTier when he was recreational director and met Doug Orr. Orr remembered him and called him when son Bobby approached eighteen and became eligible to join the Bruins. Eagleson's handling of Orr and a later involvement with Springfield players that sprang from this, sold him to hockey players everywhere and launched him.

In the summer of 1966 Boston offered young Orr a $5,000 bonus to sign a two-year contract at $7,500 for his first season and $8,000 for his second. Those numbers looked ridiculous only a few years later but they were, if anything, a little higher than standard then. When Doug Orr sought out Eagleson, the lawyer recognized he was in a position to put a big squeeze on the Bruin management whose recent dreadful teams desperately needed a blood transfusion. They were in no position to haggle over a kid who could square them with their disgruntled fans, and Eagleson was able to negotiate an $85,000 two-year contract for Orr—more than four times the original Boston offer.

His involvement with Springfield developed soon after. The Springfield situation had long been a very bad joke in hockey, largely unpublished out of deference, apparently, to Eddie Shore's stature as an all-time great player. But he'd been running his hockey clubs with Captain Queeg overtones for years, and no one ever raised a hand against him except the players whose faint cries were always unheeded by the bigdomes of hockey. Finally, midway through the 1966-67 season, the Springfield players told Shore they would play no more games for him unless he gave them proper working conditions. When Shore threatened to suspend them they called Eagleson.

"How about the league president, what does he say?" the lawyer asked.

"He said if we aren't on the ice tomorrow morning we'll be black-balled and never play hockey again."

That's when Eagleson blew his stack, he recalled later. "Then it turned out," he added incredulously, "that the league president, Jack Butterfield, is Shore's nephew!"

So he flew to Springfield and met with the players in a hotel room where they listed their complaints.

"When you hear one Shore story you smile, as people seem to have been doing for years," Eagleson grimly recounted. "When you hear ten you might still grin weakly. When you hear a hundred—and there *are* a hundred—you want to throw up. If the players were dogs you'd pick up the phone and call the humane society."

In lengthy negotiation filled with crises, Eagleson was able to settle the Springfield situation by getting Shore to stop interfering with his coach in the handling of players and even to abandon his role as medical diagnostician of their ills. Eagleson's major weapon was the threat of challenging the players' working conditions in a court of law.

The Springfield development actually triggered formation of the Players' Association. Until then there was nothing organized about his negotiations with players. He had personal clients here and there in the NHL who had retained him to handle legal work and act in an advisory capacity, mostly Toronto players he'd played lacrosse with. However, during his Springfield period he had lunch one day in Montreal with Bobby Orr, who was in town for a Boston-Montreal game. Two Boston players came to the table and invited him up to Orr's room. When he arrived he found all of the Bruins assembled there. First they told him they were in sympathy with the work he was doing at Springfield and that they wanted to handle any portion of his fee that the minor-leaguers might be lacking. Then they asked him about the possibility of forming an association. He said he'd look into it.

He had at least one client on each of the six NHL clubs by then, and through them he sounded out the rest of the players. He drew up a pledge, had it mimeographed and circulated it through his clients. It gave him authority to act as the player's agent in pursuing the formation of a union. It promised anonymity.

Within a few months he had a hundred and ten NHL names. When he met with the Chicago players Bobby Hull introduced him by saying, "This is Alan Eagleson fellows. Al's done more for hockey in two years than anybody else has done in twenty." Hull, by the way, was not one of Eagleson's personal clients.

The owners were thunderstruck when Eagleson presented them with the bad news on June 7, 1967, in Montreal that the National Hockey League Players' Association had been formed. He said later that he'd advised league president Clarence Campbell two weeks before the meeting that he had pledges from virtually all NHL players.

"And yet, many owners hadn't an inkling or refused to believe it," Eagleson told me later. "The night before the meeting Sam Pollock was convinced that none of his players had signed with us. Actually, only four hadn't, but they'd missed my meeting with Montreal players and they'd told me they'd sign." Original membership in the association was voluntary at $150 a year. Eagleson toured minor-league centres signing players across the U.S. so that he'd be ready for expansion. When it came, he had them all.

The Eagle thinks he will die young. It's not a thought that preys morbidly, only a notion that comes into his mind unexpectedly once or twice a year. "I'll be sitting in a hotel room or maybe setting off on a three or four-hour plane trip," he says, "and suddenly there it is."

At such times, he writes long and affectionate letters to his parents, his wife, and his friend Bobby Orr. A man who has great difficulty expressing affection verbally, he labours to set sentiment to paper. He carries a ton of insurance, keeps his involved financial affairs scrupulously in order. His income reaches $100,000 or more a year, he lives well, though not high, and, through various investments, can see himself reaching millionaire status—if he lives. He is always the loudest man at a party, cocky, animated, child-like in his vanity, often sophomoric though he is not a drinker. He can't, or won't, discuss the source of his apprehension but apparently because of it he lives day to day, grinning and bouncing in his unique power seat, the union strongman heading the Players' Association as executive director, the rich lawyer guiding a select group of stars to, well, to the stars.

EPILOGUE

The world of the brief case and the expensively tailored suit and the ungiving face of a lawyer is a strange one to Michael Francis Clancy. It is not the world he knew about or ever cared about in nine rollicking seasons with Frank Nighbor and Eddie Gerard and Cy Denneny and the rest of the old Senators of Ottawa or in another seven frolicking years with Conacher and Cotton and Day and the rest of the crazy Leafs of the Thirties. All King Clancy ever wanted to do was *play*. Every fall when training camp opened he'd put aside a few minutes for the boss, Connie Smythe.

"Well, King, what's it gonna be this year?"

"Whatever you've written down, Mr. Smythe. Where do I sign?"

Smythe would place a stubby finger under a figure typed into the contract.

"How does this look?"

"Looks okay to me. Gimme the pen."

Smythe remembers a fall after Clancy had retired and gone to coach the Pittsburgh Hornets, the Leaf farm club in the AHL. One night late, King phoned to report on a game.

"Oh, Jesus, boss, we were hot tonight," King chirped on the phone.

"You won, eh?"

There was a slight pause.

"Well, now, we didn't win the game but there were these four fights and we kicked the bejesus out of 'em in all four."

"'What was the score?"

"Oh, seven to one or somethin' but you'da been proud of us, boss. Not a backward step."

For all his pugnacity, Clancy couldn't lick his lips. One night in Montreal a fight broke out in a game between the Leafs and the old Maroons with one second to play. Of all available targets Clancy was injudicious enough to pick on Nels Stewart as a sparring mate, a man who often swallowed people like Clancy without a chaser. They threw off their gloves and Stewart directed a terminal persuader at Clancy, missed, and his bare fist hit the boards. When Clancy saw Stewart's face contort, he stopped scrambling, took hold of Stewart's thumb which had been knocked out of joint. He pulled on the thumb, restoring it to normal, solicitously inquired if it felt all right and, when Stewart nodded, Clancy whacked him in the nose and fled to the dressing room roaring with laughter.

Clancy rarely needed a lawyer, certainly never one to get him a raise, but, indirectly, he owes his nickname to one. His father Tom was a great football player in the 1890s, an era in which "heeling" the ball from scrimmage set play in motion. So proficient was Tom Clancy that rival teams protested he was illegally heeling the ball before it touched the ground. A lawyer was appointed to settle the argument. Lying flat on the gridiron between the lines of scrimmage, the lawyer watched Tom in action and not only exonerated him of illegal tactics but publicly proclaimed him the King of the Heelers. Thus was born the name King Clancy, inherited by Frank from his father Tom.

These days Clancy strolls the halls of the Gardens filled with the light-heartedness of the boy he's always been. He's a vice-president there, warm, talkative, loved, a man with a face like a Dublin back-alley who turned seventy-one in February of 1974. Eyebrows arched in a perpetual expression of surprise, he tells people that, to him, hockey was always *fun* and he points out that he was rarely injured. This is apt to confound anyone who notices the curve in the Clancy nose and the occasional scar on his rugged pan. "Aw, hell, I mean *injured*!" he snorts. "Sure, I lost all my teeth and busted my nose four or five times, but I mean injured so I had to miss a game. I guess I've had a hundred stitches in my face but I never was what ye'd call good lookin'. I always thought hockey was a, well, a *joyous* kind of a game. I always said you never get hurt as long as you play with a reckless abandon. It's like a good fighter; he *reels* with the punches, d'yuh see what I mean? Like, if I went into the fence I went in like a rag doll; I wasn't all tensed up. In other words, I didn't give a shit. But that's the way the game was then, you gotta remember that. Do you understand me; that's the way it was then."